ROLE OF COMPETENCY MAPPING

IN TALENT MANAGEMENT

ROLE OF COMPETENCY MAPPING

IN TALENT MANAGEMENT

Dr. Sasmita Misra

BLACK EAGLE BOOKS

2021

BLACK EAGLE BOOKS
USA address:
7464 Wisdom Lane
Dublin, OH 43016

India address:
E/312, Trident Galaxy, Kalinga Nagar,
Bhubaneswar-751003, Odisha, India

E-mail: info@blackeaglebooks.org
Website: www.blackeaglebooks.org

First International Edition Published by
BLACK EAGLE BOOKS, 2021

ROLE OF COMPETENCY MAPPING IN TALENT MANAGEMENT
by **Dr. Sasmita Misra**

Cover Design: Ezy's Publication

ISBN- 978-1-64560-192-0 (Paperback)
Library of Congress Control Number: 2021943826

Printed in The United State of America

Dedicated to my parents and my Husband Dr Sanjay and my daughter Alisha for their constant support and encouragement

Preface and acknowledgement

In order to drive excellence every organization strives hard to focus on its talent management processes and tools which will enable them to establish as the employer of choice. This book has been an attempt to answer the queries related to one such tool which helps not only in identifying talent in the organization but also enables to understand how to engage employees better. The tool explored for managing talent better in the organization has been competency mapping. The book enables the reader to study the Talent management practices prevalent in leading IT firms and how they have been using competency mapping models in their organization. The effective competencies as identified by both the HR professionals and Engineers of the respective organization.

The challenge is that times change and so does the requirement of the organization. Therefore organisations should keep working on their competency modelling and should keep updating their competency profiling techniques. The most important usage of this book is to provide a sample procedure as to how competency mapping helps in integrating the talent Management procedures of the organization. I do believe that the Talent management practices of this major IT firms will enable the readers to know how to manage Talent in the organization. The Talent Management practices of these firms would enable the readers and practitioners to craft their journey of establishing talent management in their firms. And to use the competency mapping practices as well.

This Book has been my journey of exploring the usage of the tool of competency mapping to better manage talent in the organization. In this Journey many people have contributed to my learning and experience:

1. The Group of HR professionals who keenly participated in the process
2. The entire group of executive students who helped me collect data from various HR professionals and also Engineers
3. I owe this idea of creating a book to Dr Tapan Panda, Director NMIMS, without whose encouragement my dream of authoring a book wouldn't have been possible
4. And, above all my parents and family members who have had unflinching faith in my journey and its outcome.

Foreword

I have known Dr Sasmita from my post-graduation days at Berhampur University and have always found her to be very adaptive with a passion to learn about evolving and latest HR practices. Having said that, I always felt that her ability to look at the industry practices and taking that to the classroom has been commendable. This time she has presented something unique for the practitioners as well.

HR landscape has been continuously evolving and HR practitioners aredeveloping new systems and practices across the globe. This book deals with competency mapping and its role in talent management. In this book the author has brought about a clear blend between theory and practice. She has highlighted how competency mapping and talent management practices have influenced the industry in not only hiring the best talent but also how it impacts performance management andtalent engagement at the workplace.

Competency mapping has been there for quite some time in the industry but the technicalities of creating a competency model and mapping the employees to the competencies to gain maximum advantage is yet to be fully explored by the professionals in various industries. Hence this book is going to help the practitioners, to not only understand the various competencies required in the workplace but also the ways of managing talent in the industry.

I found the book to be very insightful and interesting. This book highlights competencies on which employees are mapped in various leading IT firms. It talks *of Lominger card* which is used to map the competencies of the IT professionals that can be applied in other sectors as well. This book highlights what practitioners are doing with respect to talent management in their organizations. I hope that this book will provide insights to HR professionals to deal with talent management in their organization.

Of course, I would say that this book will definitely be of great help to the students and budding HR managers who are embarking on their journey to the corporate world.

Wishing DrSasmita all success in her quest of learning and mentoring.

DEBASIS SAHU

Sr. VP HR, Citigroup, South Asia

DEBASIS SAHU, Sr. VP HR, Citigroup, South Asia

Debasis is a Human Resource Professional with 20+ years of diverse HR &ER experience in Manufacturing, IT/ITES, BFSI and Banking with expertise in HR Business Partnering and Employee Relations.Debasis has a Masters degree In Industrial Relation and Personal Management from Berhampur University, India and Human Resources Advisory Certificate from the School of Industrial & Labour Relations, Cornell University, US. He is a certified green belt in design for six sigma.In his current role as Sr.HR Advisor for Global Functions, Citigroup, South Asia,Debasis provides end-to-end HR leadership to functions like Legal, Compliance, Finance, Internal Audit etc. In his earlier role at Citi, Debasiswas the Head of Employee Relations for Citigroup across South Asia.Prior to Citi, Debasis has worked in leading companies like OCL India Ltd., Larsen and Toubro, Dell and Bank of America (BA CONTINUUM INDIA) and has held various leadership positions in these organizations. Debasis has partnered with stakeholders across US,UK, Costa Rica, Mexico and Philippines in an onshore-off shore , matrix environment and has partnered with Sr. Business Leaders on Talent Management, Employee Relations, HR Transformation/ Change Management, Merger & Acquisitions, Diversity & Inclusion and Green field projects.

About the Book:
ROLE OF COMPETENCY MAPPING IN TALENT MANAGEMENT

This Book consists of six chapters

Chapter-1- presents the overview of the study, relevance, objectives and methodology adopted to conduct it.

Competency mapping can play a significant role in recruiting and retaining people as it gives a more accurate analysis of the job requirements, the candidate's capability, of the difference between the two, and the development and training needs to bridge the gaps. As far as meeting an individual's career aspirations are concerned, once the organization gives an employee the perspective of what is required from him to reach a particular position, it drives him to develop the competencies for the same. The author presents the relevance of the study and the research methodology adopted to draw out conclusions on the effective competencies required by professionals for managing Talent in their organization.

Chapter II- discusses the theoretical framework and review of literature is related to competency mapping, talent management, performance management and employee engagement has been undertaken to develop a perspective for the research undertaken and find out the gaps in the literature.

Chapter III presents the profile of various Indian **Information Technology (IT)** firms.

Chapter IV deals with talent management practices in the IT firms.

Chapter V analyses the perceptions of the HR personnel and engineers on talent management practices and interpretation of the data collected.

For the purpose of data analysis, the total questionnaire was divided into three clusters (construct variables)

The clusters (construct variables) were:

Competencies and tools for measuring competency mapping

Role of Competency mapping on talent management practices

Impact of talent management practices on employee engagement practices

First part was analysis of the response on the perception of HR managers as well as software engineers on the role of competency by doing cross tabulation of HR managers and technical persons.

The second part of the analysis was based on factor analysis conducted on the part B of the questionnaire which dealt with the role of competency mapping on the talent management practices.

The third part of the analysis is based on the regression analysis of various competencies on talent management practices.

The last part is based on cross tab for understanding role of talent management on various employee engagement practices.

Chapter VI The last chapter recapitulates the findings and the scope for future research.

"I really appreciate the work of Dr Sasmita on the book titled "Role of Competency Mapping in Talent Management". The best part of the book is the fact that it has a blend of both theory and practice and it is written in a very simple style which is easy to understand. The various competency mapping practices can be put to use by any MBA HR student, budding HR managers as well as industry professionals."

Thanks,
Deepak
(Dr. Deepak Sharma)
Author, HR & Legal Consultant
Coach, Faculty & Trainer
Associate Professor (HR)
NMIMS Bengaluru Campus
Mobile : +91-8826955643
email: deepak.sharma@nmims.edu
deepakshma.05@gmail.com

The ROLE OF COMPETENCY MAPPING IN TALENT MANAGEMENT provides valuable insights on a critical practice of HR management in these days, not only aimed at recruiting and retaining the right people but also bringing light to the worldwide priority of reskilling all those who would otherwise be left behind at the hands of technology and under the pressure of this global crisis. Being ready to bridge the gaps between current/future job requirements and workers´ capabilities is the stepping-stone to a new economy that re-designs work conveying productivity and inclusion; so this is an excellent tool box to address this challenge.

Thanks,
Valeria
(Valeria Fratocchi, MBA)
HR & OB Consultant
Full time OB Professor
IEEM Business School
Valeria Fratocchi
Organizational Behavior
Full time Professor

(+598) 99 254 988

Valeria Fratocchi

valeriafratocchi

IEEM
ESCUELA DE NEGOCIOS
UNIVERSIDAD DE MONTEVIDEO

Tel.: (598) 2709 7220
Lord Ponsonby 2542
Montevideo, Uruguay

www.ieem.edu.uy

Acreditado por:

AMBA
ASSOCIATION
ACCREDITED

EFMD
EPAS
ACCREDITED

Asociado a:

IESE
Business School

Executive
Education
2019
2019 - 2017
2018 - 2019
FT

Content

CHAPTER-1

INTRODUCTION

- ➤ INTRODUCTION TO COMPETENCY MAPPING AND TALENT MANAGEMENT SYSTEM

- ➤ RELEVANCE OF THE STUDY
- ➤ OBJECTIVE OF THE STUDY

- ➤ SCOPE OF THE STUDY

- ➤ HYPOTHESES
- ➤ METHODOLOGY

- ➤ ORGANIZATION OF THE STUDY
- ➤ LIMITATIONS OF THE STUDY

CHAPTER-1

AN OVERVIEW OF THE STUDY

Knowing is not enough, we must apply;

Willing is not enough we must do.   Goethe

1.1 Introduction

The traditional organization is witnessing a paradigm shift with the new technology and the availability of brain power. The world is taking a major leap in the 21st century. It is moving at a faster pace in terms of technology and boundaries; this in fact makes every organization to think on the line of aligning with the need of the hour. The traditional management which focused on productivity and efficiency were designed for 20th century economy. Today it can not operate on the same line and length. An organization commits to excellence through a carefully constructed human resources process that links together the core elements of human resources planning and then joins them to strategies, policies and action plans .A paradigm shift is taking place in Indian industry with increasing liberalization and competitiveness. While, on the one hand, global organizations with well-defined processes and practices are trying to expand their foot-hold in the country, the consumer demand within India is not expanding proportionately. To be competitive and to even retain their market-share in the local economy, companies have to look beyond Indian shores and offer products and services of global quality and prices. This requires benchmarking of practices, standards of performance and efficiency in line with the global competition. It is no longer a one-off exercise. The companies have to monitor their performance and environmental factors affecting them on a proactive and hands-on basis. The emerging imperatives are for greater deliberation, analysis and evolving of systems in all areas of operations including human resource management (HRM). The top management needs to define clear objectives and expectations.

Strategic initiatives have come to be reckoned now than ever before, and in a form that is impacting at the operational level. People are now impacted by every strategic decision and no longer have employees at the operational level claim to be insulated from the impact of deploying strategy .But ironically, business managers become too preoccupied with their competitors for existing markets, rather than seeking to create new markets, where they can occupy the competitive advantage simply by being the first ones to get there. Competition for the future is competition of opportunity share rather than market share. It is the competition to maximize the arena of sharing the future opportunities .competition for the future is not product versus product or business versus business, but the company versus company –inter-firm competition. Capable organizations are those that possess inherent strengths that are core and exceptional in nature are likely to have an edge over others. Organizations should possess the required competencies to access the new opportunity arena which may well be spread across a number of business units and it is up to the organization to bring these competencies together at an appropriate time within the organization. The investment and the time frame required to build new competencies which are necessary to access tomorrow's market, may well tax the resources and the patience of a single business unit.

The task of finding and managing talented pool of individuals has become more complex and keeping the global perspective in the mind it becomes still more challenging. Talent managers today must cope with the world of change and contrast:

- Global abundance but local scarcity of talent
- Fewer talented young people since many older people are nearing their age of retirement
- There is a rise in the demand for new skills aggravated by demographic pressures and educational shortcomings
- New methods of working and new relationships between users and suppliers of talent
- More diverse and remote or even virtual workforces, with different attitudes to work across the generations
- Steady change in the nature of work, with more and more of us working in the fuzzy world of information
- Overlaying all this trends is the art of managing and retaining the talent pool in the organization.

Finding talent is not enough if it is not aligned and motivated there is possibility that the talent pool is going to erode in the course of time. In 1997, McKinsey study coined the term War for talent. Now in the new millennium we find ourselves in the talent age- which means either you are performing beyond expectations or you are out of the industry irrespective of the stage or the level you are in. Successful companies either articulate or intuitively focused on three outcomes:

1. The identification, selection ,development and retention of the extraordinarily talented individuals/super performers .Super performers are a very small group of individuals who have demonstrated superior accomplishments ,have inspired others to attain superior accomplishments ,and who embody the core competencies and values of the organization .Their loss or absence severely retards organization growth because of their disproportionately powerful impact on current and future organization performance .

2. The identification and development of high quality replacements for a small number of positions designated as a key to current and future organizations' success. Gaps in replacement activities for key positions are highly disruptive, costly and destructive to the organization.

3. The classification of and investment in each employee based on his/her actual and/or potential for adding value to the organization .The employee group can be classified into different

categories as follows : the **super performers** who perform beyond expectation, the **performers** who exceed expectation in marginality, the **solid citizens** who meet the expectation or in other words they only do what is expected of them and there are also a group of **misfits** ,those employees who are below organizational expectations . Poor allocation of work, compensation and training and development resources can lead to unwanted turnover and morale and performance problems, particularly in super performers and performer groups.

At the heart of any successful activity lies a competence or a skill. In today's competitive world it is becoming particularly important to build on the competitive activities in business. There has been much thinking about business strategy over the last three decades, particularly regarding what competencies a business needs to have in order to compete in a specific environment. Top management has been identifying corporate core competencies and has been working to establish them throughout the organization. Human resource development (HRD) builds competency based models that drive business results.

As a highly populous democracy and an important emerging economy, India is seeking to modernize and transform its institutions without sacrificing its commitment to economic progress .With new privatization and globalization policies of the Indian government, India's work organizations have to undergo transformations in their HRM systems. Also in view of globalization and higher expectations from customers, in the next decade, organizations' performance will witness unparalleled pressures. The organizations will have to constantly innovate to stay in the market and create value for their customers. Therefore, the focus is on understanding the elements of performance that are more valuable than others and the steps organizations can take to motivate and reward their employees for success.

Whatever be the business or activity ,every organization's major challenge today is define, discover and deploy talent of every kind .To achieve this every organization must focus on talent related processes and capabilities which needs to be aligned and integrated so that they are working towards the same end. It begins with defining talent needs and mapping the competencies available within the organization. This identification of the competencies will further enable the organization to utilize their talent pool better and also help in identifying the gaps in the competencies. The identification of competencies helps in integrating all possible options and sources to discover talent and then developing and deploying talent in the right place at the right time.

1.2 Relevance of the study:

As workforce demographics change and the labor pool shrinks, the competition for talent is increasing. Attracting, hiring and retaining top talent is now critical to a company's success. Companies that effectively manage talent can not only achieve bottom line savings on employee-related costs such as hiring and turnover, but also can drive powerful top-line results as well. By aligning their sourcing activities with corporate objectives, organizations can ensure that they have the

14

right employees to execute and help the organization achieve its goals. For many organizations, however, talent management exists as a series of fragmented processes with little connection to overall corporate goals and objectives. Without that connection, companies are missing an opportunity to strengthen their human capital and are putting themselves at a strategic disadvantage in the marketplace.

Competency mapping can play a significant role in recruiting and retaining people as it gives a more accurate analysis of the job requirements, the candidate's capability, of the difference between the two, and the development and training needs to bridge the gaps. As far as meeting an individual's career aspirations are concerned, once the organization gives an employee the perspective of what is required from him to reach a particular position, it drives him to develop the competencies for the same. "Competencies enable individuals to identify and articulate what they offer-regardless of the (usually misfit) job they happen to have at the time-so that their organization (current or future) can see, value and utilize what capability is actually available," says Martin.

Lynette D'Silva, manager, learning & development, HR, Zensar Technologies,(1997) points out that competency mapping helps identify the success criteria (i.e. behavioral standards of performance excellence) required for individuals to be successful in their roles. It helps to:

- Support specific and objective assessment of their strengths, and specify targeted areas for professional development.

- Provide development tools and methods for enhancing their skills.

- Provide the basis for a more objective dialogue with their manager or team about performance, development, and career-related issues.

Therefore, if organizations select competent people, nurture a competency culture and retain successful people, then there is a good chance to create organizational success. So competency becomes the simple basis upon which all the processes are integrated.

1.3 Objectives:

The study has been conducted with the main objective of understanding the practices of competency mapping and its relevance in talent management in IT based organizations. The analysis pertains to the following specific objectives:

1. To analyze various competencies and its role in talent management;

2. To understand talent management practices in select companies;

3. To establish association between competency mapping and talent management

4. To study the relationship between talent management practices and employee engagement.

1.4 Scope of the study

As the software industry is bouncing back after a long recession, human resource managers are gearing up for another round of hectic activity. Both the boom and the recession in the industry have put a lot of stress on HR managers to manage and retain their talent pool. There was lot of talk about a proper mechanism to develop individuals and build competence.

As such the present study includes IT companies based at Hyderabad which has adopted talent management practices in the organizations. These companies are known to have best practices in the talent management practices and by adopting the practices of competency mapping in different forms and adopting talent management practices in the organization.

The study focuses on software engineers and HR managers as the talent management practices have impact both on HR managers as well as software engineers who are a part and parcel of talent management system.

1.5 Hypotheses:

H1: The employees of the IT companies significantly hold similar views on the role of preferred competencies as elements of competency mapping.

H2: The employees of the IT companies significantly hold similar views on the role of HR interventions in talent management practices.

H3: Competency mapping effectively contributes to Talent Management practices.

H4 : Effective talent management practices ensures that both the HR and the non HR employees to align with the vision and mission of the organization and it creates an element of excitement to attend to their work.

1.6 Methodology:

Research design:

This study is basically built upon live practices and outcomes in select IT firms in Hyderabad. Essentially a descriptive research design is being used to study and analyze the live cases of competency mapping practices and the resulting outcomes in the select organizations. The various factors of organizational productivity like – talent management(TM) and their association with the competency mapping practices have been substantially analyzed and results have been presented.

Sampling:

There exists two interesting paradoxes in the IT Industry- The proactiveness in adopting and practicing the latest HR practices and second being the highest attrition rate in the IT industry. This makes this study more apt to understand the reasons behind this paradox as well as to find out the role of competency mapping and its degree of association with the various talent management strategies. For the purpose of the study the researcher has taken a sample from the select IT companies which have been practicing the competency mapping procedure as well as who have the talent management approach in their human resources department.

The survey was conducted in two folds:

Primary data collection

Firstly, by circulating questionnaires to the human resources managers as well as the role holders in these select companies.

Secondly, discussions with the role holders of the company gave insight into the analysis of various results. A sample size of 128 including the HR managers as well as managers and engineers who were role holders were selected from the six major IT software industries like Infosys, Wipro, TCS, Accenture ,HCL and CSC. Necessary interviews were held with concerned officials to analyze on the hypotheses.

The views of the employees of all the IT companies were ascertained on a 10 point scale and the weight age is given as:

1-being the lowest in order of preference to 10 being the highest.

Secondary data collection:

Most of the secondary data was collected from the website of the organization and learning edge forums of IT companies.

Data interpretation and Analysis:

For the purpose of data analysis, the total questionnaire was divided into three clusters (construct variables)

The clusters (construct variables) were:

Competencies and tools for measuring competency mapping

Role of Competency mapping on talent management practices

Impact of talent management practices on employee engagement practices.

First part was analysis of the response on the perception of HR managers as well as software engineers on the role of competency by doing cross tabulation of HR managers and technical persons.

The second part of the analysis was based on factor analysis conducted on the part B of the questionnaire which dealt with the role of competency mapping on the talent management practices.

The third part of the analysis is based on the regression analysis of various competencies on talent management practices.

The last part is based on cross tab for understanding role of talent management on various employee engagement practices.

1.7 organization of the thesis

The thesis is divided into six chapters.

Chapter-1- presents the overview of the study, relevance, objectives and methodology adopted to conduct it.

Chapter II- discusses the theoretical framework and review of literature is related to competency mapping, talent management, performance management and employee engagement has been undertaken to develop a perspective for the research undertaken and find out the gaps in the literature.

Chapter III profile of various Indian IT firms.

Chapter IV deals with talent management practices in the IT firms.

Chapter V analyses the perceptions of the HR personnel and engineers on talent management practices and interpretation of the data collected.

Chapter VI The last chapter recapitulates the findings and the scope for future research.

Limitations of the study:

Data collection was very difficult in software firms especially the HR managers did not wish to reveal their companies best practices by filling up various questionnaires.

They expressed their inability to fill up the questionnaire in written format .Employees have the fear of disclosing their company's information. Questionnaire was very lengthy to fill and send it across within the specified time limit.

Secondary data collection was more difficult than primary data collection. Because all the data are available in company's intranet, which only the employees could access. Therefore most of the secondary data was collected from the annual reports of the organization.

References:

Berger, L.A. (2004c). **Four steps to creating a talent management system**. In D.R Berger &L.A. Berger . The Talent management handbook, ch.2 .New York : McGraw Hill.

Boyle, S.J. Fullerton and R.wood (1995). **'Do assessment/development centers use optimum evaluation procedures? A survey of practice in UK organizations'** International journal of selection and assessment, pp.132-40

Cooper, Kenneth carlton (2000) .**Effective competency modeling and reporting,** New york : AMA publications.

Dubois D. (1993) **competency based performance improvement, A strategy for organizational change,** Amherst, Mass: HRD press.

Hamel,Gary and C.K prahalad (1994) .**Competing for the future**, Boston: Harvard Business school .

McKinsey study (1997) **The War for Talent,** Report-October

Martin .,et.al(2000) **competency mapping –its impact on organizational success.**

CHAPTER -2

COMPETENCY MAPPING AND TALENT MANAGEMENT - THEORITICAL FRAMEWORK

- ➤ **DEFINITIONS**

- ➤ **THEORITICAL FRAMEWORK OF COMPETENCY MAPPING AND COMPETENCY MAPPING MODELS.**

- ➤ **THEORITICAL FRAMEWORK OF TALENT MANAGEMENT SYSTEM**

- ➤ **STUDIES ON COMPETENCY MAPPING**

- ➤ **DETAIL DESCRIPTION:**
  TALENT MANAGEMENT SYSTEM
  COMPETENCY MAPPING MODELS

- ➤ **TALENT MANAGEMENT AND COMPETENCY MAPPING**

2. COMPETENCY MAPPING: the first step towards talent management

The performance and productivity of the organization depends mostly on the quality of their human resource. For obvious economic and business reasons, organizations have always been concerned about the growth, competence and retention of its people. Hence employee development and talent management are essential elements of any strategic human capital management program. Thus the numbers shifted from 'numbers' to 'quality 'and from recruitment to retention. Many organizational human resource practices play a dominant role in building employee competence and commitment.

While studying about the role that competency mapping can play across different HR processes an interesting thought that arises is: Are we really managing talent? Are we really aware of our talents? Are we hired for the talents that we have or the competencies required for doing a particular job? Are all the HR processes integrated to competency mapping processes? Competence is defined as an amalgamation of knowledge, skills, ability, attitude, values, trait ,motives and self concept (Naqvi,2009)

2.1 Definition of competency mapping:

Competency mapping is a process an organization uses to identify and describe competencies that are most critical to success in a work situation or work role.

Competency mapping can be defined as a process through which one assesses and determines one's strengths as an individual worker and in some cases, as part of an organization. The individual's competencies can be measure in terms of performance standard established in the job profile itself. Thought the definition refer to individual competencies of the employees, organizations in today's scenario do map the competencies using different strategies; so that they can attract and maintain the talent within the organization.

Competency –based approaches have developed quite rapidly since their introduction 25 years ago. David C.McClleland is credited with introducing the idea of "competency" into the human resource literature. In response to a growing dissatisfaction with intelligence testing traditional job analytic approaches to personnel selection, the competence-testing movement was described by **McClelland** by study of foreign-service officers. **"Testing for Competence Rather than Intelligence"**- **McClelland's** landmark paper has continued to stir debate even after a quarter century. Competency-based approaches gained popularity and acceptance within the human resources community through the work of McClelland and his associates, particularly **Richard Boyatzis**, past president at the McBer and Company. Boyatzis is credited with popularizing the term in his book "The Competent Manager **(Woodruff**, 1991)".

Boyatzis suggested that a competency was a combination of a motive, trait, skill, aspect of one's self-image or social role, or a body of relevant knowledge. In other words a competency is any characteristic of an individual that might be related to successful performance.

Klein's (1996) offered one more definition which diverges the most from the others by suggesting that competencies are a collection of observable behaviours, or behavioural indicators. These Behavioural indicators are grouped according to a central theme, which then becomes the competency. Klein suggests that the behaviors underlie the competency; this is contrary to other definitions, which suggest that competencies underlie behaviors.

Woodruffe raised the issue of distinguishing between competence and competency and proposed that competence is performance criterion while competencies are behaviours driving the competence.

More recently, **Rowe** raised the same issue and discusses competence in terms of a skill and a standard of performance and defines competency as a behaviour needed to achieve competence. This is similar to Klein's argument that competencies are not psychological constructs thematic groups of demonstrated observable behaviours that discriminate between superior and average performance. These behaviours require no inference, assumptions, or interpretation.

Definitional and boundary delineation issues exist at a number of levels within the competency literature. This confusion exists primarily for two reasons: difference between countries and differences arising from pedagogical theories of how people learn. The former is largely historically determined and reflects differences in relationships between education and labour market in different countries. Pedagogical differences, on the other hand relate to issues of how behavioralists, cognitivists and constructivists theorists consider notions of competency. Levels of definitional confusion and differences in perspective exists. Differences in the context of competency and competence. However the gurus in this field feel very strongly that it is necessary todistinguish between competence (hence competences) and the competency (hence competencies). Disaster, they claim, will overtake anyone who confuses the two terms. Whether this is true or not, the received view of the distinction between them should be understood.

Competence Defined.

Competences describe what people need to be able to do to perform a job well or how the required results are achieved. They are about stripping the jobs down into their component parts and linking together the two basic elements of performance- what is to be done and to what standard.

Competences are concerned with effect rather than effort and with the output rather than inputs. Some people adopt what may be called the output model of competence, based on the proposition that the concept of competence is meaningful only when it is demonstrated that competences have been applied effectively.

Competences can be defined at three levels:

1. *Core competences*- these apply to the organization as a whole. They refer to what the organization

has to be good at doing if it is to succeed. This could include such factors as customer orientation, producing high quality goods or delivering high quality services, innovation, adding value through the effective use of resources and managing costs.Core competences can be linked with "balanced score card"of measuring organizational success as developed by **Kaplan and Norton.**

2. *Generic Competences*-these are shared by a group of similar jobs- financial accountants, system analysts, team leaders etc. They cover the aspects of work that they have in common, and define the shared capabilities required to deliver the results they are expected to achieve.

3. *Role-specific competences* – these are unique to a particular role. They define the special tasks that they have to be able to do; in addition to any generic competences they may share with other people carrying out broadly similar roles.

Competency defined

Competency is defined as referring to the dimensions of behaviour that lie behind competent performance. These are often called behavioural competencies, because they are intended to describe **how people behave** when they carry out their role well. When defined as competencies, these behaviours can be classified in such areas as the following: Understanding what needs to be done-critical reasoning,

strategic capability, business know- how Getting the job done- achievement drive, a pro-active approach, confidence, control, flexibility, concern for effectiveness, persuasion, and influence.Taking people with you – motivation, interpersonal skills, concern for output, persuasion, and influence.

Competencies are behaviors that individuals demonstrate when undertaking job-relevant tasks effectively within a given organizational context.

Spencer, director of research and technology worldwide at Hay/McBer, has been a font of data and wisdom about the **competencies of star performance** and the value of stars for organizational performance in co authored classic – **Competence at   work: Models for Superior Performance.**

McClelland's 1973 paper "Testing for competence Rather than Intelligence" shifted the concentration from just intelligence. He **argued** that **traditional academic aptitude, school grades and advanced credentials simply did not predict how well people would perform on the job or whether they would succeed in life.** Instead, he proposed that a set of specific competencies including empathy, self-discipline and initiative distinguished the most successful from those who were merely good to keep their jobs. His paper launched an entirely new approach to the measure of excellence, one that assesses people's competencies in terms of specific job they are doing. A "**competence** "in this tradition, **is a personal trait or set of habits that leads to more effective or superior job performance** --- in other words, **an ability that adds clear economic value to the efforts of a person on the job.**

The terms "competence" and "competency" are attributed to multiple meanings depending on the context and the perspective adopted .Although all these definitions look different on their own way, they have the following things in common

1. Competencies are Knowledge, Skill, Attitude and Other Characteristics such as personal motives, traits that are observable and measurable.
2. The underlying attributes must be observable and measurable
3. They should clearly differentiate superior performers from others for a given position.

There are two levels of job competence and two kinds of job competence models. One assesses the **threshold competencies,** those that people need in order to get the job done. These are the minimal skills needed to carry out the tasks associated with a given position. Most organizational competence models fit into this category.

The other kind of job competence model describes **distinguishing competencies,** the capabilities that set star performers apart from average ones. These are the competencies people already in a job need in order to perform superbly.

At a simplistic level, **competency models** seek to identify the ideal combination of skills, knowledge, attitudes and experience, the possession of which enables employees to become high performers with the potential to add value to the organization.

APPROACHES TO DEFINE COMPETENCY

Competency can be defined through three approaches. They are-
1. Worker- oriented
2. Work-oriented
3. Multidimensional
Worker-oriented definitions:

The behavioural characteristics of an individual that are causally related to effective and/ or superior performance in a job. This means that there is evidence that indicates that possession of the characteristic precedes and leads to effective and /or superior performance on the job.(**Boyatzis,1982**

An underlying characteristic of an individual that is casually related to criterion referenced effective and/or superior performance on the job. (**Spencer and Spencer, 1993)**

A high performance or H-competency is a relatively stable set of behaviours, which produces superior workgroup performance in more complex organizational environments.

Work-oriented definitions

Occupational competence- the ability to perform the activities within an occupation or function to the level of performance in the employment. (**Management Charter Initiative, 1990**)

The ability to perform the activities within an occupation (**Nordhaug and Gronhaug, 1994**)

An action behavior or outcome which the people should be able to demonstrate (**Training Standards Agency**)

Multidimensional definitions

The ability to apply knowledge, understanding, practical and thinking skills to achieve effective performance to the standards required in the employment. This includes solving problems and being sufficiently flexible to meet the changing demands. (**NCVQ, 1997**)

The skills, knowledge and understanding, qualities and attributes, sets of values, beliefs and attitudes which lead to effective managerial performance in a given context, situation or role (**Woodall and Winstanley, 1998**)

The conceptualizations of **Boyatzis and Spencer and Spencer** are predominantly **input-based and worker oriented and focuses on person related variables** that individuals bring to the job. Another perspective argues that competency options should be **output based or work-oriented** and considers outputs associated with effective performance. Multi-dimensional definitions tend to draw on the **best of both approaches**.

CONCEPTUALISATIONS OF THE FUNCTION OF COMPETENCY

The literature reveals that competencies are defined in terms of three distinct perspectives: competencies as individual characteristics; competencies as characteristics of organizations; and the notion those competencies as a tool to structure and facilitate communication between education and labor market.

Competencies as characteristics of individual

This perspective argues that competencies are essentially related to the characteristics of the individuals. The most important difference in emphasis here relates these characteristics can be learned or whether they are innate. The dominant view is to emphasize the trainability dimension of competency. A more traditional view emphasizes that competence and competencies are given. They argue that characteristics such as emotion, attitude and cognition originate from innate abilities and therefore cannot be learned; they can only be developed. A related perspective here is the notion that competencies do not relate to capacities, but instead to the willingness and ability of the employee to use his/ her capacities in specific situations.

Competencies as characteristics of the organization:

This perspective takes as a starting point the view that human competencies are one of the resources available to the organizations. This origin of this notion of competencies can be attributed to the work of **Prahlad and Hamel (1990)**, who analyzed the competitiveness of the organization and attributed it to the core competency of the organization.They postulated that organizations can possess unique clusters of factors

that allow the firm to be competitive and human capital is one of those factors. The resource-based view conceptualizes the organization as a collection of competencies and draws attention to the issues of learning, including knowledge accumulation and experience.

A further consideration here is whether competency frameworks should be based on current organizational priorities or should be based on current organizational priorities or should be future oriented and derived from organization's vision statement. Such a dualistic choice is dependent on whether one views competencies as a tool enabling organizational change through direct communication with employees or whether one

believes that competencies should be used as a behavioural modelling mechanism to deal with current organizational problems and difficulties.

Competency as a mode of discourse between education and labor market:

This perspective argues that competences represent a tool to improve communication in education and labor market. It conceptualizes competencies as a framing device- a model of discourse- and it in no way attempt to specify of what competencies consist. This perspective is commonly advocated in Continental Europe and to a certain extent in the UK. The need for such a discourse arises from two sets of developments.

The first relates to the changing nature of the labor market with its emphasis on flexibility, employability, the potential for obsolescence of knowledge and skills and the emergence of knowledge as a production factor. These changes in the requirements of the labor market in turn influenced views on how people are educated and trained in educational institutions.

Organizations describe, or map competencies using one or more of the following four strategies:
1. Organization-Wide (often called "core competencies" or those required for organization success)
2. Job Family or Business Unit Competency Sets
3. Position-Specific Competency Sets
4. Competency Sets defined Relative to the Level of Employee Contribution (i.e. Individual Contributor, Manager, or Organizational Leader)

it has been obsered that hard work, sincerity, knowledge, intelligence alone does not enable a person to become a star performer in his/her job altogether; there are some underlying traits coupled with the technical expertise which makes a person excel in his job. These underlying traits which plays a significant role in the individuals success has been called as competencies. Organizational psychologists have refined this understanding and formalized it as competency mapping. It has emerged as a powerful tool which has brought in significant improvement in the performance standards of the individual as well as the organization. Organization has been able to utilize their talent by understanding the competencies and giving the right person the right job. This enables the employees to put forward their best foot and involve themselves in the work processes which results in excellent output.

Hogg (1993) defined competency as "competencies are the characteristics of a manager that lead to the demonstration of skills and abilities, which result in effective performance within an occupational area".

Spencer and Spencer (1993) in their work *competence at Work* have defined competency as an underlying characteristic of an individual that is casually related to criterion –referenced effecting and/or superior performance in a job situation. An underlying characteristic itself means that it is that characteristic which is hidden but has a significant impact on the performance. Competencies are components of a job which are reflected in behavior that are observable in a workplace. Therefore in a workplace we can segregate the type of competencies required- for example those competencies which are highly essential for the job and it is essential to bring in the minimum effectiveness in the job, but does distinguish from superior performer to average performer. There are other competencies which can be listed for the job profile which can differentiate an average performer from a superior performer. Organization therefore has to craft these competencies for the job profile in its organization.

Competency mapping juxtaposes two sets of data. One set is based on organizational workflow and processes. It starts with the clear articulation of workflow and processes, including all quality and quantity requirements, inputs and outputs decision criteria and most important, internal and external customer requirements. For each step in each process, specific performance requirements are identified with all associated metrics and expectations. The other set of data is based on individual and group performance capabilities. It is collected through the utilization of a variety of assessment tools and procedures (which may be a robust 360 degree feedback process) to assess the extent to which individuals and groups can consistently demonstrate overtime the competencies required to meet the expectations. As a result of competency mapping all HR processes starting from Talent induction to talent maintenance to talent retention yield better results

Over the past 10 years, human resource and organizational development professionals have generated a lot of interest in the notion of competencies as a key element and measure of human performance.

Competencies are becoming a frequently-used and written-about vehicle for organizational applications such as:

Defining the factors for success in jobs (i.e., work) and work roles within the organization
Assessing the current performance and future development needs of persons holding jobs and roles
Mapping succession possibilities for employees within the organization
Assigning compensation grades and levels to particular jobs and roles
Selecting applicants for open positions, using competency-based interviewing techniques

In studying the competency area, one is immediately struck by the lack of uniform definitions terminology, and the resulting misunderstanding. Competency for a job can be defined as a set of human attributes that enable an employee to meet and exceed of expectations of internal as well as external customers and stakeholders. The new oxford dictionary defines competence as the power, ability, capacity to do, for a task. Oxford further states that the competence and competency are synonymous as are competences and competencies. It becomes readily apparent that if these two great dictionaries differ with respect

There are various definitions of competency but most of them refer to competence. Hogg (1993) defined competency as the characteristics of a manager that lead to the demonstration of skills and abilities which result in effective performance within an occupational area. Competency also embodies the capacity to transfer skills and abilities from one area to another.

McClelland (1973), who is touted as the "Father" of competency research, described competencies as broad collection of knowledge, skills, abilities and characteristics which included values like ethics and integrity; cognitive skills, such as thinking and problem solving; interpersonal skills like communicating and listening; embracing diversity as exemplified by tolerance and respect; and change management as demonstrated by strategic planning and risk taking. Spencer and Spencer (1993), used McClelland's work as a foundation and define competency as an underlying characteristic of an individual that is casually related to criterion referenced effective and/or superior performance in a job situation".

An analysis of the definition reveals:

- Competency is an underlying characteristic of a person. This means that it is a fairly deep and enduring part of a person's personality and can predict behavior in a wide variety of situations and job tasks.
- Competencies lead to demonstration of skills and abilities. Therefore competency must be demonstrated and hence must be observable .It must not be inferred or extrapolated.
- Causally related means that a competency causes or predicts behavior and performance.
- Criterion – Referenced means that the competency actually predicts or does something well or poorly as measured on specific criterion or standard. (p.9)

- Competencies must lead to effective performance. This means that the performance of a person with competency must be significantly better than that of a person without it. Competency therefore refers to behavior, differentiating success from merely doing the job.
- Competency also embodies the capacity to transfer skills and abilities from one area to another .A sales person may be able to deliver his sales pitch flawlessly but may be tongue -tied elsewhere. He lacks the competency of communication. Thus communication cannot be restricted to single job alone but the person must be able to carry them along. This dispels the need to differentiate between generic and functional competencies since this part of the definition excludes functional competence, which is associated with a particular job.

Another relevant definition which is widely accepted among human resources specialists in the corporate environments , "is an underlying characteristics of a person which results in effective and/or superior performance on the job" (Klemp 1980).A more detailed definition synthesized from the suggestions of several hundred experts in human resources development who attended a conference on the subject of competencies in Johannesburg in 1995 ,is "a cluster of related knowledge,skillsand attitudes that affects a major part of one's job (a role of responsibility) that correlates with performance on the job, that can be measured against well accepted standards and can be measured against well accepted standards and that can be improved via training and development.(parry1996).

Sanghi (2007) built upon Spencer and Spencer (1993) concept and postulated that there are five types of competency characteristics

These are:

- Motives- the things a person consistently thinks about or wants and that which causes action. Motives 'drive, direct or select' behavior towards certain actions or goals and away from others.
- Traits –physical characteristics and consistent responses to situations or information.
- Self concept- A person's attitudes, values or self image.
- Knowledge- information a person has in specific content areas.
- Skill- The ability to perform a certain physical or mental task.

   Knowledge and skill competencies tend to be visible and relatively 'on the surface' characteristics of the people .Self concept, trait and motive competencies are more hidden, deeper and central to personality.

   Surface knowledge and skill competencies are relatively easy to develop; training is the most effective way to secure these employee abilities. Core motive and trait competencies at the base of the personality iceberg are more difficult to assess and develop; it is the most cost effective to select these characteristics.

   It has been a general observation that hard work, sincerity, knowledge, intelligence alone does not make a person a star performer in his profession. there are other factors that help an individual to excel in his/her job .All of us have observed that during our school days the top scorer of the class need be the most intelligent or hardworking student of the class. We have also observed that the top scorer of the objective type of tests need be the top scorer in descriptive type of tests. Thus set of human qualities /attributes that makes a person star performer for a particular activity defines the competency for that activity.

Good managers are generally aware of the qualities that are necessary to perform a job effectively and they make use of their knowledge and skill to identify and train their subordinates in those qualities or attributes. Organizational psychologists have studied and refined understanding and converted it into formal process thus making it available for business application.

In organizational or business context, competency required for a particular job depends on many factors. The factors include social culture, nature of business, business environment, organizational culture and work environment, organizational structure, duties and responsibilities, nature of processes and assigned activities, attitudes and motives of colleagues, superiors and subordinates .some of these factors may change with time and thus changing competency requirements for the same job position in the organization.

Competency for any job position at a particular time is a unique set and as organization has many different job positions, managing many such sets is a difficult task. Hence for the purpose of HR management, the job competency is divided into elemental competencies.

Elemental or task competency is an ability to do a particular type of task. Job consists of many different types of tasks, thus requiring different elemental competencies. The elemental competencies can be standardized, precisely differentiated, developed into a model across the organization, and are easier to identify, study, understand, map, assess and develop.

In a like manner, the corporate leadership council (2006) defines competencies as a set of behaviors that encompasses skills, knowledge, abilities and personal attributes that taken together to critical successful work accomplishment (p.1).

Vandenbossche and Buyens (2000) organize competencies into three levels. The levels are:

- Individual. Competencies are the potential knowledge and skills of the employees; their qualification and capabilities.

- Organizational. Competency is the specific manner in which various resources are combined; the mutual combination of knowledge and skills of employees with other resources such as knowledge systems, routines, procedures and production technologies.

- Strategic. Competencies mean building and retaining competitive advantage by a unique combination of knowledge, skills ,structures ,technologies and processes.(p.292)

Davidson (2008) identified behavior, knowledge and motivation as types of competencies. He tied all of these competency types of job performance. In contrast , Sanghi (2007) contends that: competencies

29

are components of a job which are reflected in behavior that are observable in the work place . The common elements most frequently mentioned are knowledge, skills, abilities, aptitudes, personal suitability behavior and impact on performance at work....The criteria for competency are superior performance and effective performance. Only some competencies can predict performance. (p.12)

Kahane (2008) takes the middle ground and states, "competencies provide standards and a road map for effective performance" (p.71). He goes on to challenge organizations to use competencies to gain a competitive advantage. Kahane's view has been argued by Prahalad and Hamel(1990) who relates :

The most powerful way to prevail in global competition is still invisible to many companies. During the 1980's, top executives were judged on their ability to restructure, declutter and delayer their corporations. In the 1990s, they would be judged on their ability to identify ,cultivate and exploit the core competencies that make growth possible-indeed ,they'll have to rethink the concept of the corporation itself.(p.79)

Sparrow and Bognanno (1993) also supported the notion of competencies in the context of competitive advantage. They postulated that the strategic change in organizations during the 1990s reinforced the increased use of competencies. The realization that success in the new competitive environment depends largely on the ability to learn faster than the competitors and subsequently reconstruct and adapt the organization ,has focused attention on internal resources and the capabilities of the organization, such as employees' competencies, and the integration of human resources policies and practices with business strategies.(p.310)

Meyer and Semark (1996) recognized the lack of uniformity related to the meaning and application of competencies, sought to present a conceptual frame work for competencies in their work. Like their fellow researchers, these organizational scientists saw competencies as essential forces in individual, job related, and organizational contexts. In addition, in congruence, with the theories of Sparrow and Bognanno(1993) and kahane(2008), Meyer and Semark see competency as " a central issue for managers seeking competitive advantage."(p.2) the conceptual framework proposed by these authors consists of four categories and each of the categories is linked to an external driver. The categories are: 1) national competencies; 2) organizational competencies; 3) occupational competencies and 4) generic individual competencies (Meyer& Semark,1996).

Boyatzis(2008) in his treatise introducing 21st century competencies may object to his international colleagues' portrayal of the American approach to competencies as one –dimensional as he describes competencies within the context of cognition ,emotional intelligence and social intelligence. He presents competencies as behavioral manifestation of talent; as key component of a holistic theory of personality; and as objects that can be developed. This latter item is highlighted as "one of the benefits of the competency, or behavioral approach to talent is that we enter a domain of human talent that can be developed in adulthood" (p.10).

In summary ,competencies are compilations of individual's knowledge ,skills, capabilities and motives which can be utilized effectively within a particular job when the organization associates job expectations to business needs, and defines job expectations within the context of individual competencies. They are the keys to talent management allowing employers to focus on training and development, career pathing, skills inventory and assessment, succession planning, performance management, recruiting, risk analysis, resource allocation and compensation programs (Pallera, 2008). The definition of job expectations and association of such expectations to business needs is performed within the frame work of competency management models. As an introduction to such models Boyatzis (1982) relates: An individual's competencies are necessary, but not sufficient for effective performance in a job. A job competency is an underlying characteristic of a person in that it may be a motive, trait, and skill, aspect of one's self image, or a social role, or a body of knowledge which he or she uses. The existence and possession of these characteristics may or may not be known to the person. In this sense, the characteristics may or may not be known to the person. In this sense, the characteristics may be unconscious aspects of the person (i.e. he or she is not aware of them or is unable to articulate or describe them). A person's set of competencies reflect his or her capability. They are describing what he or she can do ,not necessarily what he or she does, nor does all the time regardless of the situation and the setting.

Boyatzis's concept of the relationship between job and individual competencies within an organizational context. This basic contingency theory of performance is the basis for competency. Optimum job performance happens when an individual's capability or talent is congruent with the requirements of the job within the organization (Boyatzis, 1982). This model was consistent with the Information technology business unit's concept of competency management in that the company also focused on the importance of the optimal interactions among the individual's competencies, the job requirements and the organization current and future business objectives.

Competency Management models

Competency management has been defined as the identification and closure of competency gaps in human resources necessary to implement strategic business unit decisions. It is part of people strategy, and talent management (wiethaus, 2005). It provides a systematic method to align individual performance to business strategy and goals while allowing an organization to develop core and functional competencies in order to help the company remain competitive both in the present and in the future (pallera,2008). Competencies it can be argued should arise from business needs. Lucia and Lepsinger(1999) enumerate a number of business needs addressed by competency models . These needs are :

- Clarifying job and work expectations
- Hiring the best available people
- Maximizing productivity
- Enhancing the 360 feedback process
- Adapting to change
- Aligning behavior with organizational strategies and values
- Supports Human resource Management (HRM) systems

The provision of clearly defined and consistently measured business goal –oriented competencies is critical for organizational success (Jones, 2006). A competency model describes the combination of knowledge, skills and characteristics needed to effectively perform a role in an organization and used as a human resource tool for selection, training and development, appraisal and succession planning. Identifying and mapping these competencies is rather complex. Skills can range from highly concrete proficiencies like the ability to operate a particular machine or to write a sentence, to far less tangible capabilities such as the ability to think strategically or to influence others.Sanghi (2007).

Kahane(2008) couples business strategies with competency management and states: " High performance competency management strategies at the organizational level only work if they are owned by senior management, embodied in corporate policy and managed on a daily basis".

Reasons given for companies introducing competency management are; performance, culture change, training and development, recruitment and selection, business objectives/competitiveness, career/succession planning, skill analysis, flexibility, clarity of role, and integrating HR strategy (Vandenbossche&Buyens,2000).

The benefits of competency model in the areas of HRM include: Sanghi (2007)

1. Hiring the best available people: competency models are highly useful tool to make sure that human resource systems facilitate and support a company's strategic objectives. it increases the likelihood of placing the right people into the right jobs. At the decision level, we look at succession planning to see how many of the people we have hired fall into the high potential box' (Mcillvaine 1998).

2. Productivity maximization: to maintain the same or higher productivity, it is essential that people have the specific skills, knowledge and characteristics required to be effective. By identifying relevant skill gaps, competency models help to ensure that the training and development budget will be spent wisely. competency models also allow for the development of appraisal systems that evaluate people on their use of behaviors and practices that directly contributes to competitiveness ,encouraging both the business and the individual to focus on whatever will have the greatest impact.

3. Enhancing 360 feedback process: The 360 feedback process is being increasingly used in

organizations for development, appraisal and compensation purposes. It involves a collection of perception about an individual's as internal and external customers. Competency models help to ensure that such feedback relates specifically to the competencies crucial to individual or organizational success.

4. Adapting to change: competency models provide a tool for determining exactly what skills are required to meet the different needs of the present and the probable needs of the future.

5. Aligning behavior with organizational strategies and values: A competency models can be an effective way of communicating to the workforce values of the senior management and what people should focus on in their own behavior.

Over the years many different methods of developing competency models have evolved but all of them follow McClelland's lead of determining what leads to superior performance, identifying top performers and finding out what they do. There are two principles which are followed in these models:

- Focus on the superior performers without making an assumption.
- Focus on what they do to perform the given role.

Devisch (1998) also touts competency management as an advantage to the organization and states it provides "a nucleus in the elaboration of an integrated Human resource (HR) and quality management approach . In 2005, a Hewitt associates survey studied 373 united States organizations (Effron, salob& Greenslade, 2005), twenty of these companies were designated "Top 20 companies for leaders" (CLC, 2006). The results of the survey research revealed:

- Leaders integrate competencies into HR processes
- Sixteen percent of companies consider adding competency-based performance management
- Competencies assist managers in strategic workforce planning

Based upon the available literature and Pallera's succinct observation that "A well –implemented competency management program aligns individual and business goals resulting in a more engaged, adaptive and successful workforce" (2008,p.1); it can be argued that competency management models do provide value to an organization, In the next section the development and associated benefits and challenges related to such models will be explored.

Competency management model development:

Four methods of competency management model development will be described. The authors of this methods are Lucia and Lepsinger(1999), and Sanghi(2007), all of the authors underscore the importance of aligning the development process to the business needs ,utilizing best practices as a foundation ,employing the gap analysis to identify developmental opportunities and evaluating and redefining the development process on an ongoing basis.

Rothwell and Lincoln (1999) list three approaches to competency modeling. These approaches are: 1) the borrowed approach; 2) the borrowed and tailored approach; and 3) the tailored approach (Rothwell and Lincoln, 1999, p.99). The borrowed approach is described as the easiest and least expensive approach as it simply borrows an approach from an existing organization without taking into consideration the uniqueness of the adopter. An obvious shortcoming lies in the possibility of the borrowed model not being appropriate for the borrowing of the organization. The tailored approach customizes the competency model based upon the specific organizational requirements. The combination borrowed /tailored approach very simply makes use of the available framework from an existing organization, while customizing the model to the borrower's structure, culture, and resources (human, technical, financial, informational, etc.)

Lucia and Lepsinger (1999) expanded upon these approaches to competency model by delopment by including defined steps and by describing critical elements to a successful competency management program development. This method is aimed at mitigating a number of the potential disadvantages of competency models. The recommended steps are :

1. Determine objectives and scope by
   - Identifying the business needs that the competency models will address,
   - Identifying the jobs ,functions or business units that the model will target,
   - Determining the method for developing the competency model
   - Determining the make-up of the project team.

2. Create an implementation of the goal statement that is :
   - Specific
   - Challenging ,yet realistic
   - Consistent with available resources
   - Consistent with the organizations policies and operating procedures
   - Measurable
   - Inclusive of an expected completion date

3. Develop an action plan which includes :
   - A list of project action steps
   - Identification of potential problems and their likely causes,
   - A list of preventive and contingent actions
   - A communication channel strategy.

4. Identify individuals at various performance levels(pp.51-65

Figure 1 depicts Sanghi's (2007) graphical representation of another competency model development process. This model, is like that of Lucia and Lepsinger, provides step-by step guidance as to how to develop a competency management model.

Figure-2.1 :   Linking HR processes to organizational strategy

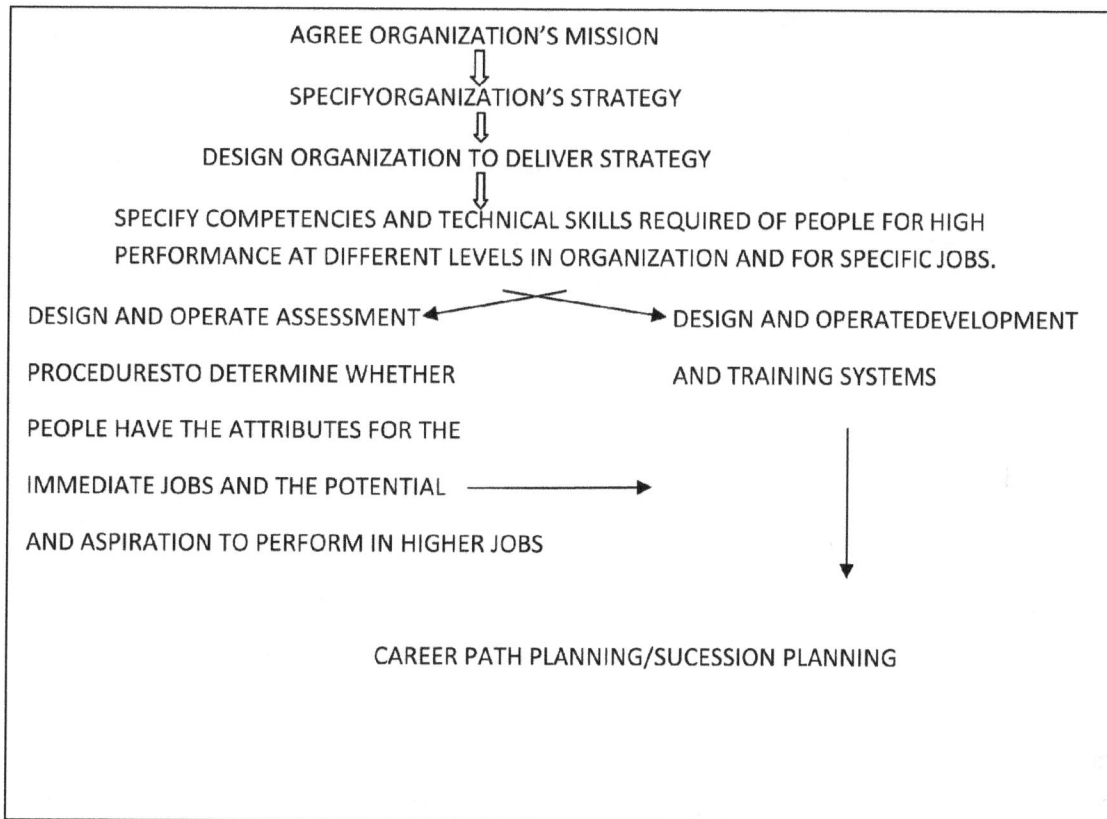

AGREE ORGANIZATION'S MISSION
⇩
SPECIFYORGANIZATION'S STRATEGY
⇩
DESIGN ORGANIZATION TO DELIVER STRATEGY
⇩
SPECIFY COMPETENCIES AND TECHNICAL SKILLS REQUIRED OF PEOPLE FOR HIGH
PERFORMANCE AT DIFFERENT LEVELS IN ORGANIZATION AND FOR SPECIFIC JOBS.

DESIGN AND OPERATE ASSESSMENT ← ╳ → DESIGN AND OPERATEDEVELOPMENT

PROCEDURESTO DETERMINE WHETHER   AND TRAINING SYSTEMS

PEOPLE HAVE THE ATTRIBUTES FOR THE

IMMEDIATE JOBS AND THE POTENTIAL ──────→

AND ASPIRATION TO PERFORM IN HIGHER JOBS

CAREER PATH PLANNING/SUCESSION PLANNING

Source: Seema Sanghi "The Handbook of competency mapping" p.21(2007).

Kanaga (2007) offers some additional guidance regarding competency model development. This organizational scholar recommends that regardless of whether the model is crafted internally or with the support of an outside vendor/consultant a number of perquisites should be considered. These precepts, as he calls them are: "define and support the purpose; take strategic direction into account; employ a rigorous process; focus the selection of the competencies; and revisit and revise the model" (pp.8-10).

Plateau Systems (2006) concurred with kanaga especially when it came to revisiting and revising the model. The steps of competency modeling process are: define your competencies; assign competencies to position; assess individuals according to their competencies; analyze gaps between individuals according to their competencies; analyze gaps between individuals required and actual competency levels; remediate through learning activities; track progress ; and refine the process(p.10

Figure-2.2: COMPETENCY MODELLING STEPS

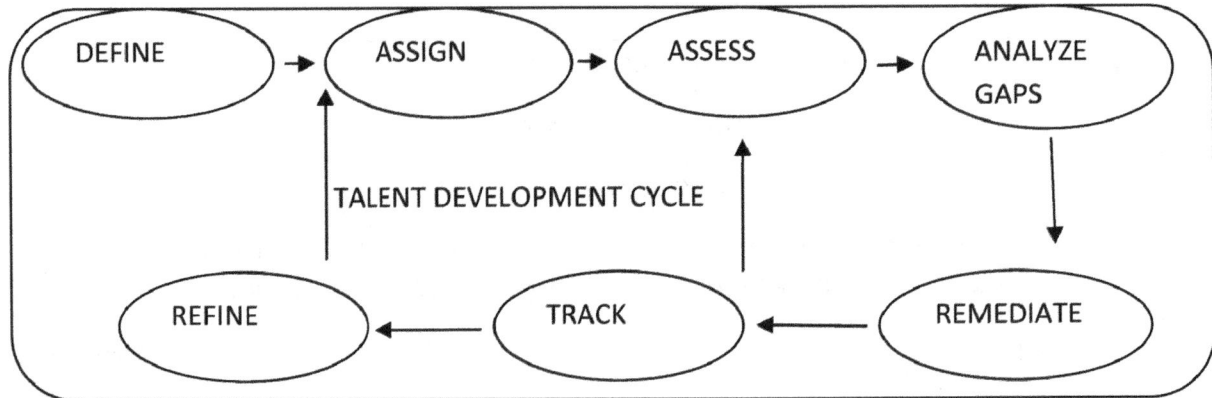

Source: *COMPETENCY MANAGEMENT: THE FOUNDATION FOR TALENT MANAGEMENT* (white paper) written by Plateau Systems ltd., 2006 p.10.

This model described that competency mapping starts with defining competencies for different job positions. Then assigning those competencies to various strata of the organization. Then individuals are communicated these competencies. The employees are then assessed on the competency parameters. Then the gaps in the competency levels are identified and communicated to the individual. The individual employees are tracked through these competencies. In every change in the role profile of the organization it is essential that they revisit the competency dictionary once again to make additions and substractions.

Understanding the shortfalls of competency models is just as important as appreciating the advantages; since the disadvantages will need to be addressed and mitigated throughout the competency management development process.

Various models:

- Job competence Assessment method- this is developed using interviews and observations of outstanding and average performers to determine the competencies that differentiates between them in critical incidents (Dubois1993).

- Modified Job competence method- This also identifies such behavioral differences, but to reduce costs .interviewees provide a written account of critical incidents (ibid.).

- Generic Overlay method- organizations purchase an off the shelf generic competency model for a specific role function(ibid.)

36

- Customized Generic model method- organizations use a tentative list of competencies that are identified internally to aid in their selection of a generic model and then validate it with the input of outstanding and average performers. (ibid.)

- Flexible job competency model method- This seeks to identify the competencies that will be required to perform effectively under different conditions in the future.

- Systems Method- this demands reflecting on not only what exemplary performers do now, or what they do overall, but also behaviors that may be important for the future. (Linkage, inc.1997).

- Accelerated competency systems method- This places the focus on the competencies that specifically support the production of output, such as an organization's products, services or information(ibid.)

The process used to develop a model must be straight forward and easy to implement. The final product must have immediate practical application, commitment and buy-in for those who will be expected to implement or change their behavior based on it. The development process should include a step to ensure that the behaviors described in the model correlate with effectiveness on the job.

The Lancaster model of managerial competencies:

The Lancaster model of managerial competencies is a universal management framework developed by Burgoyne and Stuart (1976) and first published in personnel review. The 11 qualities are separated into three groups and represent three levels: the first level forms the foundation level and comprises of two kinds of basic knowledge and information a manger may need to use in decision making and action taking. The second level focuses more on the skills and attributes of the successful manager. The third level focuses on the meta-qualities which lead to the success of the manager.

Figure-2.3: The Lancaster model of managerial competencies

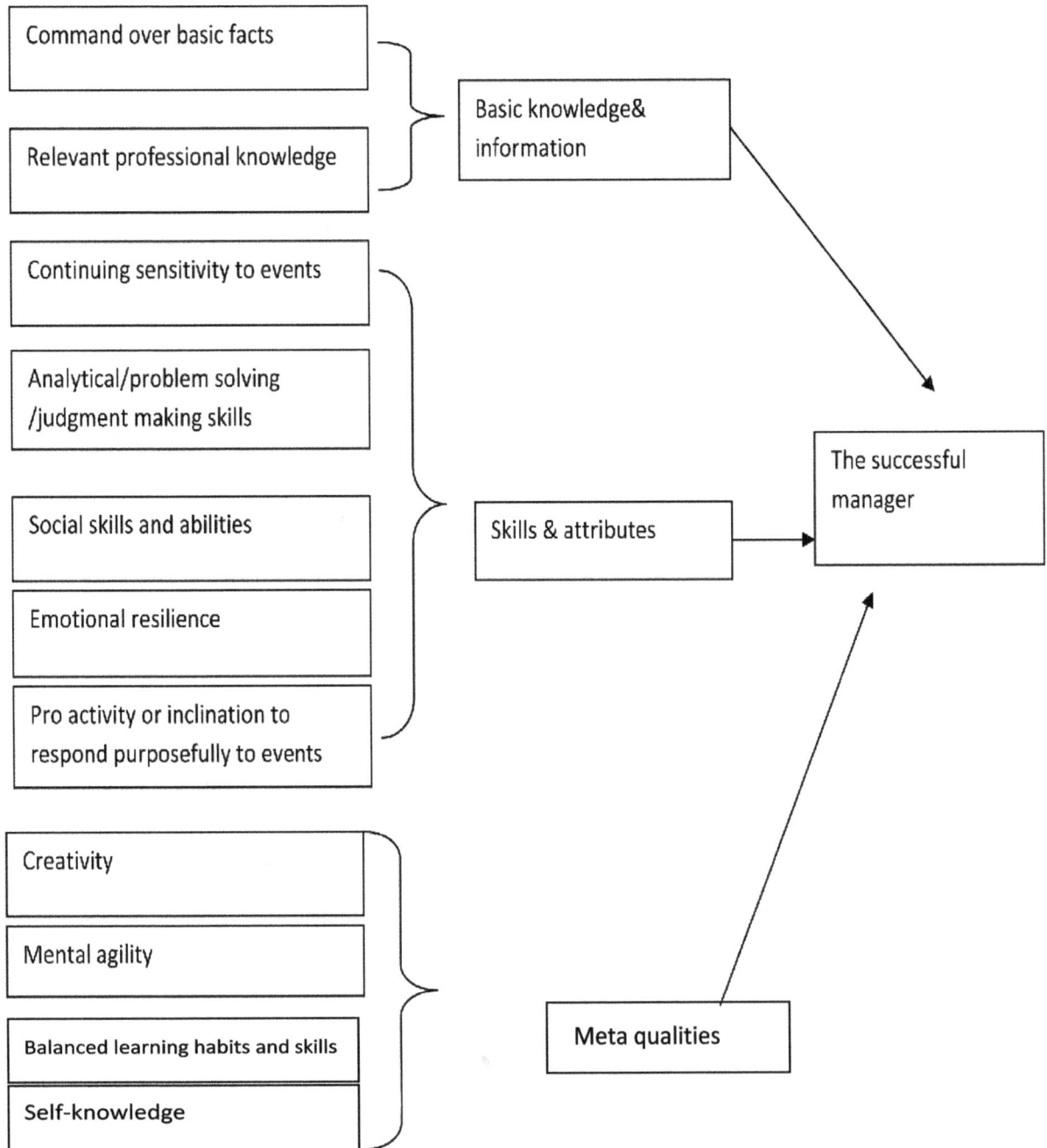

Command over basic facts		
Relevant professional knowledge	Basic knowledge& information	
Continuing sensitivity to events		The successful manager
Analytical/problem solving /judgment making skills		
Social skills and abilities	Skills & attributes	
Emotional resilience		
Pro activity or inclination to respond purposefully to events		
Creativity		
Mental agility		
Balanced learning habits and skills	Meta qualities	
Self-knowledge		

Source: Burgoyne and Stuart (1976)

Level one

Competence one: This competency states that a successful manager should understand the business and have a sound knowledge of basic facts surrounding the business such as short and long term goals, product knowledge ,and the roles and relationships between various departments .

Competence two:

This includes knowledge of a specification such as legislation ,management techniques ,sources of finance or knowledge of basic background management principle. The second category comprises specific skills and attributes that directly affect behavior and performance.

Level Two

Competence one: continuing sensitivity to events:

This means the manager is open to information and is aware of what is happening in and around him. Hard information such as figures and facts and soft information such as feelings of the people. As a result successful manager is able to respond in a suitable manner to situations as they arise.

Competence two: Analytical   , problem solving and decision making skills

A manager has the ability to analyze various events before taking decisions. These can be made by using logical optimizing techniques. At other times it means using the ability to weigh the pros and cons in what is a very ambiguous situation.

Competence three : Social skills and abilities

Burgoyne and Stuart(1976) describe interpersonal skills as one of the key features of a manager's key jobs. A successful manager needs to develop a range of skills as communicating ,delegating ,negotiating ,resolving conflict ,persuading using authority and power.

Competence four: Emotional resilience:

This is the ability to deal with the emotional stress and strain that arises as a consequence of working in situations of authority, leadership and power, targets and deadlines.

Competence five: proactivity or inclination to respond purposefully to events.

Managers ability to respond to events and situation and considers the long term aims and goals and the impact of the immediate decision. The competence also includes abilities such as dedication and commitment having a sense of mission and taking responsibility.

Level three:

Competence one: creativity

This ability to come up with unique ideas or solution and to have the insight to take up useful ideas – either your own ideas or ideas from another source.

Competence two: mental agility

This competence is concerned with being able to grasp problems quickly ,to think about several things at once to understand the whole situation quickly and to think on one set.

Competence three: balanced learning habits and skills

Successful managers according to Burgoyne et.al. exhibit independence as learners rather than depending on an authority figure capable of abstract thinking.

Competence five: self knowledge

The final competence concerns the extent to which managers are aware of their own beliefs, goals, values, feelings, behavior and the part they play in influencing their actions.

The corporate Leadership council (2005a) summarized the benefits of competency models as helping to establish clarity, consistency and connectivity in regard to performance and job expectations throughout the organization. These benefits however, are balanced by presenting some limits. The corporate Leadership council describes these criticisms in terms of challenges and relates that even though companies are implementing competency models, the effectiveness of such frameworks are limited because of the challenges .The challenges are:
- Complicated competency models overwhelm managers,
- Competencies are too current to develop future leaders,
- Competencies fail to develop future leaders,
- Competencies fail to capture organizational uniqueness,
- Abstract competencies are non actionable,
- Competencies fail to incorporate leaders perceptions(p.3)

Rankin (2005) and Sanghi(2007) both delineated possible obstacles to the successful implementation of a competency Management Program. These obstacles include:

- Purpose of a competency model is not made clear.
- Need for introducing a competency model into the current human resource system is not seen.
- Individuals are not involved in planning the development of the competency model
- High cost and reward is inadequate for supporting the effort.
- Doubt over organizational resources/follow –through to actually finish the development of implementation
- Implementation of model occurs too quickly /slowly.
- History of poorly implemented changes to human resources systems/processes.
- Concern about what "using it" really means.

For the purpose of this thesis, operational definitions of competency and competency management formulated both from the literature.

Operational definitions

Competency: A standardized requirement for an individual to properly perform a specific job which includes:

- Knowledge: consists of specific technologies, methodologies and professional acumen.
- Experience: professional, project/process, leadership, intercultural.
- Capabilities: characteristics that drive outstanding performance of a given job.

Competency management: The identification and closure of competency gaps necessary to implement strategic business unit decisions.

Job profile: specifies the mission, tasks and competencies of a position; results from assigning relevant competencies to a specific role and associating levels of proficiency to each competency; and can be used to communicate performance criteria to employees.

Levels of proficiency:

- Basic – able to work with support
- Advanced – able to work on their own
- Expert- able to coach and be a role model for others.

Gap analysis – comparison between the required competencies and the incumbent's competencies

Outcomes of the gap analysis process:

Through the gap analysis, the organization will be able to: understand the business' major training needs and untapped strengths. Propose a realistic training map (or learning plan) based upon the gap analysis for each employee.

Talent management framework- provides basis of performance evaluations; consists of results and capabilities.

Results- Based upon four areas of business goals: finance, employee, customer and process.

Capabilities: five areas which help the individual realize results-based goals.

- Edge- creates an inspiring vision of the future, make tough strategic decisions, and act with entrepreneurial spirit.
- Energy- Be fascinated by the work and initiates a continuous change and learning.
- Energize- guide and motivate your employees and develop the next generation of leaders.
- Execute- get the right things done with highest impact and quality.
- Passion- having a heartfelt ,deep and authentic excitement about our customers ,the profession and the organization.

Competency management model: use of job profiles, gap analysis results , learning plans and talent management framework to :

- Translate organization's vision and goals into expected employee behavior;
- Implement more effective recruitment ,selection and assessment methods;
- Reduce hiring costs and absenteeism/turnover rates and ensure retention of essential competencies for organizational success;
- Set more effective criteria for developing and evaluating performance;
- Identify areas for employee development that are directly linked to desired outcomes and organizational objectives.
- Focus on training costs on areas that will realize the most return on investment.

Competency models are use for performance management, career development, executive development, succession planning, recruitment, compensation, organizational design, training and development, organizational competitiveness, goal setting, job design, and achievement of great organizational effectiveness (Byham&Moyer, 1996; Davidson, 2008; Lucia& Lepsinger, 1999; Plateau systems, 2006; Rankin, 2005; state of Georgia, 2008).

Competency model experiences

The American compensation association (1996) conducted a major survey of 217 mid to large organizations to determine their use and experience with competencies. The survey pointed to wide use of competencies, but to varying degrees of rigor and application. The survey found the organizations using competencies for:

- Communicating valued behaviors and organizational culture (75% agreed competencies have a positive effect)
- "Raising the bar" of performance for all employees(59%agreed)
- Emphasizing people (rather than job) capabilities as away to gain competitive advantage (42% agreed)
- Encouraging cross functional and team behavior(34% agreed)

Close to 60% of responding organizations with competency based applications for staffing ,training and performance management had the programs in place for less than a year when the survey was conducted in1996.The report points out that competency based HR application are evolutionary rather than revolutionary, in that they are treated as add-ons to existing HR practices. "they are clearly not throwing away their existing systems ,they are using competencies as away to clarify what performance matters".

Respondents in the research study listed senior management, high performers, and functional experts as the top three sources of information to develop competencies. The study also noted that competencies tended to highlight organizational behaviors rather than job related skills. Zeroing in on these competencies which add real value to the business. (American Compensation Association, 1996)

Competency experience-private sector

Recent surveys indicate widespread use of competency based human resource models by banks, insurance companies, management consulting firms, technology companies, transportation companies, utility companies, delivery companies, retail eating outlets, manufacturing industries, and mining companies. Industry publications suggest ongoing use of competencies in private sector but the extent of use remains uncertain.

North American life (NAL) used the Hay system in 1995(Orr, 1995) to link competency, performance management and pay. They came up with a short list of 10 competencies –analytical thinking, conceptual thinking, customer focus, developing people, flexibility, information seeking, listening and understanding and responding, performance excellence, and team leadership specific to NAL using a standardized menu of competencies to survey employees and identify proficiencies relevant to each job.

Other private sector initiatives reported by Czarnecki(1995) include the finance department of McDonald's Canada which introduced competency modeling for its 50 employees and Purolator courier which used a project team to identify 10 to 30 technical competencies (e.g. Keyboard ,software skills) and five to eight behavioral competencies(e.g. time planning, initiative, telephone presence).

Winter (1996) has described how Guardian insurance uses competencies to assess and reward individual performance in terms of core competencies that reflect the company's strategic focus and priorities.

Current prospects for the competency movement in the public sector

A wide variety of generic competency models are available for performance improvement when driven by a strategic planning process in both the private and public sectors(Bryson (1995);Dror,(1997);Dubois,(1996). These models typically link organizational core competencies with employee core competencies as distinguished from employee job-specific competencies, in order to establish a direct linkage between the organization's priorities and employee behaviors. Creating effective linkages can be problematic and the above mentioned potential advantages and disadvantages of the competency approach also apply to competency programs in the public sector. For example British civil service designed a competency checklist to replace its traditional ,centrally controlled selection criteria and it resulted in a pattern of strengths and weaknesses similar to those reported in the North American Literature on competencies.); North (1993)

Bryson (1995) describes several methods by which the public and nonprofit organizations can identify their organizational core competencies as a significant output of the strategic planning process. For example, a strategic consideration of a public sector organizations strengths and weaknesses can identify its organizational core competencies in concrete terms. Improvement of organizational core competencies can then be achieved through coordinated adjustment of HRM administrative policies and practices covering all, or selected , personnel functions .In some cases even in public sector settings ,it may be important to that an organization's competency model be explicitly future oriented ,rather than implicitly historic and that it identify levels of superior strategic performance rather than levels of threshold ,minimum ,operational performance (Jacobs,1989). For example, entry level recruitment to government based organization focused on assessment of the potential could include future oriented expectations in the priority assigned to different competencies, and to design of competency assessment instruments.

Using a top-down approach, Dror's (1997) generic strategic analysis of the alternative roles of senior civil services links the core capacities of the organization with the attributes of its individual members. These are equivalent to organizational core competencies and employee core competencies, respectively. Dror's recommended future-oriented core capacities (organizational core competencies include: intervening in history ,energizing ,adjusting social architecture, risk taking ,handling complexity ,making harsh tragic choices and mobilizing support for constructive destruction.

To evaluate the potential for success of the competency movement in the public sector, it is necessary to relate inputs to outputs. At the current juncture in the history of governance, the relationship between elected officials and their bureaucracies is severely strained ,resulting in serious constraints on the strategic planning process(Caroll,1997;). The competency movement in the public sector will probably be less connected to an effective strategic planning process, and thus will be less effective than it may be in the private sector.

Many public sector organizations are experiencing ,or have experienced major changes in their strategic orientations .Snow and Snell (1993) illustrate how staffing plays a key role in the realization and consolidation of major shifts in strategy implementation function, through to a strategy formation function. An effective competency-based staffing model in the public sector will require improved methods for designing and maintaining managerial assessment and selection tools appropriate to its function or transitional state. Consultative methods, effective documentation and active strategic monitoring and maintenance is essential for the attainment and long term viability of functionally appropriate competency based staffing models in the public sector(Austin et al 1996)

The operationalization of a new staffing model can be illustrated by Dror's (1997, p.12) employee core competency of super –professionalism. The particular assessment and developmental opportunities available in each government's historical context are taken as a point of departure for a new competency –based model. The essence of Dror's super professionalism is based on practical intelligence and tacit knowledge, thus taking the middle ground mapped out by Sternberg (1995) in a recent theoretical debate on competencies.

Further analytical work is required to adapt these competitive concepts to the values production and governance functions of public sector institutions (Austin, James Hunt, 1996; Denhart, 1993; and Dror, 1997) and the articulation of methods of transferring competency approaches across governmental functions and levels. Standard capitalistic economy theory is premised on the assumption that firms are in businesses to maximize or at least make, a profit. Unlike the typical objectives of a public sector organization, this objective is unambiguous. In a rational, economic environment, the competencies that position a firm to reach this objective will be embraced and those that do not will be rejected. Moreover, certain precision tools, such as human resources accounting, can be applied to measure the extent to which this objective is being accomplished. Thus, consideration has to be given to the cost-benefit of extensive assessment for a given job versus reliance on generic competency definition. Equivalent accounting and accountability models have not been established for public sector HR activities.

As noted previously, the professional literature is quite persuasive in suggesting that competency based HRM approach should be tied to strategic objectives. The difficulty arises from the reality that while the competency based HRM approach is well founded, its applicability to government is rather difficult. The government therefore should engage in activities meant for financial gains.

A final theoretical and professional consideration in the area of industrial and organizational psychology and organizational psychology is the resurfacing of the debate between the competency movement and the standardized testing movement. The renewed debate was published in the journal, American psychologist, over twenty years after the publication of McClelland's original article on testing for competence instead of intelligence (Cowan, 1994; McClelland, 1994; Barrett, 1994; Boyatzis, 1994). The essence of the debate revolves around the professional standards required to ensure that a rigorous valid methodology in defining competencies, in designing the methods for their measurement and for their use in decision making.

Competency modeling and Assessment

A competency mapping model is an organizational framework that lists the competencies required for effective performance in a specific job, job family, organization, function or process

Understanding the competencies required should form the basis for linkage across all the talent management and development processes, from recruitment, through learning and development, to performance management. Competency frameworks are most useful when they offer a pragmatic view of the most critical and distinctive competencies on which the organization depends and when they are maintainable.

The process of competency management brings together several elements that result in a maintainable competency model. The first area is competency framework which sets the standards for us to map our talent needs the key elements of the competency framework are the competency categories we are seeking to track. These should focus on the critical competencies and common competencies required for different work groups and aim for the right balance between being pragmatic and giving sufficient insight on what is needed. Competency categories need to be exhibited, measureable and observable.

The principal competency categories usually divide into main areas:

Core competencies: common skill sets and traits that reflect the organizational values and culture, and skills need across workforce;

Functional and technical competencies – the skills and knowledge required to perform the job or tasks;

Professional competencies- Requires the behavioral aspects of competency such as personal and interpersonal skills and leadership characteristics

Fig 2.4: competency framework

Figure: competency processes (peter cheese "Talent powered organization, 2011)

As an employee progresses through the organization, their roles shift from execution and team support to managing and leading teams. Professional competencies such as leadership become more important as they progress upwards, while functional and technical competencies become less important.

After competency framework is set, the organization needs to establish standards that provide a measurable scale of proficiency for the critical competencies the organization needs for particular jobs and positions and use them as a guide to discover and develop talent in the organization. Then organizations should develop a fairly summarized data which supervisors can check off to ensure that their people have the right proficiency levels. The organization can take the help of some technologies which can automate some of the process of competency modeling and surveying. A study on Indian pharmaceutical organization, discusses a well designed talent management strategy. The purpose of this paper is to draw lessons on how building a talent management strategy based on competency profiling becomes a critical impact area within the field of strategic HRM. Findings of the study revealed the talent mindset has helped the organization in recruiting the best talent from the best pharmaceutical organizations. The attrition of the top and valued talent segment has come down. Some of the key positions have been filled through succession planning. Research limitations/implications - The case study is in a lesser known but emerging sector of the Indian economy .The case has concentrated on attracting and developing and retaining key talent, it does not concentrate on developing average talent into key talent. Practical implications - The implications lie in whether to grow talent or buy talent. What signal through a communication strategy should a HR manager give when determining for talent segmentation? How to develop talent and retain employees when there are not challenging options available in the infernal labor market? This case study provided insights to HR practitioners on how to attract, acquire and manage talent in a tight internal and external labor market. It also provides empirical support for and theoretical understanding of, the strategic HRM literature on talent management theme. (Talent management — competency development: key to global leadership .Sharma, Rakesh, Bhatnagar, Jyotsna, Industrial & Commercial Training; 2009, Vol. 41 Issue 3, p118-132, Dabur Pharmacy Limited, India, Management Development Institute).

THE OUTPUT MODEL

The most radical model and by far the most powerful in impacting current managerial education and training is the output model. It is at the heart of Management Charter Institute work. This model is primarily concerned with:

Deciding what outcomes you want managers to achieve.

MCI has analysed, defined and published generic occupational standards – called management standards – for four levels of management: supervisory, first line, middle and senior. They are what MCI calls'Benchmarks of best practice'. Generally the standards are defined in this way:

Occupational standards are not descriptions of the performance itself (specific activities or tasks), nor the means of achieving competence (knowledge and skills learned through the training program) not the means of measuring quality or achievement (assessment) nor the process by which the achievement is recognized publicly (qualifications).

Standard are 'bench marks': descriptions of the expectations of employment against which the actual performance of individuals will be compared and assessed as competent, or not competent as appropriate. In the output model, descriptions of competence are derived from a top down analysis of a job function called functional analysis. This entails a cascade of questions.

The first question for each level of management is: What is occupation's key purpose?

To achieve the organization's objectives and continuously improve

Its performance.

What key roles are entailed in fulfilling that key purpose?

Manage operations

Manage finance

Manage people

Manage information

What are the outcomes, which must be demonstrated in each of those key roles?

The outcomes are first defined as units of competence. These describe in broad terms what is expected of a competent manager is particular aspects of a job. It is these units, which are certified within **NVQs (National Vocational Qualification).**

The units of competence are then broken down further into their elements **of competence** (something you are able to do as part of that achievement).

Each element of competence is backed up by performance criteria. Onto the performance criteria are tagged range statements or indicators. These suggest the areas and circumstances within which employees must be able to perform satisfactorily against the elements of competence and provide evidence of achievement. Covering the five performance criteria are four range indicators. The elements of competence are complemented by assessment guidance. This completes the output model.

TALENT MANAGEMENT

2.1 The need, origin and growth of talent management

Talent management as a term has its origin in the year 1990s to incorporate various developments in human resources management which focused on managing the human resources or talent. The term was coined by David Watkins of Softscape published in an article in 1998; however the link between human resources development and organizational effectiveness has been established since 1970s.

The issue with many companies then was despite organizations putting tremendous effort into attracting employees to the organization; they are not able to retain their high performers within the organization. It was also observed that they spend little or no time in utilizing and developing the talent of the individuals. A talent management system therefore evolved as a strategy to be incorporated within the business strategy as well. The human resources department along with the other departments should be held responsible for implementing the talent management strategy of the organization. Companies that focus on developing talent integrate plans and processes to track and manage employee talent. The scope of talent management therefore includes:

- Sourcing ,attracting qualified competent individuals
- Managing the competent individuals by proper engagement procedures
- Mapping their future with career development opportunities & succession planning
- Retention programs

Modern technologies use competency based management to capture and utilize competencies appropriate to strategically drive an organization's long term plans.

The organizations are going for a facelift in today's scenario by having a big diverse workgroup –there is a change in the demographic patterns wherein there are an increased number of employees who are nearing their retirement age and there is dearth of young talented group to fill in those gaps. Between 40and 70% of the baby boomers are eligible for retirement. This shift is changing the pattern of the organization's way of thinking –i.e. changing the nature of employment contract such that the workers can pick from a wide variety of choices available to them. They can select from work-life balance to diversity policy-whichever suits them better. The employees are the valuable resource for the organization as they invest in their intellectual, social and emotional capital in the organization. Boole (2004) even recommends that organizations use outplacement techniques to sharpen the mutual understanding of an employee's current and future potential contribution to the organization, so that there are no misunderstandings in the career transition processes. The labor market is working in favor of the talented group altogether and therefore organizations should start redefining their nature of psychological contract and start creating a brand for themselves as an employer of choice. According to the Towers Perrin Talent report: New realities in today's workforce –workers are highly informed about

50

their options and the internet has further made the task easier by having various job search engines without risking their present position altogether. The organizations therefore have to be cautious in creating a brand for itself. They have to consciously work towards living up to the promises they have made to the employees while they were inducted to the organization itself. The organization should also be more proactive in engaging and keeping its key personnel.

Talent management has become the strategic priority for every organization in the present scenario. In order to create continuous value to stakeholders and to maintain competitive advantage, organizations must proactively manage their human capital. The shift therefore has been from efficient operations and low cost products to outstanding customer service and innovation which in turn demanded to build capabilities in the organization's human resource base. The customer centricity strategy invites employees to contribute their unique ideas and experiences in providing service to the customer. The organizations can propel towards high performance if they build in those distinctive capabilities that are key drivers for organizational success. The pace of growth of every country has been significant. Within the next 20 years by most projections there will be these developing countries who will take the lead. Adapting to this scenario requires right resources and capabilities. The idea of talent as the force that powers companies is taking centre stage. People are the key to add value to any of the organizational processes.

Modern organizations own and employ fewer of the basic inputs of the production-land, materials capital and support services than they did 20 years ago, now with the advent of new technology organization has been able to make a shift from redundant work processes to a more evolved approach in which there are interdependent parts and the production is divided not only in the units where it is produced but across the value chain altogether. As a result of this transformation there has been a shift in the source of value. Earlier the source of value was always tangible assets of the company but in today's context it is equally beneficial to attach it to the intangible assets of the organization- your employees. Branham (2005) found that recognizing the key employees on which your organization depends and attempting to understand how to better meet their needs is highly important for the organization. The company's results improved dramatically when they spent half their time on people rather than half their time on finances (Hand field – Jones et.al. 2001). It clearly projects that if you have the right people and manage them in the right way, the finances look after themselves. Mc Kinsey's report (2007) recognizes talent management as a strategic priority for organization and yet over half of the line managers are resistant to the process (Gutheridge et al.) The results of the IOMA's HR critical issues survey for 2006 identified Talent management as the top issue for 75% of the respondents Appreciation of the link between talent management and the bottom line is increasing amongst the HR fraternity. Talent management is more than just spending time looking after people and human resources management. The organizations must multiply talent by combining and recombining knowledge, skills and competencies throughout the organization to generate superior levels of effort, imagination, creativity, learning, adaptability and performance from the entire workforce. A virtuous cycle of talent multiplication is set in motion starting with defining the organizations talent needs, discover the sources of talent, and develop the talent potential and lastly deploy the talent strategically. (Sandler, 2006).

Definition of Talent management:

Talent management refers to process of identifying, maintaining and retaining the talent pool of one's organization. Companies engaging in a talent management strategy involve not only the human resources department but also all the managers across various divisions of the organization. The process of attracting and retaining talented employees is increasingly recognized as a competitive advantage for the organization as it plays a key role in strategic driver of the organization. The term talent management can be approached from two different angles; the first perspective can be about identifying high-worth individuals or the talented group, the other can be about each individuals talent is identified and utilized. The organization that have shifted their thought from only identifying high worth individuals to identifying talent in each individual and leveraging the available talent has benefitted most in the process.

Companies that engage in talent management are strategic and deliberate in how they attract, select, train promote and move employees though the organization. Research reveals that the value that this system brings into the organization has been significant in terms of revenue generated, customer satisfaction, quality, productivity cost, and market capitalization.

The major aspects of talent management therefore can be listed as follows:

- Develop assessment tools and scales which can identify competencies
- Develop training and development application tools
- Evaluate each employee using assessment tools
- Engage them for better motivated workforce
- Talent retention strategy

It is therefore imperative for the organization to identify and categorize the employees into certain subcategories also. Berger and Berger (2004) had categorized the talented employees into three categories: super keepers-a small category of workers who demonstrates superior accomplishments, inspire others to high achievement, and embody institutional core competencies and values. The second category is that of keepers- those who exceed expectations for value creation and third category are the solid citizens- those who meet expectations for creating value. With greater number of companies vying for the talented workforce organizations can certainly not lose on their talent. No matter whatever is the stage of the organization there will always be a demand for super keepers, keepers and solid citizens to man the key positions of the organizations.

2.2 Studies on Talent Management

The environment for most organizations today is global, complex, dynamic, highly competitive, and extremely volatile, and is likely to remain so for years to come. In addition to these external conditions, most organizations are also facing several global challenges including those related to: talent flow; the managing of two generations of employees, viz., older or mature workers and younger workers; and a shortage of needed competencies. One major result of these challenges for organizations is that they have to be global and that they have to be systematic in managing their human capital if they wish to have any hope of gaining and sustaining a competitive advantage in the years ahead. Many human resource practitioners and consultants (HR professionals) are now recognizing this, especially those that operate globally, the multinational enterprises. Academics are also showing a strong interest as evidenced by their work in the new area referred to as "global talent management". In this article we review that academic work and attempt to organize that literature by creating an integrative framework for understanding and advancing further research in global talent management. To guide this research our framework highlights several selected challenges in global talent management, and several drivers of those challenges. It also highlights the potential role of IHRM activities in addressing those selected challenges. A discussion of possible criteria of global talent management effectiveness completes the framework. Hopefully this integrative framework may guide further academic research on global talent management and might also inform the work of HR professionals. (Tarique, Ibraiz1 &Schuler, Randall Apr2010)

Talent management has a direct and quantifiable connection to overall business risk management, business improvement and cost management. In fact, there are serious potential pitfalls in not having the right people with the right skills in the right jobs at the right time. An amalgam of forces is bringing talent management to the forefront of today's human resource risk concerns-forces that include the ongoing crisis in financial and economic markets, changing business strategies, ups and downs in recruitment as well as retention and an aging workforce. But perhaps the most powerful force at play is globalization. With many organizations now viewing the entire world, not just a single country or region, as the milieu in which they conduct business, managing talent optimally is an increasingly complex and critical goal. The most basic talent management programs focus almost entirely on filling open positions with qualified individuals. But at the other end of the continuum, and far more likely to contribute to an organization's success, is a fully integrated approach that addresses all segments of the talent management life cycle-recruitment, development, retention and transition-and aligns each segment with the organization's vision, mission and values. Also, any organization that maintains a global presence needs to maintain a truly global perspective, striving for consistent implementation of an integrated talent management program throughout the world (Leisy, Bill and Pyron, Dina,**Talent Management Takes On New Urgency.** Compensation & Benefits Review; (Jul/Aug2009).

Talent Management refers to the skills of attracting highly skilled workers of integrating new workers, and developing and retaining current workers to meet current and future business objectives. Companies engaging in a talent management strategy shift the responsibility of employees from the human resources department to all managers throughout the organization .The process of attracting and retaining profitable employees, as it is increasingly more competitive between firms and of strategic importance has come to be known as "the war for Talent".

The talent management process may differ between organizations, some common understanding of what we mean by talent management is necessary if it is to be conceptualized and researched.

Hence the definition as given by Blass, (2007): talent management is the additional a management, processes and opportunities that are made available to people in the organization who are considered to be talent.

The impact of talent management may vary from industry to industry and work place to workplace. Industries such as PR, consulting and other professional services stand or fall by the people they recruit and retain and hence may have a larger pool of "high potentials within their organizations still need a solid talent base on which to build the organization. Regardless of the sector, industry or organization, talent management appears to be an important consideration when the future of the organization is contemplated. However, moving from this strategic realization to an operational talent management process is something that many organizations are struggling with.

The strategic perspective shapes the way in which talent management is viewed, implemented and operationalised, so that the same activity can result in a different action and /or outcome depending on the perspective employed.

There is the process perspective which proposes that it includes all processes needed to optimize people within the organization Farley, (2005) as they truly believe that the future success of the company is based on having the right talent –so managing and nurturing talent is part of the everyday process of organizational life.

There is the cultural perspective that believes talent management is a mindset Creeman, (2004) and that you must believe that talent is needed for success this can be seen where every individual is dependent on their talent for success due to the nature of the market in which they operate, and is typical of organizations where there is a "free internal labor market, with assignments being allocated according to how well they performed on their last assignment. Alternatively this can be an organization where the development of every individual's talent is paramount and appreciated, and allowing people to explore and develop their talent becomes a part of the work routine. (Michaels et.al., 2001)

There is the competitive perspective which is underpinned by the belief that the talent management is about identifying talented people, finding out what they want, and giving it to them –if not ,your competitors will (woodruffe,2003). This tends to be default perspective if no other perspective is taken, if only as a retention strategy. It is also seen as in the professional services firms where they generally adopt the competitive approach because their business proposition is based on the talents of their people.

There is the developmental perspective that proposes that the talent management is about accelerated development paths for the highest potential employees applying the same personal development process to everyone in the organization, but accelerating the process for high potentials. Hence the focus is on developing high potentials or talents more quickly than others .Wilcox (2005),

There is the more general HR perspective which claims talent management is about having the right people matched to the right jobs at the right time, and doing the right things This is often identified with companies currently experiencing rapid growth which to some extent is driving the talent management system, and once they become more prominent in organizations taking this approach. (Mucha, 2004).

Finally there is the change management perspective which uses the talent management process as a driver of change in the organization, using the talent management system as a part of the wider strategic HR initiative for organizational change (Lawler, 2005).

There are six dimensions that contribute to how talent is identified and defined in an organization:

- Size of the talent pool - the number of people considered in the talent pool. The extremes are only 1% of employees through to all 100% of employees.
- Entry criteria- Is it easy to meet the criteria to enter the talent pool. The extremes are very easy where can be considered for entry at any time through to very difficult where certain criteria needs to be met to qualify entry.
- Decision process the number of people involved in deciding the classification of talent. The extremes in this dimension are concentrated decision making, usually resulting in it being the line manager, through to distributed decision making of some form.
- Permanency of definition- the labeling of certain category as talent is dependent on how permanent is the classification. The extremes here are 'once talent- always talent' through to the label of talent being transient.
- Recruitment as a source of talent- it also depends from where the organization fills up its key vacant roles.

  The extremes here are all internal candidates through to all the external candidates.

Transparency- the talent management system is also dependent on how transparent the system is. The extremes are that it is fully transparent with everyone appreciating how the system works and their personal talent classification; through to the system being transparent, sometimes to the point that individuals don't even know there is a system in place.

The following seven dimensions impact on how talent is developed in the organization:

- Development path- it says that once people are identified as talent what necessary steps the organization takes to develop the talented lot. By an accelerated path whereby they receive the same development as everyone else only faster ,through to a completely differentiated ,bespoke route that is designed to meet that individual's needs.
- Development focus- organizations' focus should be on identifying the strengths and weakness of the identified talent
- Support- the organization should provide the support to the talent pool in nurturing their fullest potential
- Influence on career- organizations should identify the point of influence for the talent in the organization. This can range from the individual themselves, to their line manager, senior management teams, HR and peers across the organization.
- Connected conversations- the organizations should encourage the talented individuals to have connected conversations about their career options. The extremes here are just their line managers through to anyone they wish to talk to in the organization.
- Organizational values- the organization should pay more emphasis in creating such set of values which will help motivate those in the talent pool. In some organizations managers are motivated by challenge and are used to dedicate service and dedication.
- Risk- the amount of risk the organization is prepared to tolerate has an important impact on the outcomes of the talent management system.

Finally there are five dimensions that impact on the structure and systems that support the talent management process:

- Performance management – performance assessment to performance management helps in determining the outcomes and outputs that individuals achieve over a period of time which has significant relationship in the results and behaviors.
- Talent Management processes- the way talent management systems and structures are made explicit or implicit determines whether people will contribute to the success of the system or the structure. If the system is explicit, it means the system and structures are open and everybody is aware that there is a process and how it works.
- Use of Technology- the role of technology should be supportive of the system. Organizations can be either IT dependent or IT independent such that it is largely paper based has an influence on the type of talent that they look for.
- Systems flexibility- whether the organization has prescriptive or static system or it is evolving and changing has a direct impact on the talent management process.
- Ownership of talent- whether the organization has local ownership or there is shared ownership around the organization has a significant role in the way the talent management process is carried out in the organization.

The results of IOMA's critical issues survey for 2006identified talent management as the top issue for 75% of respondents (Sandler, 2006), suggesting that appreciation of this link with the bottom line increasing. The best talent strategies show executives the talent implications of the business strategy; accurately forecast talent needs and gaps in type (skill sets) and number(head count); provide information on human capital programs to allow correct decisions to be made ;and lead in upgrading the organization's talent portfolio (Sandler, 2006). This in turn leads to succession planning.

Identifying Talent in the organization:

The crucial question which today's organization faces is how to discover the talent the organization needs and how to attract them to your organization. This question is more complex because the need to source talent from increasingly diverse and unfamiliar talent pools. A few years ago organizations might have concentrated their efforts on some kinds of expertise on certain business schools, or leading international companies, or global IT hotspots and other specialist clusters. Today the rapid growth and spread of talent, knowledge and technology make it not just harder but also distinctly foolish to narrow your choices. The global talent market has made the workforce diversity inevitable. Successful companies are those that do not wait to be forced into it but actually embrace it as a source of advantage. Diversity should become your biggest asset. Therefore the key process of discovery of talent is to

1. Identify the specific competencies the organization is looking for
2. Ensuring that all recruitment channels and processes are geared to seeking out the specific talent you need;
3. Establish and sustain distinctive employer brand that can appeal to different segments of the talent market;
4. Promote word of mouth in establishing your reputation as an employer;
5. Make every part of the recruitment process attractive and effective for the applicants;
6. Match the promises made in the recruitment process to the reality of working for your company, from the first day one.

Talent is precious to the company —and to everyone else's. It is also precious to itself: people are becoming much more aware of their value, and in the markets with significant talent shortages, the employees are becoming aware of that every day. That is one of the major reasons for which organizations put much effort into the recruitment processes and that effort is particularly rewarding. Economic changes have created the new phenomenon called as knowledge worker. This new phenomena has transformed the concept of labor as an anonymous commodity with readily interchangeable units, into talent, a new kind of productive resource, far more difficult to replace.

Yet the very qualities that make knowledge workers such a vital strategic resource make them very much harder to incorporate into a conventional supply chain model. Therefore it is highly essential for the organization to look beyond simple head count. The organization need to create a clear picture of the specific combinations of knowledge ,skills and attitudes that are available in the organization as present supply of talent and match that against the specific combination one needs for its organization in future. Managers in more conventional businesses also have to be able to understand their talent needs at the level of specific and general competencies that are necessary to fulfill the tasks and jobs required. They have to model the competencies to map out where the requirements are as they look ahead, and where the gaps are today and in the near future. Cheese, et.al .(2011)

.2 b.Recruiting talent

There is an inherent conflict with recruiting as to whether to recruit for a better workforce today or to plan for the workforce of the future. Ideally both are covered, but the Aberdeen group report that over half of the respondents to their survey are still operating a reactive ,emergency driven recruitment strategy ,rather than identifying the critical jobs in the company and having processes in place to ensure that any potential gaps are covered (Aberdeen Group,2005). Recruitment processes are vital –if people don't like the process they won't come (Bannister, 2005). Chowdhury (2002) suggests that talent is treated as a customer when being recruited and then as a preferred supplier once hired. The important factor is getting the right caliber of people to want to work for you. ideally the organization should establish themselves as the employer of choice and your recruitment practices will address both the tangibles and intangibles of the employment process, giving the potential recruits a feel for the culture, environment and colleagues with whom they will be working as well as details of the compensation and benefits offered(Branham,2005)

New ways of recruiting are also looming large .In the third quarter of 2003, Monster.com had 16.7 million unique visitors, and 30.7 million active resumes online (frank and Taylor, 2004) and the recruitment market is becoming global. Morton et.al(2005) report that in the U.S and Europe only 10% of current graduates have science and engineering degrees, while in India and china the figure is over 40%. Given this, where is the innovation more likely to occur? Organizations need to know the market they are recruiting in and actively source the talent they are after.

Von Seldeneck (2004) suggests a more proactive approach. He suggests identifying the good competition and who their key people are, and then luring them to one's organization. To convince these talented individuals you need some motivational factors which will lure them to the organization. It is therefore essential to start by making a survey on what appeals the talent markets today and how the organization establishes them as the most sought after brand. The appeal of organization to potential recruits begins at a general industry level. Some industries are seen by people today as very appealing and some are not. There are market workforce surveys of graduates of employees that give a good indication of how particular industry is perceived. Accenture carries out regular surveys of graduates in order to understand what they are looking for. For the most recent survey in2005 which covered five major countries and over1600 responses, graduates were asked a series of questions about what industries they found most and least attractive. There are some surprises in there for industry sectors, which urgently need to discover what it makes them unattractive. In some cases concern centers on environmental issues and social responsibility. In other cases it may be because the industry is seen as dull or unappealing to the new generation of graduates and school leavers. Insurance appears to be suffering from this perception which may or may not be fair, but which has been recognized. Generation Y looks for early responsibility and ability to shape their own jobs, investment in their training and diversity of experience and even things like casual dress environments and informality. These are things that organizations in any industry could provide.

2.2 .c. Employer branding:

Minchington   (2005) defines Employer branding as "the image of the organization as a great place to work for in   the minds of the current employees and the key stake holders in the external markets (clients ,customers and other key stake holders in the organization)"

Strong employer brand has employer Value proposition (EVP's) defined and communicated to all the major stake holders of the organization through the actions and behaviors and evoke both emotive (e.g., I feel good about working here) and tangible benefits (this company cares about my career growth) for both current and both prospective employees. The EVP reflects the brand image of the organization which it wants to portray in front of its customers and the major stakeholders of the organization.

Typically there are two types of employer branding exercises one is for prospective employees and the other for the current set of employees. In case of the former, the employer branding initiatives are targeted at building mind share in potential recruits about the company as a preferred place to work. This can be in the form of communication through advertisements, and in case of the latter it is to create a value chain within the organization so that the employee identifies himself/herself in creating value for the organization.

There are four dimensions for establishing this brand:

1.   Brand image and reputation

2.   Management of performance

3.   Culture and environment

4.   Employment package

Brand image and reputation:

The component which distinguishes one brand from the other so far as employer branding is concerned is **visionary leadership**. An important dimension to successful Employer branding is the role played by an organization's leaders. Visible direction set by leaders is a vital component in showcasing to employees the desired behaviors and culture. Organizations which try to encourage employees to understand and engage with their employer brand will invariably fail if their leaders are not actively living the brand themselves. Another argument is that any successful employer brand comes from within the guts of an organization – based on the innate culture, values and traditions of the workforce. It is not artificial, based on an expensive branding consultancy's musings or simplistic focus groups findings. But what if an organization wants to move its culture on – changing behavior and the way people understand experience and relate to what their employer stands for?

Some may say this is the 'cop-out' answer. However, to shape a successful employer brand which supports your organization's strategic goals you have to set a marker in the sand. You need to define what kind of culture, values and behavior will help deliver the organization's goals. And you have to get leaders to be very clear about what kind of organization they want to lead. The leaders should know where they want to reach. The visionary leader should understand that culture shift happens through a smooth transition rather than sudden shift from what was existing to what they wish to build as an ideal organization. The leader should be able to emulate the ideologies of the organization through which it wishes to convey strongly to the role players that this is where you need to bend the rules and carve a world class organization worthy of anybody's dream.

Management of performance:

This requires the committed and sincere effort of the senior management in creating a valuable customer as well as rendering value to the customer- because customer defines value. Therefore it is highly essential to understand at each level of the organization the specific roles that they are expected to perform and the kind of performance they are expected to deliver. This is a misconception that Employer brands are associated values that are the exclusive preserve of HR or internal communication teams; this will, more likely than not, end up as meaningless words translated into glossy posters, mouse mats and expensive videos. This is where organizations get it wrong. In fact the whole of the organization and each and every unit of the organization contribute to the creation of the value based culture of the organization.

Factors through which management of performance can be enriched:

- Setting standards
- Communicating the expectation to the Role players
- Empowering them to find the Best way of doing a certain activity
- Assessing them on their competencies
- Helping them to improve their performance incrementally.

Culture and Environment:

Culture of the organization symptomatically reflects the beliefs and values it holds dear to make the organization scale new heights. It has to be flexible and   tailored to meet the dynamic environment of the organization. The employees should be given a space to think and imbibe the values into their day to day activity so that they become trend setters of the organization.

Roger Harrison (1986) has identified four broad categories in which organizational culture can be classified. Any organization, he argues has a blend of these types of culture, though there some types may be characteristic of some organization more than others. Each of these types of culture has its strengths and limitations, as well as its dark or shadow side, where culture strength can become a limitation. He suggests that organizational excellence is achieved through exploiting the dynamic tension between the strengths of these different types of culture.

Factors that affect the direction in which the culture travels –

- How richly the networks within the organization are connected
- The diversity of mind set of the other people within the network
- How quickly or otherwise, the active information flows through the system.
- How power differences are used
- How anxiety is contained.

To reach this state, you have to recognize that formal and informal systems co-exist. The informal networks themselves must generate their own order and change. The role of the senior manager is to articulate ideals, open ended challenges capable of different interpretations, umbrella concepts and metaphors.

Employment Package:

The notion of employer brand starts from what the employee knows about the organization and secondly how he feels about it. How emotionally engaged are employees in your organization? And how positive is their understanding and experience of what your organization stands for?

By knowing the answers to both these questions, organizations can see how many of their employees are ambassadors for the brand. These 'ambassadors' are people who both 'understand' and are 'emotionally engaged'.

The employer brand should then be built on understanding the characteristics of the people who are likely to succeed in the organization and expressing the brand in a way that attracts more of those people. Therefore the organization must accentuate qualities which everyone working for would accept as part of the basic character of the company and which fosters their personal success: they might be things like swift recognition for outstanding performance or particular care with working conditions or high quality relationships at work.

2.2.d. Talent development: The rise of the celebrated knowledge workers is a reflection of changing skills requirements in the workforce. As businesses continually apply new techniques, new processes and new growth models and work in new locations their need for up skilling becomes constant and continuous. The American Society for Training and Development has estimated that no fewer than 75% of the existing American workforces will need retraining over the next 10 years .This estimate could even prove to be optimistic as globalization and the advancement of technology are such forces for change, and the competitive advantage of organizations and indeed even of countries is now more and more dependent on the skills of their workforces.

The knowledge economy constantly redefines the skills it demands from current workforces. In particular it requires ever-greater competencies associated with information technology, to a point where it has become a basic currency of knowledge workers. In a recent studies on adult competencies and learning (such as OECD 2006b), on which these competent draw), the OECD has observed that the facility to learn new skills is itself becoming a critical competence. This is undoubtedly true, and it can be extrapolated to the organization itself. A talent powered organization is also a learning organization: it has mastered how to invest in learning and development, and knowledge management capabilities, and use them to accelerate skills building and thereby improve competitiveness in all its critical workforces. To become a talent –powered organization, you must multiply talent by developing and deploying the talent identified. Talent development and deployment are key capabilities that support talent multiplication and competitiveness.

Career development efforts in large corporations are too often limited to programmes that target people with high potential and future leaders. Given the demands of knowledge work and the increased strategic importance of human capital, broad investments in employee capability development should be a top priority for all firms. The question of who becomes responsible for managing one's career underlies much of the talent debate. The Gratton & Ghosal (2003) idea of the "volunteer' employee puts the emphasis firmly on the employee. It is their career and they will choose where to invest their time to develop it. Alternatively talent management approach wants individuals to stay within the organization wants to take responsibility for ensuring that the individual is developed and ready for the career move, and they want to guide the career path of the individual in the direction that they need. There is fine balance that needs to be achieved. In order to perform, the organization has become dependent on the talent the individual possesses giving the individual the balance that needs the organization as a work community in order to develop and use their talents shifting the power back to the employer. Hence the employer needs to be reshaped on reciprocal terms (Schoemaker & Jonker, 2004).

Electrolux company views career management as a dual responsibility. Each manager is responsible for developing his or her people, and each individual is responsible for seeking out new challenges and actively managing his or her career within the open labor market within the group (Pollitt, 2004). Tsui&Wu (2005) call this mutual investment where they offered inducements from the company and the expected contributions of the individual are both high, so a long –term relationship is formed on the basis of a contract, rather than the commitment and loyalty ideals of the previous century.

If organizations want to manage the careers of their talent they need to clearly articulate the ways in which their roles will change, both laterally and hierarchically, based on the organization's requirements, and what the behavioral implications of that will be. This provides clarity with regard to shared anchored points, and helps high potentials navigate through transitions and undertake appropriate development with a clear understanding of what they need to do differently to be successful as their role changes. (Watkins, 2003). Mentoring provides both professional guidance and psychosocial support to employees, and despite the fact that most senior managers currently in post did not receive mentoring as part of their career development and management of others (Scheck McAlearney, 2005). Central to the idea of career development is the role of competence development itself.

Workforce development is a critical competency for all organizations in the 21st century, but it is especially vital in businesses and sectors where employees' knowledge, skills and capabilities are the main tools for creating value. Talent powered organizations understand this and prioritize learning and development. Whether the focus is on individual competence or organizational competence, developing competence within the organization is key to creating a talent management system. Berger (2004c) argues that an organization should develop a list of its core competencies and assessment tools for measuring them; assess everyone against them and forecast potential; and finally prepare action plans to ensure that the core competencies rather than the future leaders per se, in an effort to find people who can do the jobs brilliantly ,while Romans(2005) redesigned his entire organization using the human capital pipeline systems thinking model, based entirely on a system of role competencies rather than individual competencies.

Talent management needs an organizational commitment to continuous professional development (Clarke, 2001). This will be visible through the range developmental experiences offered within the organization, moving away from the traditional classroom training –based model ,to include stringing together a range of meaningful experiences to build character. These could include coaching, issue development meetings, job rotation, and interim assignments, taskforce assignments, extracurricular activities and so forth (Krewson, 2004) argue that corporate universities can help by linking learning and strategy, and preparing employees for future challenges.

Deploying talent is becoming an increasingly strategic capability, with the proliferation of possible ways to organize work and access talent .Talent powered organizations understand the deployment is not just about getting the work done .It is about developing the available talent to increase your organizational capabilities and expand your strategic opportunities .

The way an organization deploys its talent will have an enormous impact on employee engagement. Talent management is an espoused and enacted commitment to implementing an integrated, strategic and technology enabled approach to human resource management (HRM). This commitment stems in part from the widely shared belief that human resources are the organization's primary source of competitive advantage; an essential asset that is becoming an increasingly short supply. The benefits of an effectively implemented talent management strategy include improved employee recruitment and retention rates, and enhanced employee engagement. These outcomes in turn have been associated with improved operational and financial performance. In a study conducted by Hughes, Julia Christensen, Evelina, (International Journal of Contemporary Hospitality Management (2008), "Talent management: A strategy for improving employee recruitment, retention and engagement within hospitality organizations") the external and internal drivers and restraints for talent management are many. Of particular importance is senior management understanding and commitment. Practical implications - Hospitality organizations interested in implementing a talent management strategy would be well advised to: define what is meant by talent management; ensure CEO commitment; align talent management with the strategic goals of the organization; establish talent assessment, data management and analysis systems; ensure clear line management accountability; and conduct an audit of all HRM practices in relation to evidence-based best practices. This article will be of value to anyone seeking to better understand talent management or to improve employee recruitment, retention and engagement.

2.2.e. Employee engagement:

The essential component of talent management is to have a human capital strategy to address the new global workforce ,approaches to recruitment that recognize talent market diversity, skills development and learning that best develop talent , and the ability to deploy talent to best advantage. But we still have more to do to achieve the high performance that any global organization requires. This is where engagement comes in.

Talent is the engine of the modern organization, and engagement the ingredient that can transform the organization's output. Engagement is a concept incorporating many subsidiary meaning. It says about motivation, commitment, passion, desire, ambition, trust, empathy, solidarity, inspiration and selflessness. It is the quality that persuades people to align their own interests with their organizations. It is what it makes them want to work, put the proverbial best foot forward, to go the proverbial extra mile.

Motivational studies have been a long time favorite area of research for psychologists, from the early pioneers such as Abraham Maslow, whose famous "hierarchy of needs" developed in the early 1940s (Maslow,1943) still has resonance for many business people today. Recent studies have demonstrated the linkage between engagement and performance. For example, the Corporate Leadership council report of 2004 showed that the highly engaged employees achieved performance 20% above average. A Towers Perrin study in 2005 concluded after several years of surveys showing the link between engagement and performance, that a 5 percent increase in total employee engagement correlated to a 0.7 percent increase in operating margin.

The most comprehensive report was the ISR Employee Engagement report in 2006(2006b) .It reported that organizations with highly engaged workforces performed up to 50% better than those with low engagement. Based on surveys of over 664,000 employees worldwide, the study analyzed companies' operating income, net income and earnings per share (EPS) over a 12 month period:

- In terms of operating income ,the high- engagement companies improved by19 % whereas the low engagement companies declined by 33%
- Net income for high engagement companies rose by 13% for low engagement companies it fell by 4%.
- In the high engagement companies EPS grew by 28%; in the low engagement companies it fell by 11 %.(Management issues News Online, 2006).

The concept of engagement was introduced by Bill Kahn who defined it as "simultaneous employment and expression of a person's preferred self" in task behaviors that promote connections to work and to others, personal presence (physical, cognitive and emotional), and active full role performances' (1990). Engagement is a measure of the degree to which people express their identity at work-not only who they are but who they would like to be. Therefore organizations should focus on the strategic role of line managers in building engagement. Organizations should make them responsible for building engagement and give them training and support they need to do it. To succeed on this the organization has to ensure that the line managers themselves are engaged. The line managers need a clear strategy, created and sustained by senior leaders and their role in delivering it.

Employee engagement is personified by the passion and energy employees have to give of their best to the organization to serve the customer. It is all about the willingness and ability of employees to give sustained discretionary effort to help their organization succeed.

Engagement is characterized by employees being committed to the organization, believing in what it stands for and being prepared to go above and beyond what is expected of them to deliver outstanding service to the customer. Employee engagement is more a psychological contract than a physical one. It is something the employee has to offer. Employees make a choice about how they behave and the extent to which they are engaged. Engaged employees feel inspired by their work, they are customer focused in their approach, and they care about the future of the company and are prepared to invest their own effort to see that the organization succeeds.

Engagement can be viewed as how positively the employee:

1. Thinks about the organization
2. Feels about the organization
3. Is proactive in relation to achieving organizational goals for customers, colleagues and other stakeholders.

In other words, it is about the degree to which employees perform their role in a positive and proactive manner. The three aspects which can be noted about engagement are having an employee who feels thinks and does wholeheartedly the role assigned. Engagement therefore is about how employees think rationally about their employers, what they feel about them, their emotional connection, as well as what they do and say as a result in relation to their employees and their customers. Employee engagement has been of importance in today's scenario for two reasons: the increasing power of the customer and the increasing power of the employee.

Definitions of engagement have primarily been offered by consulting houses or in practitioner publications. Perhaps the most extensively used definition of an engaged worker was offered by the Gallup organization. They define an engaged employee as a worker who is fully involved in and enthusiastic about his or her work (Tritch, 2003). HR Magazine's February cover story (Bates, 2004) focused on employee engagement and its role in the workplace. Engagement was essentially defined as "an innate human desire to contribute something of value in workplace." Crawford (2006) defined engagement as a measure of the energy and passion workers have for their organization. Gubman (2004) defined engagement as a heightened personal attachment to the organization. Harley, Lee, and Robinson (2005), while not specifically defining the term, did identify a profile of an "engaged work" and also listed various aspects of engagement that have been used within organizations the measure engagement. Konrad (2006), while not providing a definition, discussed engagement as having a cognitive, an emotional, and a behavioral aspect. Seijts and Crim (2006) defined an engaged worker as one who is "fully involved in, and enthusiastic about, his or her work."

There is not much agreement on exactly what employee engagement is, or how to make it happen .LinkedIn, the social networking site, hosts online discussion groups focuses on employee engagement, and a recent discussion question was, "in ten words or less, name what you believe are or could be the three most effective drivers of engagement." 124 LinkedIn members have posted a wide range of answers, including: creating conversation where none existed, work gratification, purpose, compelling vision, camaraderie, personal connection, inclusion, feedback, caring and cash. The range of responses is interesting and instructive, but it doesn't give managers much help on how to engage their employees. For that, we need to look at the science of engagement – what it is, why it's important, and how to maximize it.

The most comprehensive report published by ISR Employee engagement report in 2006(2006b).It is reported that organizations with highly engaged workforces performed up to 50% better than those with low engagement. Based on surveys of over 664, 000 employees worldwide, the study analyzed companies' operating income, net income and earnings per share (EPS) over a 12 –month period:

- In terms of operating income ,the high engagement companies improved by 19% whereas the low engagement companies declined by 33%
- Net income for high engagement companies rose by 13% for low engagement companies it fell by 4%.
- In the high engagement companies EPS grew by 28% In the low engagement companies it fell by 11 %.(Management issues News Online, 2006).

Employee engagement is defined as a heightened connection to work, the organization, the mission, or co-workers .it's necessarily about happy employees, although it would be nice if employees were happy, at least most of the time. Engaged employees find personal meaning and pride in their work. They believe that their organizations value them. In return, engaged employees are more likely to go above the minimum and expend "discretionary effort" to deliver performance. Another way to put it is that "engaged employees plan to stay for what they give; the disengaged stay for what they get."

With the change and restructuring inevitable for many organizations, one of the biggest challenges currently facing companies is employee engagement. Smart organizations understand that an engaged workforce results in better business performance, so many are placing greater emphasis on measuring employee engagement and implementing strategies to keep staff happy. Evidence of high levels of interest in employee well-being is more difficult to find on a global basis but there is evidence that interest is growing, at least in some countries. For example, in the UK, The Chartered Institute of Personnel and Development (CIPD) reported a very large increase from (26-42 percent), over a one-year period, in the number of employers with an employee wellbeing strategy or similar approach (CIPD, 2007a). In addition to Indications of heightened interest within the organizations, there is also significant interest at national government level in well –being. Research evidence suggests that high levels of psychological well-being are directly correlated with performance. Wright and Cropanzano (2000) report two field studies which demonstrate positive relationships between levels of psychological wellbeing and job performance. These studies show that people with higher levels of psychological well-being perform better at work than those with psychological well-being; indeed, the results from Wright and Cropanzano (2000) show that well being is a stronger predictor of job performance than job satisfaction.

As well as the research by Wright and Cropanzano (2000), linking psychological well-being with performance, Donald et.al. (2005) in a study of 16,000 employees found that almost 25% of the variance in reported levels of employee productivity was predicted by psychological well-being, the perceived " commitment of the organization of the employee" and the resources and communication". Using meta-analysis techniques Harter *etal.* (2002) analyzed data from nearly 8,000 separate business units in 36 companies. They found significant relationships between scores on an employee survey and business unit level outcomes, such as customer satisfaction, productivity, profitability, employee turnover and sickness/absence levels. Their research reports are particularly interesting as they illustrate the potential relationships between psychological well-being and employee engagement.

For employees, psychological well-being is linked to important individual outcomes, including a range of mental and physical health issues, with lower levels of psychological wellbeing linked to poorer health. The impact of job strain on the individual has been heavily reported by researcher (Cooper and Quick, 1999). The impact of Job strain on the individual has been heavily reported by researcher Cooper and Quick, 1999. A series of research studies (Ferrie *etal* ,2005; Griffin *etal* .,2007) have explored the relationships between job conditions ,individual health and other outcomes in a study of government employees.

In fact, although there is some broad agreement about the type of factors included in "employee engagement", there is a lack of clarity about its definition and measurement, Robinson *etal* (2004, p.9) give a definition of engagement as," A positive attitude held by the employee towards the organization and its values . An engaged employee is aware of business context, and works with colleagues to improve performance within the job for the benefit of the organization.....". In general, the items in most engagement surveys focus on the aspects of engagement that are most obviously related to "positive" employee behavior, and cover established psychological concepts such as organizational citizenship(Organ and Paine,1999) and organizational commitment and attachment(Meyer,1997). For example, the Utrecht Work

Engagement Survey (Schaufeli et al., 2006) concentrates on three factors: vigor, dedication and absorption. The Gallup Workplace Audit (see Harter et al., 2002) focuses on factors such as clarity – knowing what's expected and control (input and opportunity) By and large practitioners and researchers views of engagement embody the three core concepts of Attachment, Commitment and Organizational Citizenship. These concepts reflect a focus on the aspects of engagement that are likely to be most directly involved in driving positive employee behavior. As such, they reflect a focus on "Narrow Engagement" – i.e. the factors that are of most direct interest to employers and organizations, since they describe positive employee behavior that is likely to lead to more effective performance and confer direct benefits on the organization.

Typical questions in (narrow) employee engagement surveys are:

- The goals of my organization make me feel that my job is important.
- I am committed to this organization.
- My opinions are listened to by my bosses at work.
- I am enthusiastic about the job I do.
- At work, I am prepared to work hard, even when things do not go well.

The Narrow Engagement approach reflects a "commitment/citizenship" model of engagement, in which employees' commitment and citizenship are seen as important factors in the overall success of the organization. In addition to this focus on "narrow engagement", many engagement questionnaires also include at least a few items that focus on employee psychological well-being (e.g. "I enjoy my work and feel happy at work") – but, by and large, they do not distinguish between employee psychological well-being and the narrow engagement factors. Of course, narrow (strong commitment and good citizenship) engagement is important for the organization, but in some ways it is less important for employees. There are certainly benefits to employees from being committed to their work and feeling positive about the organization that they work for, but the long-term benefit for employees "themselves" is closely linked to personal psychological well being.

Another study, of 50 global companies, also found that the firms with high levels of employee engagement produced dramatically better results than companies with low levels of In three key metrics –income, income growth and earnings per share –the high engagement organizations performed dramatically better by up to 43%. Most employees however are not very engaged .For example:

- The polling firm's engagement survey data, reflecting the views of millions of (mostly private sector) employees are engaged, while 29% of employees are engaged, while 54% are not engaged and 17% are actively disengaged.

- A consulting firm surveyed more than 17,000 public and nonprofit sector employees and found that only 16% of employees are highly engaged, and 19% disengaged.

The concepts of goal-setting, optimism, and employee engagement as mechanisms to improving employee performance have all been discussed fairly extensively in the management literature. Goal setting has been explored in terms of both motivational impact toward improving performance and as being integral parts of management systems or processes designed to improve performance. Though fewer studies exist concerning optimism in the workplace, evidence certainly exists linking the concept to improvement in worker performance. An article titled "The relationship among goal setting, Optimism, and engagement: the impact on Employee performance" By (Bobby Medlin, USC Upstate

Ken Green, Jr., Sam Houston State University, Allied economics International conference, 2008)

Since the Gallup organization's development of the Q12(a survey instrument to measure employee engagement) almost a decade ago, articles in the area of employee engagement –ranging from the benefits of increased employee engagement to ways to improve the level of engagement-has increased and intensified dramatically. Numerous studies (Locke, 1968; Latham and Yukl, 1975; Matsui, et al, 1987; Tubbs, 1986, 1993; Knight et al, 2001; Dweck et al., 1993; Sujan et al., 1994) have pointed to effective goal setting's impact on employee performance. Many management systems or processes (MBO, TQM, and continuous improvement initiatives for example) all feature goal setting as a critical element in improving performance. Gallup's Q12 survey instrument features 12 questions that are used to measure the level of engagement of an employee. Of these twelve drivers of employee engagement, four are related to the idea of goal-goal setting.

Improving individual performance of workers is a critical challenge for all managers. Research indicates that high levels of optimism can lead to improved employee performance. Hiring optimists and creating optimistic subcultures (Green, et al., 2004) are two mechanisms to do this. This study identifies engagement as another means to enhance worker optimism. In addition, it identifies structured, formal goal setting processes as an additional mechanism for managers to improve the level of engagement of their employees.

Engagement can be assessed either indirectly or directly. Indirect assessment involves using data like employee performance, turnover, missed time, accidents, etc., to measure engagement. It isn't a big leap of faith to conclude that an agency with a lot of poor performers, high turnover or excessive employee sick time may have some engagement issues. If we have to establish through this method that high engagement will result in lower turnover, less missed time, better performance, and then this is not the right way of looking at it. Let's us look at high turnover .It could be that an organization with high turnover, but it could also be that an organization with high turnover doesn't pay its employees enough to keep them, or has a poor selection process that results in bad job fits, or has lots of baby boomers who are retiring because it's time for them to move on to the next stages of their lives.

That's why direct measurement, through surveys is the more valid and reliable way to assess engagement. It is more involved than simply looking at already existing data, but it's worth the time and effort to accurately measure engagement.

There are approaches to building employee engagement that are based on strong scientific evidence. For example, one firm's work is based on 30 years of research involving more than 17 million employees. These results, which have been reported in publications such as the Harvard Business Review, have isolated 12 core survey questions that predict employee engagement and therefore work group performance.

- I know what is expected of me at work
- I have materials and equipment I need to do my work right.
- At work, I have the opportunity to do what I do best every day.
- In the last seven days ,I have received recognition or praise for doing good work
- My supervisor ,or someone at work seems to care about me as person
- There is someone at work who encourages my development.
- At work, my opinions seem to count.
- The mission or purpose of my organization makes me feel my job is important.
- My associates or fellow employees are committed to doing quality work.
- I have a best friend at work
- In the last six months, someone at work has talked to me about my progress.
- This last year, I have had the opportunities at work to learn and grow.

In a study conducted by Simeon S. Simon "Essentials of employee engagement" (2008), engagement is linked to three essential forces in the organization-attrition, productivity and profitability. Ultimately the productivity is what is expected by the company from employees. An engaged employee carry out what is expected of him, having the focus and goal clear and bring success to the organization. Profitability is the result of actively engaged workforce.

Engagement challenges

- Engagement levels decline as employees get older –until they reach the oldest group (60 plus) where levels suddenly rise and show this oldest group to be the most engaged of all
- Managers and professionals tend to have higher engagement levels than their colleagues in supporting roles. Although people in the latter group appear to owe greater loyalty to their profession than to the organization in which they practice their craft.

- Engagement levels decline as the length of service increases
- Having an accident or injury at work or experiencing harassment (particularly if the manager is the source of harassment) both has a big negative impact on engagement.
- Employees who have a personal development plan, and who have received a formal performance appraisal within the past year, have significantly higher engagement levels than those who have not.

Building blocks of job engagement:
- Good quality management
- Two way communication
- Effective internal co-operation
- A development focus
- Commitment to wellbeing
- Clear, accessible HR policies and practices, to which managers at all levels are committed.

Driving forces of engagement:

Research shows that committed employees perform better. Study data indicates that opinions about, and experiences of many aspects of working life are strongly correlated with engagement levels. However the strongest driver of all is a sense of feeling valued and involved. This has several key components:
- Involvement in decision making
- The extent to which employees feel that he/she is able to voice his/her ideas managers listen to these views and values employees contribution.
- The opportunities employees have to develop in their jobs
- The extent to which the organization for employees health and well being

Key measures to control Employee Disengagement:
- Offer challenging, meaningful, assignments to the employees.
- Provide scope for advancements.
- Communicate clear vision and direction.
- Recognize the employee's performance output and motivate
- Exhibit team spirit
- Maintain credibility and high ethical standards
- Develop belief in the employees and they start developing belief in the organization.

Simeon S. Simon "Essentials of employee engagement" (2008), point out that the leaders who would like to build employee engagement try to lift the fellow employees of the organization, being an example in everything they do. These leaders as is observed in the study are always transparent, doing everything in complete transparency whereby other employees are able to believe and put their trust in them. These leaders are able to exhibit the spirit of endurance, patience, long suffering and temperance in everything they do and are able to convince others in their decision making .it is observed that these leaders were able to spot the talents and potential hidden in each employee and bring them out by careful nurturing. Such people boost the employee morale and employee engagement. They are able to exercise leadership skills, being able to counsel employees strategically with regard to employee's personal, family and work related problems. They would try to provide comfortable work environment improving quality of work-life of employees through participation and other means.

The companies that do not address the employee's insecurity are likely to be surprised to see the destructive consequences. It has been observed that even though there are good policies in place in the employee manuals but the management capability to engage the workforce and to implement the policies practically is very difficult. This is true because the management looks at tangent focusing on corporate benefit alone. Employees feel that they are expected to offer loyalty to their employer but they do not receive an equal commitment from the employer to protect their jobs. Managers are so focused on their corporate survival that they seem to have to have a limited bandwidth to attend to attend to the employees feeling of injustice. In such a scenario it is observed that in order to generate the sense of belongingness from the employees, managers must maintain transparency in all the dealings apart from good policy manuals.

Survey in the US over the last few years show that indices like loyalty and trust have collapsed from the 80% levels to 30% levels .More than half of the respondents feel a sense of stagnation and disinterest in their work. The recession has increased uncertainty simultaneously with a perceived "onslaught "by managers to increase workforce productivity.

In India too, it has been observed from the hyper cases of industrial action recently that after many decades of relative labor tranquility company executives have been killed. Strikes have occurred at Gurgaon-Manesar, Chennai and Bangalore.

Employees in the emerging markets are deeply concerned about inflation, food and insecurity. Prices of essential commodities have already increased supply. Food experts predict that the rise in food prices is only the beginning of a serious, new threat. Universally, employees are worried lot. All of these are alarming trends and needs to be addressed .Employees feel engaged or disengaged at the transactional level within departments.

Therefore the subject of employee engagement needs to be driven down the company by the CEO .There is a general lack of awareness of the problem down the line. It is also mixed up with the general economic downturn. Poor employee engagement must be understood as a precursor to some other problem which is brewing. That is why there needs to be top level engagement. If enough employees feel disengaged, the consequences will certainly be disruptive. Operating managers have to act .it cannot be left to the HR managers alone.

There must be the action to measure and track employee engagement .Techniques are available and excellent companies already track their employee engagement scores. However the extent to which such companies act on the results is unclear. Operating managers need refresher training on empathy and listening skills .Unions have been quite for over two decades now. A whole new generation of managers has taken leadership roles without any direct experience of dealing with employee discontent. Listening skills are difficult to develop especially when manager's career thus far has not required him to do much of it. There is need for powerful conversation at the operating level, where employees feel they have been listened to even if all their suggestions have not been accepted.

The top leadership of any company must institutionalize ways to connect directly with the lower level employees. Many Tata companies practice a monthly dialogue or two way webcast. Many formal and informal models of listening downwards have been practiced. It is observed that if companies practice this earnestly there is significant improvement in the engagement levels of the employee.

Therefore conclusions can be drawn as to what organization can learn from the recent research and improve and maintain employee engagement procedure.

Measuring employee engagement is complex and it is not always easy to gain an accurate measurement without employee surveys. Employee engagement can be usefully defined in terms of "say, stay ,strive":

- Say. This is a measure of how likely an employee is to be an advocate of the organization. The employee should perceive the work atmosphere to be friendly and welcoming so that they can advocate for the organization in front of new entrants.

- Stay. Commitment is the key, so it is vital to measure the employee's loyalty to the business. The employees should feel that they are a part and parcel of the organization and they remain in the organization. It all depends on how long they envisage working for in the organization.

- Strive. The employees should be more than satisfied in the work that they are doing. This area measures whether employees would be prepared to go "over and above" the call of duty to ensure organizational success.

Using these principles of say, stay and strive as a basis for assessing the level of employee engagement, can be useful for organizations. It is therefore important to understand the "Employee life cycle" as proposed by Kate Pritchard (2008) vol.22,no.6 Emerald group publishing Limited; it is important to understand the different needs and levels of engagement of employees at every stage of their career-from a potential employee, right through to becoming an ex-employee, and every step along the way.Bearing this in mind can ensure that the organizations are able to adapt their practices to suit different employee needs .

FIGURE. 2.5. Employee life cycle:

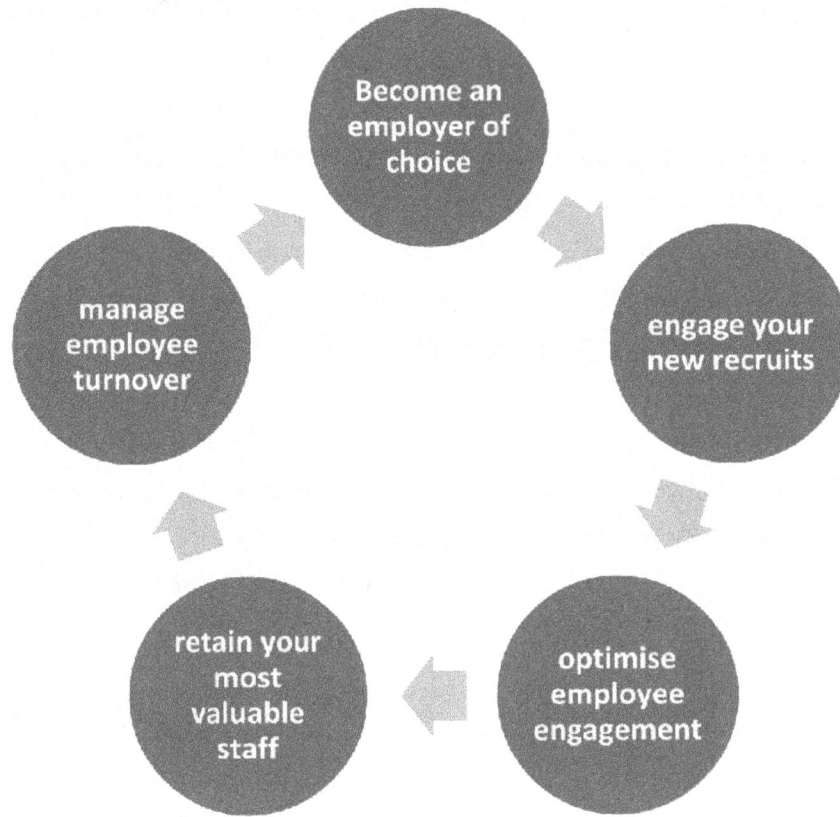

Giving consideration to creating a strong and attractive employer brand can engage potential employees, and turn them into members of your workforce. Understanding joiners can ensure they want to say, stay and strive and similarly working on ways to keep most valued staff happy is crucial for retention. It can be equally as important to consider ex-employees and use their feed back to shape the organization to ensure better levels of employee engagement for retained staff. This employee life cycle model can be used by organization to improve the employee/employer relationship at each stage of the lifecycle.

A well designed employee survey is another tool which can help to provide a good picture of how employees are feeling, which is particularly relevant during times of upheaval or restructuring, when it is crucial that employees remain focused and engaged. Employers should aim to carry out regular research as employee engagement is transitory, very much affected by changes within the workforce and organization. However it is not enough to establish the level of employee engagement and measuring employee opinion. Any resulting information needs to be analyzed thoroughly and ultimately used to drive action that leads to organizational improvement. It is only through action that managers can address problem areas and keep employees engaged and effective. It is clear that regular monitoring of staff opinions is crucial to all organizations, particularly during times of rapid change. By carrying out surveys and bearing in mind the fundamental principles of engagement as well as

74

understanding the employee lifecycle, managers in organizations can discover ways to manage inevitable changes while keeping employees engaged.

2.2. f. Succession planning and Talent Management:

Succession planning activity itself should be clearly linked to the organizational strategy. An organization needs to know where it is going in order to plan what it needs to get there, and link HR strategy and processes to business results (Farley, 2005).

Successful succession management integrates talent management with organizational strategic planning and anticipates changes in management. It is more than just replacement planning, and creates a culture of learning and development at all levels, building a structural development process for top managers and providing a range of practical tools for employee advancement. A variety of technological solutions can help including monster.com, resumix and Talent Smart, the latter offering 360 degree multi-rater assessments (Hartley, 2004).

Carey (2004) argues that good succession planning is a culture more than an activity. It involves the board, exposes top managers to the board, encourages future CEOs to gain exposure outside with media and investors and so forth in an ongoing real time process that becomes predictable. Part of the difficulty is that talent identification and measures of potential are generally decisions made subjectively on judgments rather than objectively on facts (Carrington, 2004) .It is not just a case of relying on past performance to predict future performance. Dalziel (2004) argues that past performance indicators lead to the Peter Principle (People who promoted to their level of incompetence) rather than where decisions are made on the recognition of the self confidence ,self awareness and emotional fortitude needed by people ,who will deal with high pressure situations even handedly. Heinen &O'Neill (2004) also stress the difference between potential and promotability, arguing that the first needs development in order for the second to be successful. Michaels et al. (2001) argue that a certain part of talent eludes description.

At Intel employees who are recognized as talented are given by management experience at an early stage by working in teams of ten with peers and managing each other's performance before they actually have to manage a department (Sandler, 2003). Wilcox (2005) also advocates giving people early and realistic previews of various senior jobs as it helps employees self select. Conger& Fulmer (2003) acknowledge the failure to master the more general competencies such as public relations as a cause of failure of leadership, and advocate grooming individuals for linchpin positions. Marshall (2005) argues that you need to identify the key people to take over in the event that a key person is "hit by a bus", and that these potential successors then need to be kept in the loop about all the key things to do with the job role they may one day fulfill. Hence succession is a deliberate process, to the extent that some organizations make it a requirement that a successor is in place before the promotion is offered.

2.2.g.Retaining Talent:

Business has always been dependent on talent to drive performance. But as the war for talent heats up the competition for talented employees is at an all time high. Driving widespread adoption of a talent management mindset and utilizing the second generation of the web are vital to success. Phillips ("Tapping into the next talent generation", Strategic HR Review; 2008, Vol. 7 Issue 3, p26-31) outlines methods that organizations can use to attract and retain talent to beat the competition. The paper demonstrates the efficiencies that can be gained by focusing on a talent management system implementation at DeticaDFl. The findings of the paper focused on the fact that Talent is defined as an ability or quality possessed by a person in a particular field or activity In business it is also recognized as the only true and sustainable competitive advantage. As the criticality of attracting and retaining the best people has increased, so has the necessity to manage talent holistically on a unified and business-centric talent management platform. Talent management is evolving to become a series of complex HR processes combined to make sure you have the right staff, in the right role, doing the right things. Talent management is emerging as a fundamental element of business management. With this in mind, this feature will look at the need for talent management and how organizations need to adapt their mindset and processes if they are to attract and retain the next generation of talent. Arguably the economic downturn at the start of this decade has caused many employees to stay in jobs as long hours, lower pay and benefits coupled with their perception of ungrateful and greedy senior leadership propels disgruntled employees to leave as more opportunities become available. (Mucha, 2004).

The 2005 what's working survey conducted by Mercer Human consulting found that 50% of employees who thought that their organizations could meet their long-term career objectives were thinking of leaving, while this number more than halved for employees who felt that their organizations could. Similarly being given good opportunities for continuous learning reduced the number thinking of leaving from57% to 32% (Mercer, 2005). However, it does not at all seem to be about opportunities. A Gallup study of 80,000 managers concluded that the greatest drivers of employee engagement and retention are intangible, mostly related to the way a manager treats their employees (Branham, 2005).

In fortune 500 organizations, female executives are leaving at twice the rate of men because of their frustration with the work environment (Dickinson Shephard &Betof, 2004) resulting in 77% of new business in the USA being opened by women. Changes employers could have made to keep these women in their employment were inclusion, a more flexible environment, feedback and career planning. In short, they felt underutilized.

Gandossy& Kao(2004) report that half of all employees are disengaged at work, and employee engagement was cited at the second most important issue for 2006 (behind talent management) In the IOMA HR critical issues survey (Sandler,2006). Mucha (2004) argues that you want people in the "sweet spot" where the work they do well, the work they enjoy doing, and the work that is essential to the organization overlap, its employees will demonstrate their best work and leadership.

Equally, good people leave when poor performance and continual underperformers are not redressed (Digeorgio, 2004), although facing up to low performers is not an easy or pleasant task (Handfield-Jones et al., 2001). While nobody likes to discipline or dismiss people, equally nobody likes to discipline or dismiss people. Carrington (2004) recognizes that the need to address underperformers rather than simply being polite is a significant culture change in most organizations, but one that is necessary if you want the good people to stay.

As well as losing talent, organizations lose knowledge .Kermally (2004) notes that a significant proportion of knowledge in an organizations in a tacit form, and so when staff leave, the organization is losing a massive amount of tacit knowledge. Some organizations are becoming clever at retaining this tacit knowledge and talent even after it has left or retired from the organization. Tulgan (2002) suggests creating a SWAT team of unassigned internal talent who can be moved around wherever and whenever they are needed, as long as they are available as a means of keeping talent in the organizations who perhaps feel ready to move on from their job but there is nowhere yet available for them to go. Rather than lose them from the organization to the competition, keeping them in-house in a SWAT team can offer them the variety and challenge they are seeking ,while retaining their knowledge and skill.

The challenge of global talent management is critical to firm success. Even with the global economic slowdown of 2008 and 2009, there are continuing challenges in attracting, managing, and retaining talent, especially in the developing regions of the world where economic activity has outpaced the availability of skilled employees To examine this situation, Tymon, Walter and Stumpf, Stephen(Journal of World Business; Apr2010, Vol. 45 Issue 2, p109-121) developed and tested a model of talent management across 28 Indian firms involving 4811 professional-level employees. The intrinsic rewards experienced are a critical element in employee retention, satisfaction with the organization, and career success. They explored four antecedents of intrinsic rewards: the social responsibility of the employer, pride in the organization, manager support, and performance management (PM). They found support for the importance of intrinsic rewards as a mediating variable, as well as for the moderating role of certain hygiene factors. The research suggests multinational, international, and national employers may have non-pecuniary mechanisms to promote retention and employee satisfaction, even in challenging labor market environments and concluded by proposing implications for research and global HRM practices. In another study conducted by Cheese, Peter (Strategic HR Review; 2008, Vol. 7 Issue 4, p25-31) discusses the importance of talent management to the strategic success, to identify the challenges in building talent power and to explore how to overcome those challenges. Talent is now the key to strategic success, but is conversely getting harder to find and easier to lose. In tackling these issues, every organization must deal with a world of change and variability. The paper asserts that an organization needs to put in place key processes in order to retain and actively multiply talent. They include: maintaining visible leadership that is focused on talent; encouraging and rewarding line managers for nurturing talent; and modernizing HR and training to identify, develop and deploy talent the best effect. The paper discusses the importance of talent management to strategic success, in order to identify the challenges in building talent power and to explore how to overcome those challenges. Organizations are becoming relentless in managing and developing their key talent. This is a view, however, largely based on anecdote rather than reliable empirical evidence. Utilizing data from 260 multinational enterprises (MNEs), this paper helps redress this deficit. Specifically, this paper explores the extent to which MNEs engage in global talent management (GTM) and deciphers some of the factors which may explain the use and non-use of GTM practices. In so doing, we find that although a significant number of MNEs have systems and mechanisms in place to strategically identify and develop their talent many more seemingly adopt an ad hoc or haphazard approach. For instance, less than half of all MNEs have both global succession planning and formal management development programs for their high-potentials. Consequently it seems that there is a considerable distance yet to be travelled to arrive at a universal appreciation of the need to strategically manage one's key employees. The authors found the size of the MNE has a significant effect on GTM system usage—larger MNEs are more likely to undertake GTM. Other significant, positive influences include whether products or services are standardized regionally or globally, and if the MNE has a global human resources policy formation body. Of considerable interest is the finding that MNEs operating in the low-tech/low-cost sectors are significantly more likely to have formal global systems to identify and develop high-potentials the barriers to effective global talent management: The example of corporate élites in MNEs. (Mellahi, Kamell K.mellahi &Collings, David; Journal of World Business; (2010).

Cynics might argue that talent management is just another HR fad, but few fads seem to have turned themselves into a new tranche in the labor market. The roots of talent management can perhaps be traced back to the downsizing and outsourcing trends in the 1990s, including the slimming down of graduate recruitment schemes (Carrington, 2004). Talent management shifts the focus of HRM away from people as resources towards people being men and women who need towards people being men and women who need to be appreciated and valued for who they are (Casse, 1994) and hence it completely refocuses the activities of HRM away from command and control towards a model of shared success. In many organizations, HR has already moved beyond simply being a purveyor of talent to becoming an integral part of the talent management process by extending its activities such as leadership assessment (Sandler, 2004).

Identifying talent and making sure it gets to the top is not enough–unless the value that a talent management system offers can be shown, it is likely to be shelved. Lawler (2005) argues that HR can and should add more value to corporations by being a business partner, focusing HR as a business in its own right and reviewing what products it has to offer. He identifies three types of services to offer: basic administrative services and transactions; business partner services and systems; and strategic partner role contributing to business strategy through considerations regarding human capital. Building on the idea of the knowledge economy ,Ulrich &Small wood (2005) see the emerging focus on intangibles in the economy as an opening of the way for HR professionals to more readily link their work with shareholder value ,providing the vital link with strategy that may previously have been overlooked.

While Farley (2005) may agree with Lawler's views, he is realistic about HR being in a difficult position in many organizations, having a strong mandate without the credibility to fulfill it, and so he challenges HR to be held accountable for its investments, as is the case with any other business function. Farley sees ensuring HR operational processes excellence as a critical success factor for managing talent processes. This requires a shift from the discrete thinking of individual processes to using data and technology to support the measuring and reviewing of information to determine the relationships between business goals and the people.

2. Performance management and talent management.

As organizations undergo changes in systems, structures and attitudes, they modify the workplace experience often positively for many and negatively for some. Effective organizations use such experience –positive or negative as sources of continuous learning .Vibrant organizations appropriately capture this learning and act to systematically use it while reviewing both the design as well as functioning of their systems, processes and attitudes. Most contemporary organizations possess some of the following features:

- A diversity of locations, units, programs, projects, sectors and specialized disciplines.
- Dramatically varying rules that govern day-to-day operations in different segments
- Complex cultural interactions
- Varied tasks and problems
- Decentralizations- meaning that a lot of power vests in the localized managerial levels
- Interdependence and dynamism-what one segment of the organization does ,affects the total organization and vice versa
- Globalized to the core.

Such organizations according to Prem chadha, (2003) aspire to provide high quality goods and services to highly–discerning and differentiated customers, clients or other kinds of stakeholders. They understand that abiding organizational excellence rest only on excellence in the performance of individual managers, who may be located next to each other, or miles apart-whether frontline stars ,backroom boys and girls.

Performance management is a way of systematically managing all such people for innovation, goal focus, productivity and satisfaction-it is a goal –congruent win-win plan. Its main aim is to ensure success for all managers and all the teams-who believe in its approach, and implement it with sincerity and commitment. The manager's success must reflect in the organization bottom –line in terms of fulfillment of its planned goals.

Performance Management defined

According to Michael Armstrong, (2006), Performance management can be defined as a systematic process for improving organizational performance by developing the performance of individuals and teams. It is a means of getting better results by understanding and managing performance within an agreed framework of planned goals, standards and competency requirements. Processes exist for establishing shared understanding about what is to be achieved, and for managing and developing people in a way that increases the probability that it will be achieved in the short and longer term. It focuses people on doing the right things by clarifying their goals .it is owned and driven by management.

Armstrong and A. Baron, *performance management: the new Realities.* Institute of personnel and Development, London, (1998)define performance management as a strategic and integrated approach to delivering sustained success to organizations by improving performance of the people who work in them and by developing the capabilities of teams and individual contributors. They consider performance management as strategic since it concerns the achievement of longer-term organizational goals and effective organizational functioning in its relevant external environment. It is integrated, because it affects four types of integration:

- Vertical- aligning objectives at the organization, team and individual levels. Vertical integration is achieved when well –aligned, interlocking objectives, cascading from organizational goals are agreed upon at the work team and individual levels. Yet, individuals and teams formulate their own goals within the broad framework of organizational purposes and values, when objectives are agreed upon through ongoing dialogues between senior managers and their subordinates and are unilaterally set.

- Functional- focusing functional energies and strategies onto tasks into different parts of the organization.

- Human resource – linking different human resource management sub systems like people management and task monitoring, job design, human resource development and task monitoring, job design, human resource development and motivation and the appraisal and reward sub-systems to achieve goal and task-related synergies towards optimum performance.

- Goals- attempting congruence between individual needs and aspirations of managers with goals and objectives of the organization.

    Armstrong's formulation of performance management concerns, ethical principles suggested by Winstanley& Stuart-Smith, *Policing performance: the ethics of performance management.* Personnel Review,(1996), and IRS Management Review, *Performance Management,* (1996) listed key areas of performance management:

- Transparency- in the sense that parties at the organizational ,team and individual levels ,affected by performance improvement decisions emerging from performance management processes, through -

Planning performance expectations from individual managers in advance.

Organizing work appropriately

Effectively guiding and thereafter equitably and empathetically monitoring and reviewing performance against known standards at pre-determined intervals have access to the basis upon which these decisions are made.

- Manager's development- in the sense of addressing core competencies of the organization and specific capabilities of teams and individuals –treated as partners in the enterprise whose interests are respected and who have a voice on matters that concern them."

- Mutual Respect- among parties involved in performance management processes –in the sense of respect for the team as well as individual member and organizational needs and preoccupations ,at the same time ' recognizing that that they will not always coincide; and by treating people not only as a means to other ends but also as ends in themselves.

- Fairness and equity in all procedures and due satisfaction of the needs and expectations of the organization's stakeholders must obviate the perception of prejudice to any party involved in performance management –owners ,management ,managers, customers ,suppliers and the general public.

- Organizational climate- in which a continuing dialogue between the managers and their subordinates helps share information on the organization's mission ,values and objectives,' define mutual expectations of what is to be achieved and a framework for managing and developing people to ensure that it will be achieved.

The overall aim of performance management is to establish a high performance culture in which individuals and team take responsibility for the continuous improvement of business processes and for their own skills and contributions within a framework provided by effective leadership.

Specifically, performance management is about aligning individual objectives to organizational objectives and ensuring that individuals uphold corporate core values .It provides for expectations to be defined and agreed in terms of role responsibilities and accountabilities(expected to do) ,skills(expected to have)and behaviors (expected to be) . The aim is to develop the capacity of people to meet and exceed expectations and to achieve their full potential to the benefit of themselves and the organization. Importantly, performance management is concerned with ensuring that the support and guidance people need to develop and improve are readily available.

The following are the aims of performance management as expressed by a variety of organizations (sourceIRS, 2003):

- Empowering, motivating and rewarding employees to do their best. *Armstrong World Industries*

- Focusing employee's tasks on the right things and doing them right. Aligning everyone's individual goals to the goals of the organization. *Eli Lilly& co.*

- Proactively managing and resourcing performance against agreed accountabilities and

81

objectives. *ICI Paints*.

- The process and behaviors by which managers manage the performance of their people to deliver a high-achieving organization. *Standard Chartered Bank*
- Maximizing the potential of individuals and teams to benefit themselves and the organization, focusing on achievement of their objectives.

The research conducted by the CIPD in 2003 (Armstrong and Baron, 2004) elicited the following views from practitioners about performance management:

- The line managers should recognize performance management as a useful contribution to the management of their teams rather than as their chore.
- Managing performance is about coaching, guiding, motivating and rewarding colleagues to help unleash potential and improve organizational performance. Where it works well it is built on excellent leadership and high quality coaching relationships between managers and teams.
- Performance management is designed to ensure that what we do is guided by our values and is relevant to the purposes of the organization.

The research conducted by CIPD in 1997 (Armstrong and Baron, 1998) obtained the following additional views from practitioners about performance management:

- A managers tool which helps managers to manage
- Driven by corporate purpose and values.
- To obtain solutions that work.
- Only interested in things you can do something about and get a visible improvement.
- Focus on changing behavior rather than paper work.
- It's about how we manage people-it's not a system.
- Performance management is a process of management and focuses on what managers do
- Based on accepted principles but operates flexibly.
- Focus on development not pay

Success depends on what the organization is and needs to in its performance culture.

Process of performance management:

The three parts of performance management are-

- Planning manager's performance and development, that is concluding a performance and development agreement.
- Monitoring and mentoring manager's development
- Reviewing.

Planning is done at the beginning of the year; monitoring and mentoring is done throughout the year and reviewing at the end of the year, when it is also time to plan afresh for yet another year. Each one of these phases require concrete actions to be taken by the manager and the subordinate, both of them providing appropriate inputs ,while keeping the whole process in perspective.

These three phases also work in an action research mode. Planning, monitoring and review happen all through the year: more pointedly at times of the periodic review during the monitoring and mentoring phase. As such the three phases are dynamic and they continuously interact .The relevance and feasibility in a changing context where all events or influences may not be adequately foreseen. Similarly, the criteria and standards used during appraisal, while reviewing are largely developed and rehearsed during the year. This process becomes participatory since the review meeting, where it happens, involves the subordinates and the managers. That is the way in which the standards and criteria for relative assessment of manager's performance evolve. The following figure gives the process of performance management:

FIGURE. 2.6: PERFORMANCE MANAGEMENT PROCESS

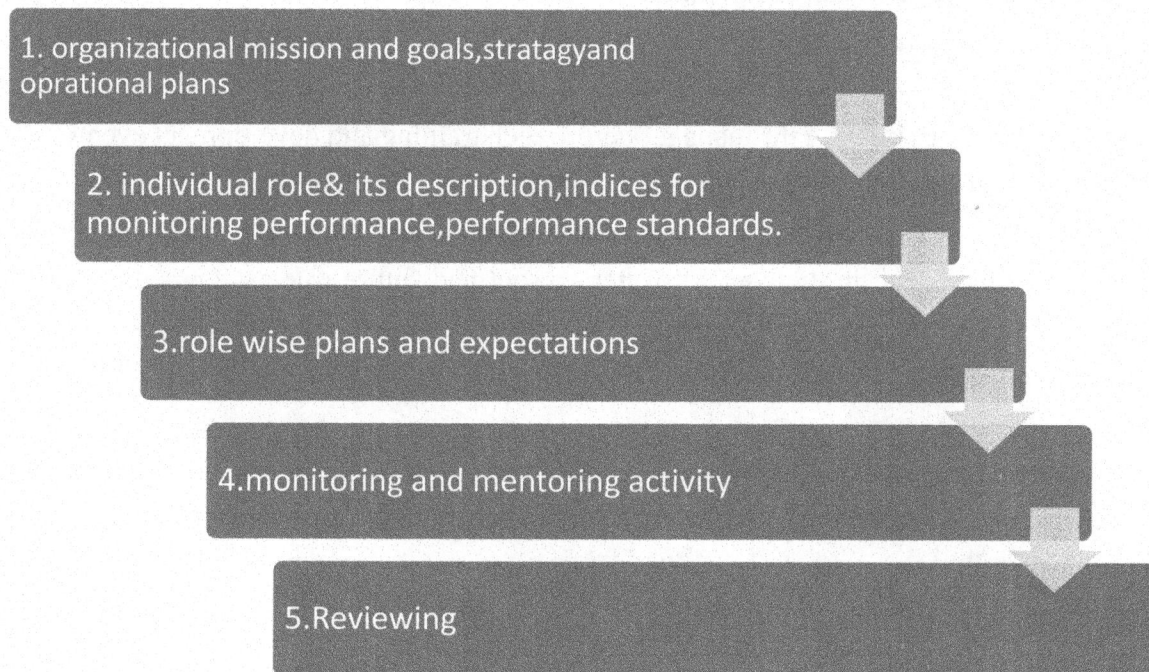

1. organizational mission and goals,stratagyand oprational plans

2. individual role& its description,indices for monitoring performance,performance standards.

3.role wise plans and expectations

4.monitoring and mentoring activity

5.Reviewing

Source: Prem chadha,performance management ,(2003)

Individual roles, their descriptions, indices for monitoring performance and performance standards naturally cascade from the organizational Mission, goals, strategy and operational plans. Since performance management attempts to improve the quality of collaboration among people in the organization, role wise performance plans and expectations must flow from both:

a) The organization's mission, strategy and operational plans and

b) The individual manager's roles and indices of her contribution to the organizational process in the form of performance standards and indicators.

These two are cardinal inputs into the individual manager's performance plan. It is important that the performance plans extract all that is relevant to the plan period from the manager's role description during the year and allow the manager to focus totally on the performance plan. Performance plans of all the managers in the organization must, ultimately, add up to the organizational goals to be achieved during the year.

Manager's performance and development plans feed into the monitoring and mentoring activities. Without a cogent plan for task accomplishment, there is no benchmark to gauge achievement against and to monitor the manager's progress in achieving her goals. Mentoring and development draws its direction from both the development plan and the role requirements. Only when manager's performs, does her potential for the assigned role reveal itself. That is the manager can determine what combination of individual manager's unique competencies and skills will help the manager's develop and grow in the organization and where the critical gaps or opportunities for helping manager realize her full potential.

Mentoring also involves briefing the manager before each training and development event-on the job and off the job, and debriefing after each such event. Briefing helps each such manager focus on the learning agenda from the specific event and debriefing helps the manager crystallize her learning achieved during the event, in the context of her present and future role assignments and help the manager crystallize her learning achieved during the event, in the context of the present and future role assignments and help its internalization by providing for its earliest use in the day-today work situation.

Performance review or stocktaking-periodic or annual attempts to continuously assess the extent to which the work as well as learning opportunities has been optimally availed by the manager. Inputs to review come from the performance plan and the monitoring and mentoring records.

Stocktaking, including appraisal, provides several inputs to future performance plans: for reviewing task assignments; for reviewing task system and tools; for more deeply understanding the manager's task environment.-within the organization as well as outside. And for reviewing the manager's future tasks and responsibilities .the hope is that both the organization as well as the individual manager's benefit out of this process and performance management helps spiral manager's performance and development.

A study conducted by André A. de Waal, Vincent Coevert, *The effect of performance management on the organizational results of a bank,* International Journal of Productivity & Performance Management, (2007) revealed that the striking issue in this case study is the different effects the introduction of the new performance management system had in the two commercial divisions of the bank branch. However, only the Private Clients division improved its results significantly while those of the Business Clients division only improved slightly. After analysis, it turned out that this difference was due to the way the new system was used. The divisional manager of the Business Clients division paid virtually no attention to the behavioral factors of importance to the successful implementation of performance management, with detrimental effects. Practical implications of the study revealed during the implementation of a performance management system an organization has to expressly pay attention to fostering and improving the behavioral factors of performance management, in order to increase the chance if a successfully implemented and used system. Originality/value - This article describes the results of a study that explored the impact and working of a new performance management system in a branch of a bank, and thereby sheds light on the important role behavioral factors play in the successful implementation and use of performance management.

In another study conducted by De Waal, André&etal. International Journal of Operations & Production Management (2009) the paper identified whether there exists a relationship between the level of completeness of a strategic performance management (SPM) system implementation and the advantages and disadvantages an organization experiences from this system. Advantages and disadvantages encountered during the implementation and use of an SPM system are collected from the literature and tested during extensive interviews at 17 prominent Dutch organizations (with 52 interviewees in total). During the interviews the level of completeness of the SPM system implementation is also assessed. Subsequently, the advantages, disadvantages and level of SPM system implementation completeness are related. The research results show that organizations that have fully completed the SPM implementation gain more financial and non-financial advantages and experience less disadvantages than organizations that are still in the process of implementing such a system. Organizations that have almost completed the implementation of the SPM system already gain qualitative advantages from this system, but they experience fewer financial advantages. Practical implications points out that Management now knows which advantages are to be expected at which stage of SPM implementation completeness, and can use the research results to convince staff that an SPM system will only yield full benefits to the organization when it has been completely implemented. The study brings out the need for efficient and effective SPM systems has increased over the past decade and the successful implementation and use of these systems have become of paramount importance to organizations. In this respect, one issue has been underexposed in the literature thus far, namely: the relationship between the level of completeness of the SPM implementation and the benefits organizations experience. This paper provided an overview of the main advantages and disadvantages to be expected at various stages of SPM implementation completeness.

In a study conducted by Marchand, Marie; Raymond, Louis. International Journal of Operations & Production Management, (2008) it was found that the knowledge developed in IS (Information System) research in the form of IS theories, models and methods can be applied in research on PMS, particularly in empirical studies that analyze the individual and organizational behaviors associated with the PMS phenomenon. The research benefits of an IS based approach are illustrated through a PMS usage model founded on IS theory. In so doing, a contribution is made to the PMS research field by reinforcing its theoretical and empirical foundations. Originality/value -- This study proposes a novel and demonstrably useful IS-based perspective, including an improved conceptualization and definition of PMS.

Performance management system: a powerful tool to achieve organizational goals by Gunaratne, K. Asoka; Du Plessis, (2007) presents that Performance management is a system and not simply a once a year meeting to review the past year's performance and set goals for the next year. Setting goals, preparing performance plans, conducting reviews, tracking behaviors, gathering data, and writing evaluations are all activities of a performance management system that requires time, commitment and skills. This article discusses a performance management system employed by a Fortune 500 company and how its employees rated the individual facets of the system, as well as their overall satisfaction with the total system on completion of the fifth year of implementation. It elucidates how the organization aligned the performance management system with the organizational system and articulated the company business objectives to the individual goals. The results of the study show that implementing a performance management system that people understand and believe in will provide a powerful foundation for the employees to achieve their ambitions and organizations to achieve their key financial goals.

In another study conducted by Morgan, Robert,(2006) "Making the Most of Performance Management Systems"it was observed that too many companies invest in performance management programs to little or no avail. Developing talent is a concern that plagues HR managers at big and small businesses alike. Whereas large corporations often have a widespread, diverse workforce that is difficult to contain, smaller firms rarely have the necessary resources to implement an effective system. But at the end of the day, they are all competing for the same talent. Too often, firms isolate tactics such as succession planning, career path development and training even though all of these are key to developing a workforce and supporting the overall business strategy. Essentially, performance management is only effective when it's part of an organization-wide talent management strategy. This article delves into how to go about implementing such systems and the impact successful initiatives can have on a business.

Performance management systems by Furnham, Adrian. (2004), looks at the theory and practice of performance management systems (PMS) in organizations. It discusses the reasons why these systems are introduced and the problems and issues that arise in using PMS effectively. Although a basic management requirement in all types of organizations, nevertheless PMS almost universally work poorly and are negatively viewed by both managers and managed. The paper discusses ten common criticisms of PMS and considers whether they are justified. It also looks at how PMS may be affected by changing concepts and new issues arising from current organizational changes in the nature of work and work roles.

"Getting the most from your performance management system" by: Davis, Patricia; Rogers, Robert W. Catalyst (2005) offers organizations several pieces of advice on how to get the most from their performance management system. The authors note that organizations need to determine the reasons why they are not realizing satisfying results from their performance management system. The rest of this article discusses the key factors that contribute to a successful performance management system.

"Making the Case for Critical Realism: Examining the Implementation of Automated Performance Management Systems" by: Dobson, Phillip; Myles, John; Jackson, Paul. (2007) seeks to address the dearth of practical examples of research in the area by proposing that critical realism be adopted as the underlying research philosophy for enterprise systems evaluation. We address some of the implications of adopting such an approach by discussing the evaluation and implementation of a number of automated performance measurement systems (APMS). Such systems are a recent evolution within the context of enterprise information systems. They collect operational data from integrated systems to generate values for key performance indicators, which are delivered directly to senior management. The creation and delivery of these data are fully automated, precluding manual intervention by middle or line management. Whilst these systems appear to be a logical progression in the exploitation of the available rich, real-time data, the statistics for APMS projects are disappointing. An understanding of the reasons is elusive and little researched. We describe how critical realism can provide a useful "under laborer "for such research, by "clearing the ground a little … removing some of the rubbish that lies in the way of knowledge" (Locke, 1894, p. 14). The implications of such an under laboring role are investigated. Whilst the research is still underway, the article indicates how a critical realist foundation is assisting the research process.

Business Performance Management Systems by: Corbitt, Terry(2004) offers information on business performance management (BPM) systems. The systems are designed to link the operational data with top-level planning, monitoring and reporting. BPM enables operational information to be fed into strategic planning, scenario testing and forecasting. It also enables companies to benchmark performance against competitors. Although it depends much on technology, effective BPM is not only a question of software. There are packages that claim to do all things but information technology always comes second to strategy management and processes. A good BPM system should do several things. First, it must plan and measure things that drive value. Second, it must align processes for planning, budgeting, forecasting and reporting in order to formulate, communicate and monitor strategy. Third, it must give people an incentive to do the right things and exploit the technology. Cartesis director John Taylor said the software element of BPM is small, unlike enterprise resource planning systems which are largely software. BPM often involves changing the way in which the head office interacts with local offices and subsidiaries. There is usually some process change involved and that is where many of the benefits emerge.

Implementing a new performance management system within a project-based organization: A case study by Mei-I Cheng; Andrew Dainty; David Moore(2007) the paper seeks to show that implementing change initiatives in organizations is extremely problematic, particularly in relation to human resource management (HRM) initiatives. The challenges inherent in implementing new HRM systems and procedures is arguably more acute in project-based organizations where temporary teams and geographically dispersed employees render the coherent implementation of new systems and procedures problematic. This paper presents the findings of case study research in which the implementation of a new performance management system for improving individual project manager performance is evaluated. A framework is developed for guiding the implementation of similar change initiatives in other project-based organizations. A longitudinal case study methodology was adopted for the study. This enabled the ways in which resistance to change was manifested, and to be explored, and the actions necessary to circumvent barriers to its use discerned. The final framework is derived from a review of change strategies in other industries and sectors as well as from the case study findings. Findings - The paper finds that barriers to implementing new performance solutions stemmed from a lack of senior management commitment and support ingrained working practices and an absence of appropriate training interventions.

In one particular study it was found that performance management was greatly influenced by behavioral factors. The study also highlighted on the significance of human element in performance management "Behavioral factors important for the successful implementation and use of performance management systems" by Waal, André A. de. (2003)

Competency based performance management system :(CBPMS):

Competence and competency approaches allied to competence –based assessment and related pay are being used by growing number of companies. Utilization includes applying national frameworks /such as Management Charter Initiative in the UK ,or internally generated organizational core competencies ,generic and role specific competencies and behaviourally anchored competencies.

A Guide to Developing a Competency-Based Performance-Management System by Martone, David (2003) Focuses on development and implementation of a competency-based performance-management system that involves establishing the skills and behaviors that employees need to achieve specific goals. Benefits of establishing a competency-based performance-management system; Key elements that should be considered in designing and implementing a competency-based performance-management system; Cultural and organizational competencies at various organizational levels

An important consideration is where the application of competencies fits within the performance management process. Roberts(1997) links competencies to the initial stages of the recruitment and selection process, which he contends should be ruthlessly streamlined if it is to be effective. Among various suggested approaches, he includes:

- Definition of key competencies-personal attributes knowledge, experience, skills and values-to meet the organization's long-term needs.
- Combining a range of selection techniques and methods to obtain reliable data on all core competencies
- Feeding the information gained into the induction, appraisal and development of the employees.

Employee Workplace Effectiveness: Implications for Performance Management Practices

This article discusses the implications for senior managers and human resource management (HRM) specialists of operating a performance management system that takes into account employee workplace effectiveness. Performance management systems need to be compatible with, and complemented by, other HRM systems. If sub-par employee performance is diagnosed to reflect shortcomings of organizational culture, this is a call to top management to indicate, through acts of leadership, their commitment to building a culture that expects and values citizenship, emotional labor and intelligence, and ethics. At the level of organization, collective capabilities, such as gaining the trust of customers, or arriving at tailored solutions through cross-functional collaboration, may reflect core competencies that draw upon the non-task performance domains to provide sustained competitive advantage. A major contemporary challenge for strategic HRM is to realize the full gamut of capabilities and core competencies of organizations and their members. It is suggested that in order to achieve this, employee performance management systems should not focus narrowly on task performance, should emphasize employee development rather than control, and should consider judgments from all sides about employees' actual and potential contributions in the supporting performance domains of citizenship, emotions, and ethics. Yuk Lan Wong; Snell, Robin Stanley.(2003)

Fig:2.7 :Competency based performance management system:

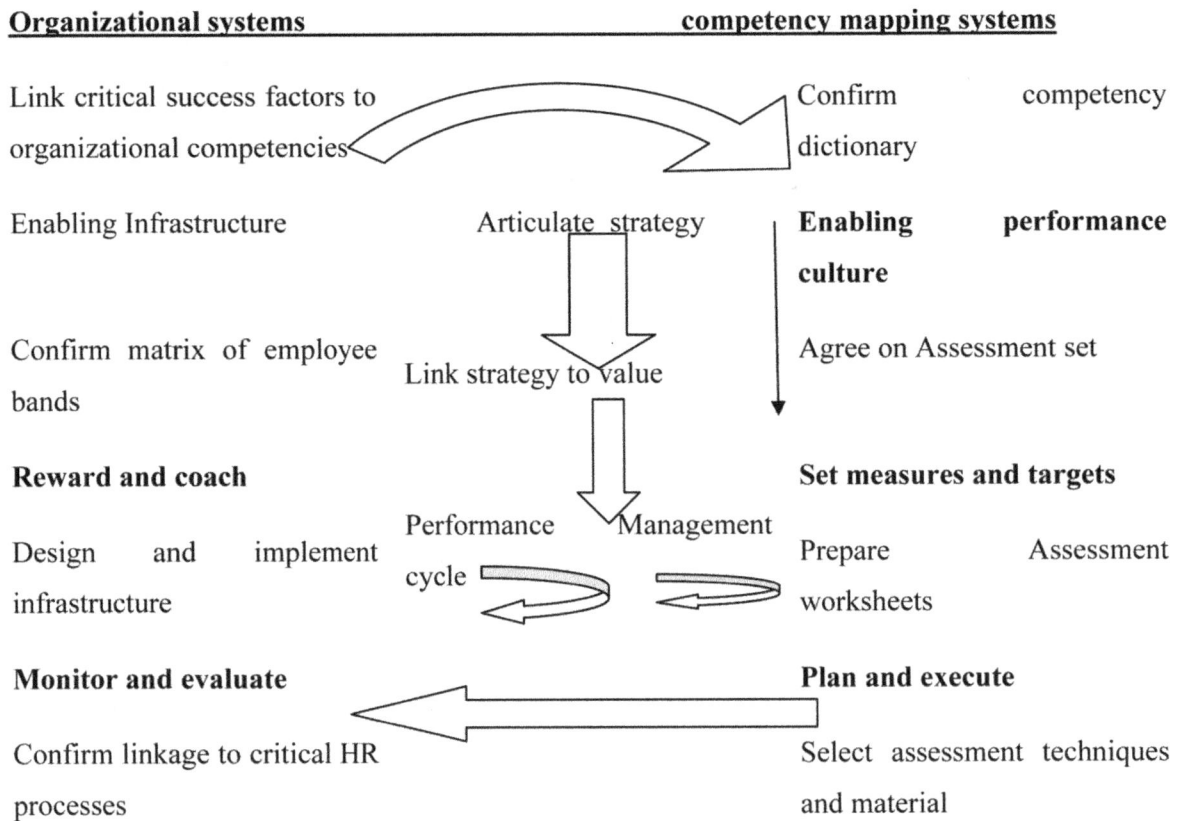

Organizational systems   **competency mapping systems**

Link critical success factors to   Confirm   competency
organizational competencies   dictionary

Enabling Infrastructure   Articulate strategy   **Enabling   performance**
                                                              culture

Confirm matrix of employee   Link strategy to value   Agree on Assessment set
bands

Reward and coach   **Set measures and targets**

Design   and   implement   Performance Management   Prepare   Assessment
infrastructure   cycle   worksheets

Monitor and evaluate   **Plan and execute**

Confirm linkage to critical HR   Select assessment techniques
processes   and material

Competency based performance management at the core involves (CBPMS)

1. People are more effective in a culture with a vision, a common purpose and a reason for existence. The importance of vision cannot be understated. The concrete possibilities that are thrown up in an open ended vision statement are often missed for its dream like articulation. But in the dream like articulation are the power of people link, the bondage, the spirit and a super ordinate goal. At the minimum vision should encompass value based articulation to include long term business direction ,focus on the core competence of the organization, concern for the stakeholders and in particular customers and employees, performance standards and benchmarks and should be collaborative and supportive. Effective vision statements challenge and stretch the organization. The PMS linkages are evident in the individual /team goals that are congruent with the corporate vision. The will to perform is inspired by the cohesive and pervading vision statement.

2. Built into the organizational existence is the power of values. The thread of beliefs, norms, practices, concerns and goals shared, imbibed over time and used as a base for shaping behavior, the corporate invincible, the ethos so very fundamental for survival.

3. Values are possible in several forms but the core human values, although it exists in the soul of the organization needs speaking. They could be respect, value and dignity for the individual, care in consonance with nature, trust, mutuality, openness and transparency, integrity, equality, work ethos, positive attitude and standing by people in good and bad times. The binding values make many things simply unspoken, make things happen automatically.

4. At the operative level, starts the business mission and strategic management, the core purpose of the organization, the clarity relevant for business goals, need for competencies, the direction to compete, the plans, aspirations, resource allocation, target setting and results. All with a measurable destination. The basics of planning deals with converting the vision, mission into operative plans at the top management level, at the management planning stage and into key tasks and core benchmarks at the operative stage. Planning establishes the journey and the milestones

Role of performance management system in talent management system:

The Talent Management system (TMS) is an effective tool for creating a symbiotic relationship between talent and organization to dramatically accelerate performance improvements.

Performance management is the process of creating a work environment to perform to the best of one's abilities. Performance management is a whole –work system that begins when a job is defined as needed. A performance management system includes selection, job description, setting performance standards, providing effective orientation, education and training with on-going coaching and feedback. By conducting quarterly performance and rewarding people for their contribution to organization also helps in their career development, coupled with exit interviews to understand why valued employees leave the organization. Infosys has a comprehensive and integrated role-based performance management system. It is a combination of task and competency evaluation based on predefined parameters for each role. This system integrates with the reward systems as well as with the training systems. (Farah Naqvi 2009).

Significance of clarity in setting goals on the performance of the workforce Tools for Talent by: Hartley, Darin E(2004)This article describes some of the major phases of talent management and then takes a look at tools and technology that are facilitating this process. The phrase talent management is used loosely and often interchangeably across a wide array of terms such as succession planning, human capital management, resource planning, and employee performance management. Finding the right people for open positions in an organization is a task not to be taken lightly. The organization gets better and the person is passionate about what he or she does. That's the most desired state when recruiting people

Balanced scorecard as a performance management tool.

1. The balanced scorecard approach may require some substantial changes in culture within the organization. The balanced scorecard requires understanding, commitment and support from the very top of the business down. The balanced scorecard will evolve. As culture changes and develops to accept the new approach and members of the organization mature within the new culture, the organization will find new things to measure, new goals in different areas, to make the balanced scorecard even more balanced and effective in supporting a living, growing, viable organization. Different organizations have quite different needs, market areas, people, products and services, and will end Practical implications - The balanced scorecard is balanced in another dimension - not just a balance of measures of essential areas of the business, but also a balance of goals versus accountability. If people do not accept accountability for achievement of the balanced measures and goals of the balanced scorecard, there is no balanced scorecard. The people of the organization are the key to the success of the balanced scorecard system. Chavan, Meena.(2009).

The significance of High performance work systems:

Can high performance work systems really lead to better performance? The effect of HPWS on firm performance is empirically tested using data collected from publicly listed companies in Taiwan, as well as multinational companies' branch offices in Taiwan. Findings — Initial factor analysis on HPWS practices supports this conceptual scheme. Using the structural equation modeling technique (AMOS 4.0) better-performing firms were found to invest in more sophisticated HRM practices, which further enhanced organizational performance. While most previous research on HPWS involves regression-like analyses, this study tries a different approach, with the structural modeling technique, to verify HPWS' relationship with firm performance. Hsi-An Shih; Yun-Hwa Chiang; Chu-Chun Hsu. (2006).

Articulating appraisal system effectiveness based on managerial cognitions.

In another study it was found how managers see, interpret and make sense of their performance management system experiences and recommend the way forward for both policy and practice, in what makes effective appraisal systems. The study applied the repertory grid to elicit the personal constructs of how managers make sense of their appraisal experiences. The cognitive mapping methodology allows the researcher to go deep into the respondents' "theories in use" to provide new insights on how they "think". This, in turn, allows a better understanding of the language managers use to make sense of the experiences. Findings--Core conceptual dimensions, cognitive maps and cluster diagrams were generated, providing implications for research, practice and new directions for future research. Research limitations/implications--Although the application of the grid technique was time-resuming, the finer grain level of analysis provided a deeper appreciation of managers' "theories in use". The study provides a cross-sectional view of the current state of managerial cognitions. Findings open up new ways of thinking and new way of doing in appraisal research and practice. Practical implications--The findings provided very meaningful insights on what managers look for in appraisal system effectiveness, along with the documentation of how they make connections between their own elicited personal constructs on system effectiveness. Originality/value--The paper makes a modest contribution to both theory and practice from the perspective of managerial cognitions about the entire appraisal systems using a method originating from clinical psychology. Wright, Robert P.; Cheung, Frenda K. K.(2006)

What do People Want from their Jobs? The Big Five, core self-evaluations and work motivation by: Bipp, Tanja (2010), If people are differentially motivated on the basis of individual differences, this implies important practical consequences with respect to staffing decisions and the selection of the right motivational techniques for managers. In two different samples (students facing graduation vs full-time employees), the relationships between personality traits and the preference for job characteristics concerning either extrinsic (job environment) or intrinsic job features (work itself) were investigated. Two personality traits [openness to experience and core self-evaluations (CSE)] were consistently found to be positively related to the preference concerning work characteristics, and CSE showed incremental validity with regard to intrinsic work motivation factors (e.g., experienced meaningfulness, autonomy). Furthermore, age was differentially linked to those job characteristics. The results are discussed with regards to the optimal Person–Job Fit and the practical utility of the personality constructs.

Best Practices for Performance Management. HR Magazine, (2006) this article discusses the findings of the benchmark report from Aberdeen Group, regarding best practices for performance management. Best-in-class companies that are doing the best job of employee performance management pay special attention to salaried individual contributors and, to a somewhat lesser extent, their managers. They also concentrate on vertical goal alignment, measured performance and frequent feedback.

Performance Management. by: Bersin, Josh. Training, Jun2006, highlighted the role of performance culture on the productivity of a company. In today's economic world productivity is the prime goal of any company. A study shows that the companies having better techniques for managing employee performance were 50 to 60 percent more efficient than those that do not have such good system. The benefits of employee performance management provide the mechanism to deal with the poor performing employees. Lack of such management always keeps employees away from understanding how their success is measured for themselves and the organization. If a poor performer is accepted then it is considered that mediocrity is acceptable, imparting a negative influence on the productivity and morale of co-workers. The result comes in the form of low productivity level of organization and diminished credibility of managers. The remedy lies in creating a performance culture which creates a sense of employee accountability and commitment. It also presents the ideas on performance culture by leading business executives including Jack Welch, Michael Dell, James Kilts and Elisabeth Fleuriot.;(2010)

How to Close the Gap between Corporate Goals and Employee Performance(2004)-Provides information on how to close the gap between corporate goals and employee performance. Challenges faced by human resources and compensation managers in aligning employee and organization goals; Relationship of employee performance management with enterprise performance management;

Today's companies no longer succeed by frequent introduction of new products or use of first-class technology alone. Companies have realized that they must also seek sustaining competitive advantage from the effective management of human resources. Today's world-class companies such as Nokia employ effective employee performance management (PM) practices. They have realized that seeking sustaining competitive advantage from the effective management of human resources is of utmost importance. Until today, however, there has existed little understanding about how these companies manage the performance of their critical personnel group, the expatriate employees. A key finding of the case study of Nokia Telecommunications Inc. is that the performance of different types of expatriates in varying situations is, and should he, managed dissimilarly. Reflecting this finding, it is suggested that companies should develop alternative PM tools. As this study examined expatriate performance management in a Finnish company that is large, highly internationalized, and uses hundreds of expatriates, future research could benefit by focusing on expatriate PM issues in smaller and less internationalized companies having fewer expatriates. Tahvanainen, Marja (2000).

2.5 Gaps in literature

The emergence of the concept of Talent management has made HR professionals to think more strategically and meet the organizational requirements more effectively. Though human resource professionals used to be more focused on hiring and firing issues; the modern corporate world expects the HR professionals to take a little bit more ownership on talent management issues rather than only designing the system of human resource management.

As per the literature review Talent management can be defined as the "integrated process of ensuring that an organization has a continuous supply of highly productive individuals in the right job at the right time."

What has been observed as a gap in the literature is that there has to be an integrated approach for talent management -starting from identifying the competencies required for the various job profiles and clearly developing the behavioral indicators for handling the job proficiently. After identifying the competencies required for performing a particular job, the individuals needs to be mapped according to the competencies. Organizations can utilize these competencies mapping for better recruitment and selection procedure and also branding themselves for attracting the best talents in the industry. These brands simplify decision making and communicate the value they create for their customer's .Likewise, employees also identify themselves with certain organizations especially in the light of forecasted labor shortage. The employees can be better engaged and this leads to better understanding and involvement in the work processes as well as the organizations. The performance management system can then swing into action for identifying the highly productive individuals and in the right job at the right time. If any coaching and mentoring needs to be done then the individuals can be guided through the process for having a highly productive workforce which leads to employee satisfaction and decline in employee attrition rates.

Though there is a tremendous change in the talent management approach – but still the observation has it that the integrated approach towards managing the high potential workgroup is missing. The present study is to focus on establishing relationship between the various HR processes and then establishing that how a competency based HR process can bring about a significant difference in the workplace. Even though organizations are aware of the need for human talent they were neglecting it all these years without giving it a comprehensive look. Therefore it is imperative for the organizations today to develop adequate and appropriate plans and put in efforts to attract the best pool of talents and also retain the current employees.

References:

Anstey, Edgar (1989). *Reminiscences for wartime Army psychologists*", The Psychologists, vol. 2, November, pp.475-78.

Boyle, S.J.Fullerton and R.Wood (1995). *"Do Assessments /development centres use optimum evaluation procedures? A survey of practice in UK organizations'* International Journal of selection and Assessment 3(2),pp.132-140

Burgoyne,J.G. and R.Stuart (1976) . *"The nature ,use and Acquisition of Managerial skills and other attributes'*,Personnel review ,5(4) , pp.19-29

Boyatzis,Richard E. (1982), *"The competent manager".* New York, NY: Jhon wiley ,

Boyatzis ,Richard E. ., Scott.s.Cowen ,and David A. Kolb . (1995) , *"Innovation in professional education".* San Francisco, CA.

Bipp, Tanja. , (Mar2010), International Journal of Selection & Assessment, Vol. 18 Issue 1, p28-39

Bersin, Josh,(Jun2006),Performance Management, Training, Vol. 43 Issue 6, p7-7, 1p;

Best Practices for Performance Management. HRMagazine, Oct2006, Vol. 51 Issue 10, p16-16

Chavan, Meena, (2009), The balanced scorecard: a new challenge. Journal of Management Development, Vol. 28 Issue 5, p393-406

Cernuşca, Lucian1 luciancernusca@gmail.com Dima, Cristina2 cristina@data.no Source:Revista da Faculdade de Ciências Humanas e Sociais; 2007, Issue 4, p162-171

Corbitt, Terry, Mar2004, Business Performance Management Systems, , Vol. 48 Issue 3, p22-23.

De Waal, André; Kourtit, Karima; Nijkamp, Peter. (2009) International Journal of Operations & Production Management, Vol. 29 Issue 12, p1242-1265.

Davis, Patricia; Rogers, Robert W, (Summer2005) *"Getting the most from your performance management system"*, Vol. 34 Issue 2, p13-16.

Dobson, Phillip; Myles, John; Jackson, Paul. (Apr-Jun2007), *"Making the Case for Critical Realism: Examining the Implementation of Automated Performance Management Systems"* Information Resources Management Journal, Vol. 20 Issue 2, p138-1

Furnham, Adrian., (2004) European Business Journal 2nd Quarter, Vol. 16 Issue 2, and p83-94,

Gunaratne, K. Asoka; Du Plessis, Andries J. Journal of Global Business & Technology, Mar(2007) , Vol. 3 Issue 1, p17-28,

Hay Mc Ber, (October 1997) **Competency Study Database**

Hsi-An Shih; Yun-Hwa Chiang; (2006) Chu-Chun Hsu. International Journal of Manpower, Vol. 27 Issue 8, p741-763, 23p, 3

Mc Clleland ,David C(1973) . *"Testing for competency Rather than Intelligence"* , American Psychologist,28 ,January , pp.18-20.

McClleland ,David C. " *Identifying competencies with the behavioural event interviews"* Psychological science .Vol.9,no.5, September 1998

Management charter initiative 1990.

Management issues News Online (2006) *Employee engagement gives big boost to the bottom line, 7 June* (online) http:// www. Managementissues.com /2006/8/24/research/ employee-engagement –gives –big boost to the bottom-line .asp (accessed 21 july 2012)

Maslow ,Abraham H (1943) *A theory of motivation, Psychological Review* 50,pp 370-96

Mc Kinsey (2005) – *"Addressing china's Looming Talent shortage"* report- October

Martone, David, (Autumn2003) A Guide to Developing a Competency-Based Performance-Management System Employment Relations Today (Wiley), Vol. 30 Issue 3, p23-32.

Mei-I Cheng; Andrew Dainty; David Moore., (Jan2007), *Implementing a new performance management system within a project-based organization: A case study* International Journal of

Productivity & Performance Management, Vol. 56

Marchand, Marie; Raymond, Louis. (2008)International Journal of Operations & Production Management, , Vol. 28 Issue 7, p663-686

Morgan, Robert, Compensation & Benefits Review, (Sep/Oct2006), Vol. 38 Issue 5, p22-27.

Naqvi, Farah,(Jan2009), . ICFAI Journal of Management Research Vol. 8 Issue 1, p85-94,

Nath, Rabindra; Raheja, Rajat.(Apr-Sep2001) Journal of Services Research, , Vol. 1 Issue 1, p25

Bersin, Josh.,(Jun2006), "**Performance Management Training**". Vol. 43 Issue 6, p7-7, 1p;

Resource Management International Digest, (Aug2004), "*Pay for performance* report. Vol. 4 Issue 8, p1-15, 4p

Spencer ,Legde M. and Sigme M. spencer (1993) . *competence at Work* ,Newyork : Jhon Wiley & Sons Inc.

Hartley, Darin E.T+D, (Apr2004) *Significance of clarity in setting goals on the performance of the workforce Tools for Talent.*

T.V. Rao* and Sumeet Varghese TVRLS, February (2009), Ahmedabad, Indian Human Resource Development , 15–34 .Vol. 12, No. 1

Woodruffe,c, (2003). *To have and to hold: Getting your organization onto talented People CVs* .Training Journal ,May :pp: 20-24

Kaplan, RobertS and Norton,David P(2004) *Strategy Maps : converting intangible assets into intangible outcomes,* Harvard Business SchoolPress , Boston, Mass

Wright, Robert P.; Cheung, Frenda K. K. (2007), Personnel Review, Vol. 36.

Yuk Lan Wong; Snell, Robin Stanley. (Winter2003). Journal of General Management, Vol. 29 Issue 2, p53-69.

Chapter-III

3.1 Emergence of IT industries

Information technology (IT) industry has become one of the most robust industries in the world. IT is concerned with technology to treat information. The acquisition, processing, storage and dissemination of vocal, pictorial, textual and numerical information by a microelectronics-based combination of computing and telecommunication are its main fields. The term in its modern sense first appeared in a 1958 article published in the Harvard Business Review, in which authors Leavitt and Whisler commented that "the new technology does not yet have a single established name. Some of the modern and emerging fields of information technology are next generation web technologies, bioinformatics, cloud computing, global information systems, large scale knowledge bases, etc. Advancements are mainly driven in the field of computer science.

IT is the area of managing technology and spans a wide variety of areas that include computer software, information systems, computer hardware, programming languages but are not limited to things such as processes, data constructs. In short, anything that renders data, information or perceived knowledge in any visual format whatsoever, via any multimedia distribution mechanism, is considered part of the IT domain. IT provides businesses with four sets of core services to help execute the business strategy: business process automation, providing information, connecting with customers, and productivity tools.

Managers and business firms invest in information technology and systems because they provide real economic value to the business. The decision to build or maintain an information system assumes that the returns on this investment will be superior to other investments in buildings, money or machinery.

The IT era, beginning in the early 1980s refocused the use of information technology on the knowledge worker. Financial analysts, stock brokers and production planners used PC work stations, primarily for what-if types of analysis.

In the mid-80s, another major shift occurred. Instead of managing data processing alone, MIS management discovered new application portfolios. Besides the traditional data processing portfolio, application portfolio for office automation, micro computing, and computer assisted design and robotics emerged. All these portfolios were characterized by different stages of evolution, with data processing at a fairly mature stage of evolution compared with other technologies.

In the network era, the move towards using information technology to leverage business results is becoming most pronounced. If major productivity improvements are to occur, Nolan argues, new technology must be introduced along with new forms of organizational structure. Information technology alone will not enable organizations to achieve the business results they seek, but information technology combined with new forms organizational structure will bring about dramatic productivity improvements.

Nolan predicts that information technology, combined with networked forms of organizing people and their work, will create a 10-fold productivity increases. The networked form of organization will create opportunities for multidisciplinary teams to accomplish projects. Traditional departmental barriers will be blurred and new methods of accomplishing tasks will emerge as work is reengineered.

Edgar Schein has proposed a framework depicting the evolution of new information technology within organizations that provides a holistic view of the organizational change process. In some ways, his theory is similar to Nolan's stage theory. Schein's phases include 1) investment or project initiation,2) technology learning and adaptation 3) management control and widespread technology transfer.

In the investment phase, the organization decides to invest in a new information technology such as office automation. If this new technology seems to have merit, this initial phase leads to the second phase, technology learning and adaptation. However if users are not involved in the initial selection system selection or if vendor related problems occur, stagnation A may occur. Stagnation A, which may result from significant cost overruns, poor project management, and unanticipated technological problems delays further evolution of new information technology indefinitely.

In successful projects, the introduction of information technology leads to the second phase –trying the technology- during which users learn how to use the technology for tasks beyond those initially planned. For example, microcomputers may be introduced for word processing during project initiation. Experimentation with word processing and database software may lead secretaries to set up mailing list, files and office record keeping systems. Experimentation with word processing and database software may lead secretaries to set up mailing list files and office record keeping systems .Experimentation causes new technology to be used in ways different from those originally planned and brings about unforeseen benefits.

If users have an opportunity to develop a better understanding of new technology and its benefits during phase 2, the organization will move into phase 3.However, premature controls can cause failure to learn how to use new technology and lead to stagnation B. stagnation B occurred in an organization that introduced work, and the organization had no motivation to expand   the scope of office automation to new tasks based on its experience with the mailing application. Because of the premature focus on cutting clerical costs, the organization was unable to reap the potential benefits of expanded uses of office automation.

Phase-3 –management control –occurs when the organization recognizes the importance of the technology and introduces precise controls over systems development and implementation that help to ensure the cost effectiveness and success of the application that result. If this phase is successful, the organization then begins to transfer this application to other groups within the organization.
However if excessive controls are introduced, stagnation C results. Stagnation c may inhibit further

transfer of the technology into other organizational units. For example, in one organization a local area network was established within a research department. To justify the network, its users focused on paperwork reduction and operational efficiency. As, a result, the enthusiasm for innovation was a lost, and the new technology failed to be transferred to other offices throughout the organization. Stagnation C may also lead to surreptitious experimentation with altogether different technologies causing evolution beginning with phase 1 again.

If technology is successfully implemented, Phase 4 –widespread technology transfer- should occur. During this phase, a technology such as local area network is transferred to other parts of the organization. Technical expertise should be transferred by user analysts and technical support personnel along with the technology itself.

The stage evolution of new technology assimilation creates new challenges for MIS management because organizations may be in different phases of growth for different types of technologies. For example, success with the development of on-line transactions systems may put an organization in phase 4 with regard to data processing technology. Gradual assimilation of word processing may result in a phase 3 evolution in office automation. Finally, the introduction of software supporting the development of expert systems may put the organization in phase 1 in the development of artificial intelligence. Each phase requires different types of management techniques and control strategies. Improper management and premature controls may create the various forms of stagnation that retard further development.

The stage theory also points out that some of the disorderliness accompanying experimentation with new information technology may be necessary.

3.2 IT sector in India

The definitions of statistics and statisticians succinctly sum up the figures for the Indian IT industry in FY10. Though a 7% growth (in rupee terms would not excite analysts used to 20% or more growth rates (last year it grew 19%),what the numbers do not reveal the resilience of the industry the gains it had made over the years ,the brand equity it has built and most importantly the capabilities it had developed that relatively insulated it from the impact of the worst global recession in recent memory.

While the emergence of the IT sector as India's sunrise industry was a direct fallout of globalization .The good news was how the Indian IT industry emerged relatively unscathed; from whatever angle it is viewed ,be it the 7% growth in rupee terms or a more realistic 5% growth in dollar terms(perhaps more suitable in this era of globalization)these results in a recessionary year were quite encouraging.

The domestic sector grew 9%, while exports recorded a 6% growth, in rupee terms .quite understandable, considering that exports were predominantly dependent on the US and Europe –economies which bore the brunt of the recession. The domestic share(33%) of the overall pie continued increasing ,albeit by a single point only .And despite the slowing down of the domestic growth rate(from 12% in FY09),the resilience of this 121237 crore industry ensured that more and more global MNCs were keen to take a share of the pie.

Information and communication technology is the key to boost the country's global competitiveness, says a World economic forum study. India's success in the IT-BPO domain over the past decade has been exemplary. Total export revenue earned by this sector grew from $1.8bn in 1997-98 to $46.3bn in 2008-2010at CAGRof 35%. The Industry has been engine of growth for the Indian economy, quadrupling its share of GDP numbers and exports to 4% and 16% respectively.

While contributing to the GDP numbers nd exports, this growth has had multiplying effect too. Direct employment in the IT services and BPO segment touched nearly 2.2 by 2008-2009, translating into the creation of about 8mn indirect jobs in diverse fields.

Still the country has not been able to tap the full potential of the ICT sector as penetration remains extremely low by International standards.

The challenge of the ICT use is most visible in the large gap between ICT services accounting for 90% of ICT GDP and ICT manufacturing. Consequently, India's high level of network readiness has not translated into higher levels of usage; the national policy environment is yet to be molded to facilitate development of new technologies.

There is however a silver lining. The Gartner report for 2010 says India centric IT services companies will represent 20% of the leading cloud aggregators in the market at the end of 2012.

Globally, the network is becoming all-pervasive as an increasing awareness of the transformational role that network connectivity can play has set the tone for the growth of the networking market in India. As rural India achieves the last mile connectivity it presents a huge opportunity for the IT sector .IT services banking, financial services and Insurance (BFSI) and telecom will continue owing to be the key market adopters, while the government is likely to emerge as a big spender owing to the various e-governance and SWAN initiatives. Technology investments to bridge the digital divide and drive inclusive growth in rural and semi urban India are likely to gain momentum. Wireless for last mile connectivity in rural India and unwiring our cities will be the focus in emerging markets like ours. The advent of 3G in India has given the much needed impetus to the mobile value added services .Increased bandwidth will help improve the quality of video services which will in turn spur the growth for collaborative technologies such as tele presence. Healthcare and educational sectors will continue to drive the growth of IT in India, with medical facilities being delivered over the internet and distance learning being imparted over the internet to students in remote areas.ICT development in the energy sector also looks promising .Smart grid solutions for transmission and distribution automation, security ,business and home energy management coupled with smart meter communications will save huge amounts of energy and facilitate accurate distribution as per demand.

In essence therefore, continued investments by both the private and the public sectors will hold the key to the growth of the IT sector in India over the next decade.

With end of 2010, Indian IT has closed a successful decade .it was an eventful decade –for the industry recovered two economic recessions. India discovered and enabled new business models that necessitated new learning. India further established the position as a global powerhouse in the IT industry. The next decade appears full of opportunities for IT outsourcing as the industry continues to mature to a point where the benefit from the labor arbitrage is being strongly complemented by the improved efficiency, effectiveness and innovation that companies are delivering .Taken together, these two factors will continue to stimulate companies to reconsider what is core to their business and what should be outsourced.

Four irrefutable and interconnected forces gaining strength worldwide, requiring organizations across industries to rethink how work should be conducted. Work of all forms is migrating to its right location worldwide allowing companies to leverage expertise anywhere and everywhere it resides; digital natives ,both as employees and customers are creating new social and operating norms for companies worldwide; new virtualized platforms are enabling collaboration within organization and outside the organization leading to new ways of working ,managing and innovating. Cloud computing, social networking, broadband and mobility are enabling new business and technology models that improve operational flexibility and knowledge sharing. Together, these forces will make work increasingly dynamic, allowing organizations especially in knowledge –intensive industries, to shift tasks to places where talent and the cost advantage can improve outcomes and business performance. In response, organizations will be required to gain a deeper understanding of differentiating knowledge embedded processes that drive business effectiveness, competitive differentiation and growth.

To achieve new ways of working, organizations will need more scalable and flexible IT systems and processes that allow knowledge to be captured and applied by virtual teams inside and outside the conventional organizational structure. This is area where Indian IT industry will discover unprecedented opportunities to scale up the value chain by building newer capabilities and broadening its services horizon.

The steps taken by IT industry, though hard for everyone in the short term, worked well for the individual firms as well as sector. The IT sector experienced temporary decline in profit margin because of high expenses on marketing, sales, and resourcing. In 2011 though, IT sector seems to have achieved a stable rate. This rate is certainly not the glamorous rate of the past decade. But this is reasonably good growth rate, a rate that is usually characterized by a stable industry. An analysis of the IT firms will enable us to know how the overall sector is performing, how the valuation and what should be our take on IT sector as a whole. To understand this we can analyze the performance of

3 large firms, Infosys, TCS, and Wipro. 2   Medium firms, HCL Technologies, Tech Mahindra & Mphasis, and 2 small firms, Mindtree and Polaris. We will study their market numbers, financials, and

few ratios. Let's look at their revenue and profit numbers. All numbers are in Crore of Rupees.

Large companies: TCS, Infosys, Wipro

These companies have done tremendously well in last 5 years despite slowdown in developed world market. They have been able to steer largely unscathed from the US recession. The reason is that these firms, while still majorly focused on United States market, started finding other avenues to expand. These efforts have paid them very well.

However, if you look at revenue growth versus net profit growth, except TCS, both Infosys and Wipro has not been able to grow their bottom line the same way they did their top line. The other important factor is their net profit margin. TCS and Infosys maintained their net profit margin at healthy 24.14% and 27.78%. Wipro's net profit margin is 18.40%.

Inference

Looking at the PEG ratio which is nothing but PE ratio divided by the growth rate. All the three companies are overpriced at the current price. Now being overpriced is not such a bad thing if the companies are expected to grow at a higher rate but the growth rate has subdued in recent years. In fact the last 2 years growth rate is 14%, 12%, and 11% CAGR for TCS, Infosys, and Wipro respectively. Looking at all these parameters, Infosys looks extremely overpriced. TCS and Wipro too are overpriced.

Medium companies: HCL Technologies, Tech Mahindra, Mphasis

Tech Mahindra has performed worse in growth rate as well as average net profit margin. The net profit growth rate (CAGR) of Tech Mahindra is misleading because of a huge cost in 2007 which lowered the base net profit number. Hence in this case, we looked at operating profit CAGR.

Mphasis and HCL technologies look good bet as far as PEG ratio is concerned. It tells us there is scope for price appreciation.

Inference

While Mphasis and HCL technologies look good when you look at last 5 years numbers, their growth in last 2 years have been at a CAGR of 11.47% and 4.9%. Mphasis looks attractive at this price if we assume that it will continue the same performance in next few years. This is less likely. In fact the net profit increase in all three firms in last 1 year, it has gone down.

Small companies: Mindtree, Polaris

Mindtree and Polaris have done pretty considering the fact that they came to the real competition with service companies pretty late. Looking at their numbers, both have managed to produce a decent margin. As far as PEG ratio is concerned, Mindtree certainly looks expensive.

Inference

Mindtree has a good brand owing to its founders Subroto Bagchi & team. His articles and books have been a source of inspiration to a lot of people. The mindtree team has been able to build a name for it which is a great achievement. This is the reason why Mindtree is overpriced. Mindtree, at the same time, has been able to grow at 22% in last 2 years which is amazing growth. This is the highest growth in last 2 years among all the 8 companies studied here.

Polaris, on the other hand looks fairly priced. In fact Polaris is the only company in the last 5 companies that has been able to increase its net profit in the year 2011. I think this could be a good bet if Polaris is able to sign some decent business deals in next few quarters.

Overall Analysis

IT sector companies, especially the well-known brands, are overpriced. This is quite acceptable as the Nifty at PE ratio of 20+ can be easily termed overpriced. However this is not the bubble phase yet. Remember the last bubble phase occurred when Nifty crossed 26+. The problem is that there doesn't seem to be any trigger that can catapult the market in bull phase and enable investors to earn profit on these stocks.

Mphasis, Polaris, and Mindtree could be good bet if the prices further decline by 20%. At the current price, they look fairly priced but their last few quarters results are too volatile to really comment on the stability of the trend.

In a country as diverse and complex as India, the odds of understanding what ICT in india will evolve into is at best calculated prediction. With the growing momentum of cloud computing we are at the cusp of the next evolution in IT services delivery –everything as a service .The next wave will be driven by a new model of computing. Instead of installing packaged software applications on their computers, people and business will use their web browsers to access a wide range of cloud services available on demand on the internet.

A major reason for this spending is the modernization drive that the PSU banks have been undergoing since the last couple of years. While most of the foreign and multinational banks were still reeling under the pressure of the slowdown, PSU banks went on a heightened spending drive that majorly bolstered the demand coming from this sector.

FY11 is expected to be the year of services across verticals .While hardware and software spends are just beginning to get back on track after this unpleasant tryst with slowdown ,services that managed to have a decent run even amid turbulent times is gathering further momentum. During the slowdown, two trends that gained a lot of traction were managed services and the hosted model. Because these options involved little or no CAPEX investment, the OPEX model became a rage with Indian enterprises across verticals. Software deployment and consultation services also became high spending points for CIO'S. Spending on IT is expected to increase by more than 10% in the coming year. The outlook for services thus is rosier than hardware and software. However the services scenario in India is still laced with challenges. While most of the large organizations and MNC's are spending more on network integration and software deployment, there is comparative silence on the part of the mid sized organizations.

Companies now perceive information technology as not just a cost head ,but a key enabler which helps organizations achieve competitive advantage.

3.3. INFOSYS- PROFILE

A multinational technology based organization headquartered at Bangalore, Infosys Technologies limited, is easily reputed to be one of India's largest IT company .The Company has nine development centers in India alone and spans an entire range of over 30 offices worldwide. The company Infosys and its subsidiaries together employ slightly over 80,501 professionals according to figures provided on September 30, 2007. The company's annual revenue for Fiscal year 2006-2007 has exceeded US$3.1 billion and it has a market

capitalization of over US$30 billion.

The company Infosys was established in July2, 1981 in Pune by NR Narayan Murthy along with Nandan Nilekeni,N.S Raghavan,S.D shibhulal ,Kris Gopalakrishnan,Ashok Arora and K.Dinesh and subsequently Raghavan was the first employee of the company . N.R.Narayan Murthy started the organization with the registered name "Infosys Consultants Pvt.Ltd." and the registered office of the company was established at Raghavan's house in Matunga. After that in 1983,the company moved to Bangalore,which is the capital of Karnataka . Infosys got its first International client in 1987 which has Data Basics Corporation based in the United States.

The year 1999 saw Infosys attain SEI-CMM level 5 ranking and then became the first national level company which was listed on NASDAQ. Infosys in the year 2001 was rated as the Best employer of India by Business Today magazine ,and subsequently in the year 2002 ,the business world magazine named Infosys as "India's Most Respected Company" The company also Global MAKE which is actually abbreviated form for the Most admired Knowledge Enterprises Award. Consecutively for 2003,2004 and 2005. This was a record in itself since it was the only Indian company which won this award and was inducted into Global Hall of Fame for this reason.

3.3.a. Initiatives taken by Infosys:

In the year 1996, Infosys had created Infosys foundation In Karnataka state, and has been operating in the areas of Social rehabilitation and rural up liftment, healthcare, arts, education and culture. Ever since the foundation has expanded its operation In the state of Maharastra, Tamil Nadu, Andhra Pradesh, Punjab and Orissa. The organization Infosys foundation is chaired by Mrs. Sudha Murthy. Since the year 2004, the company Infosys has been involved in a series of initiatives which will help consolidate and formalize some of its academic relationships on a worldwide basis all under an Umbrella program known as ACE or Academic Entente. The company remains in touch with all its important stakeholders in the academic conferences and University events ,Case studies ,research collaboration and hosting study trips to the Infosys Development Centers as well as running the InStep Global Internship program,which recognizes the fact that this message extends beyond campuses to shareholders ,partners ,customers and also other stake holders who are in some way associated with academia.

Today Infosys is a global leader in the 'next generation' of IT and consulting with revenues of $6.35 billion (LTM Q1-FY12). Infosys defines designs and delivers technology-enabled business solutions that help Global 2000 companies win in a Flat World. Infosys also provides a complete range of services by leveraging their domain and business expertise and strategic alliances with leading technology providers.

Infosys' offerings span business and technology consulting, application services, systems integration, product engineering, custom software development, maintenance, re-engineering, independent testing and validation services, IT infrastructure services and business process outsourcing. Infosys pioneered the Global Delivery Model (GDM), which emerged as a disruptive force in the industry leading to the rise of offshore outsourcing. The GDM is based on the principle of taking work to the location where the best talent is available, where it makes the best economic sense, with the least amount of acceptable risk.

Key Executive Directors:

S.No	Name	Designation
1	K V Kamath	Chairman
3	S D Shibulal	CEO& Managing Director
2	NR Ravikrishnan	Company Secretary
4	Deepak M Satwalekar	Director
5	Omkar Goswami	Director
6	Sridar A lyengar	Director
7	David L Boyles	Director
8	Jeffrey S Lehman	Director
9	R Seshasayee	Director
10	Ann Fudge	Director
11	Ravi Venkatesan	Director
12	Srinath Batni	Director
13	V Balakrishnan	Director
14	B G Srinivas	Director
15	Ashok Vemuri	Director
16	S Gopalakrishnan	Executive Chairman

3.3.b.Infosys value system:

They believe that each customer should go with a delighted experience that their expectations have been met consistently. The drive of Infosys is to set standards in the business transactions and be an exemplar for the industry and themselves, to be ethical, sincere and open in all the transactions, to be objective and transaction oriented, and thereby earn trust and respect and to strive relentlessly, constantly improve themselves ,their teams, their services and products to become the best. Infosys takes pride in building strategic long-term client relationships.

3.3.c.A magnet for best global talent:

Over 97% of their revenues come from existing customers. Fortune Magazine identified Infosys among the top companies that "inspire, nurture and empower a new generation of global leaders. "They are committed to remain among the Industry's leading employers. Infosys has global presence through its 50 offices and development centers spread across India, China Australia, the Czech Republic, Poland, the UK, Canada and Japan. Infosys and its subsidiaries have 133,560 employees as on June 30, 2011. Infosys's Finacle is Universal banking solution that caters to core banking, e-banking, Islamic banking, treasury, wealth management and CRM requirements of retail, corporate and global banks. It is used by over 106 banks across 61countries,namely UK US, China, Taiwan, Hong Kong, India, Zimbabwe, Saudi Arabia, Maldives, Nepal, etc

Software Engineering & Technology Labs (SETLabs) is the research arm of Infosys. it is at the forefront of anticipating and shaping the evolution of technology and its impact on business. Infosys SET Labs undertakes targeted R&D to address your business problems. Our researchers are engaged in cutting-edge research to share insights with clients. We focus on research areas such as Malleable Architecture, Pervasive Access, Flexible Processes and Personalized Information. These areas constitute the fundamental business technology components of a progressive, information-centered enterprise.

3.3.d.Infosys focus on quality:

At Infosys they constantly benchmark their services and processes against globally recognized quality standards. Their certifications include SEI-CMMI Level 5, CMM Level 5, PCMM LEVEL5, TL 9000 and ISO 9001-2000. In February 2007, Infosys BPO was certified for e SCM level 4.0, the e sourcing Capability Model for service providers developed by a consortium led by Carnegie Mellon University's information Technology services qualification centre.

3.3.e.Innovation, Speed and Excellence in Execution:

They were the first companies to develop and deploy a global delivery model and attain the SEI-CMM Level 5 certification in the offshore and onsite operations. They manage growth by investing in infrastructure and by rapidly recruiting, training and deploying new professionals. They have 44 global development centers, the majority of which are located in India. They also have development centers in Australia, Canada, China, Japan, and Mauritius and at multiple locations   in the United States and Europe .

3.3.f.Industry Leadership

Their history is marked by a series of initiatives. They were the first Indian company to list on a US stock exchange and the first Indian company to be added to NASDAQ 100 index in December 2006. They were recently listed on the Global DOW. Infosys was ranked no.14 among the most respected companies in the world by Reputation Institute's Global Pulse 2008. Infosys in the year 2001 was rated as the Best employer of India by Business Today magazine ,and subsequently in the year 2002 ,the business world magazine named Infosys as "India's Most Respected Company" The company also Global MAKE which is actually abbreviated form for the Most admired Knowledge Enterprises Award. Consecutively for 2003,2004 and 2005. This was a record in itself since it was the only Indian company which won this award and was inducted into Global Hall of Fame for this reason.

ir history is marked by a series of initiatives. They were the first Indian company to list on a US stock exchange and the first Indian company to be added to NASDAQ 100 index in December 2006. They were recently listed on the Global DOW. Infosys was ranked no.14 among the most respected companies in the world by Reputation Institute's Global Pulse 2008. Infosys in the year 2001 was rated as the Best employer of India by Business Today magazine ,and subsequently in the year 2002 ,the business world magazine named Infosys as "India's Most Respected Company" The company also Global MAKE which is actually abbreviated form for the Most admired Knowledge Enterprises Award. Consecutively for 2003,2004 and 2005. This was a record in itself since it was the only Indian company which won this award and was inducted into Global Hall of Fame for this reason.

3.3.g.Products and Services offered by the company:

IT Services

- Application Services
- Architecture Services
- Enterprise Quality Services
- Independent Validation Services
- Information Management Services
- Infrastructure Services
- Packaged Application Services

- SOA Services
- Systems Integration Services

Engineering Services

- Product Engineering
- Manufacturing Process and Plant Solutions
- Lifecycle Management
- Consulting Services
- Information & Technology Strategies
- Product Innovation
- Next Generation Commerce
- Core Process Excellence
- Learning & Complex Change

BPO Services

- Business Platforms
- Customer Service Outsourcing
- Finance and Accounting
- Human Resource Outsourcing
- Knowledge Services
- Legal Services
- Order Management
- Sourcing and Procurement Outsourcing

Product and Platforms

- Collaborative Analytics
- Finacle
- Infosys ActiveDesk
- Infosys mConnect
- Infosys Unified Communications and Collaboration (UC)

Subsidiaries of the company:

- Infosys BPO
- Infosys Consulting
- Infosys Australia
- Infosys China
- Infosys Mexico

3.3.h.Global sourcing

Addressing Catch 22 situations in global sourcing

In a majority of global sourcing initiatives, the biggest challenge is to reconcile disparate objectives into feasible solution. For instance, how does one ensure a quick transition with minimum disruption? Or mitigate risk while maximizing saving? They show us how such issues can be addressed during a global sourcing initiative.

Captive centers in India and china: A reality check

An Infosys survey of captive centers in India and China that sought to understand their role in meeting sourcing needs revealed that they adopted a portfolio approach to outsourcing. The survey also pointed out that the centers established strong party vendor relationship with work being distributed between India and China based on their special capabilities.

3.3. i.Global delivery model

Infosys pioneered the global delivery model (GDM) to ensure the distribution of application and business process lifecycle activities and resources, while ensuring their integration. The Key drivers of their Global Delivery Model are:

Processes: Infosys relies on processes to consistently high quality solutions while executing engagements from multiple locations. Their values, vision and policies form the first level of the three tiered process architecture. They are implemented through process execution at the next level. These processes are defined by clear ownership using the "entry ,Task ,Verification ,exit" (ETVX) paradigm along with clearly defined roles and responsibilities.

Figure 3.1 Process Map of Infosys

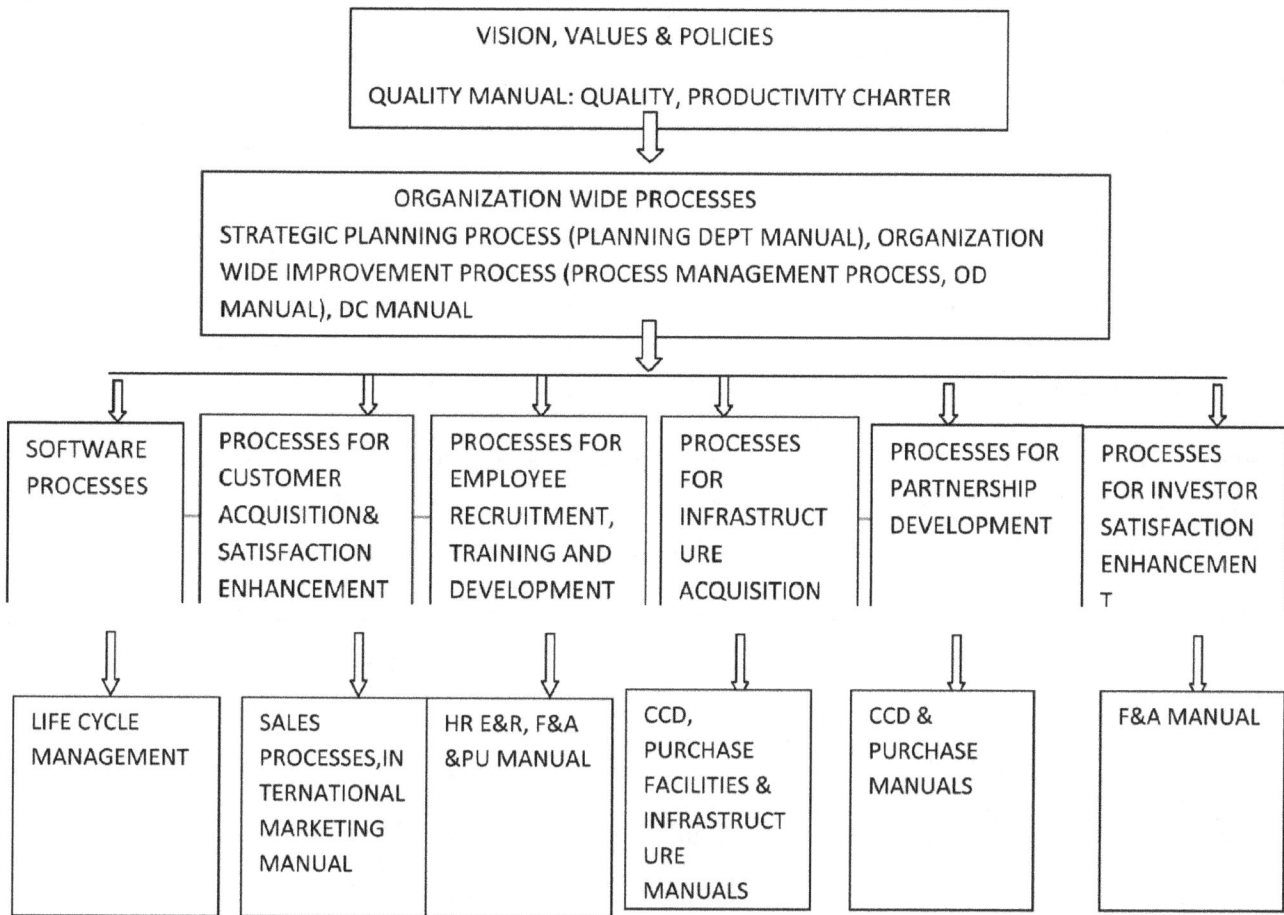

Source: www.infosys.com

3.3.j. Quality system documentation:

Quality System Documentation (QSD) listed Infosys best practices in the form of processes . The QSD provides a vast repository of detailed procedures ,templates ,standards,guidelines and check lists . The QSD is updated every four months.

3.3.k.Body of knowledge :

The Infosys Body of Knowledge (BOK) is a forum to share knowledge gained from experience. It is a central repository of experiential knowledge that can be tapped by Peers at Infosys.

3.3.l.Process Assets:

The repository of Process assets facilitates the dissemination of "engagement learning"across Infosys. A process asset is information gleaned from an engagement that can be roused during future engagements a.Process database:

The process database is a software engineering database to study the processes at Infosys with respect to productivity and quality can be expected when following the process.

a.   Tools Repository:

The tools repository is a centralized repository containing a list of tools that have been evaluated.

3.3.m.Quality:

Quality is ensured across all the processes , interfaces and outputs –in Management ,core and support processes . it helps them deliver long-term excellence ,and ultimately ,predictability of returns , through the Global Delivery Model (GDM) ,to all stakeholders.

They improve "Execution Excellence" through continuous productivity improvement. They have continuously benchmarked their processes against World –class standards and models such as ISO 9001 – Tick IT , SEI-CMM, ISO 20000, ISO27000, AS9100,TL 9000 and ISO 14001.

Regular and rigorous assessments are conducted by reputed external assesors . Their process performance has emerged as better than that of their peers. Infosys has embarked on several strategic improvement initiatives:

- Baldridge –based assessment of units for business excellence
- Organization –wide reuse and tools initiatives for productivity improvement
- Patent application filed for PROSO , their project scheduling model
- Program management framework to enable execution of large deals
- Proactive risk assessment model and approach to mitigate execution risks
- eSCM level4 certification of Infosys BPO by the IT services Qualification center (ITSqc) at Carnegie Mellon university.
- Internal quality certification to equip their team members with required skill sets quickly.

Tools

The practice project management philosophy of Infosys is bolstered by the use of robust tools. They keep the largest and most complex projects on track with the following tools:

Integrated Project Management:

Integrated Project Management (IPM) is Infosys' web- based tool for engagement management. It facilitates efficient and effective project management and addresses the functionality of a typical professional services automation framework. IPM supports the Infosys Global Delivery Model and SEI CMM Level 5 processes .

Process database :

The process database captures all project performance related metrics at Infosys. This data is used as a framework to construct the organization's process-capability baseline ,which is used by project leaders to estimate effort, schedule tasks and predict defect levels during the engagement-planning phase.

Influx

Inflix is the Infosys methodology used to define effective IT solutions for enterprise initiatives . it maps the business process view for all IT initiatives . it maps the business process view for all IT initiaves , making it possible to understand the impact of IT on specific processes. Its framework is based on the digital concept of an extended organization that includes suppliers ,customers and partners . InFlux allows the people to study the roles of different systems and entities and how they function.

PRISM

Project reviews by Infosys Senior management (PRISM) is a web based intranet tool to automate the workflow for reviews ,in line with engagement schedules and plans. The PRISM tool is a review mechanism that offers a clear pictureof engagement risks involved for a client as well as Infosys. It also drives process improvement and sharing of best practices.

Knowledge Management:

Infosys provides end-to-end workforce collaboration and knowledge management services including KnowledgeManagement Process Consulting, Collaboration and knowledge Management Applications,Portals ,Content Management, Document Management ,Enterprise Application Integration,security and Workflow. Their Knowledge Management services helps in assessing needs ,evaluate technologies and recommend solutions in the context of business problems.

They are at the forefront of introducing new methodologies and practices of knowledge sharing and adoption. They have launched blogs and customized Wiki solutions to enable communities to collaborate across geographical, time and project boundaries.

Centers of Excellence:

Their Centers of Excellence (COE) focus on extending technology competence in convergence, data warehouse and business intelligence, grid computing, J2EE, Microsoft and SOA.

Global Internships:

Instep, Infosys internship program, enables undergraduate, graduate and PhD. Students to work on live technical and business projects .

3.3.n.Engagements:

Infosys SETlabs engages clients through workshops ,research projects ,joint publications and deployment opportunities.

3.3.o.Environmental Conservation:

Infosys had developed a culture of environment conservation and is working with customers to develop sustainable products and services.

Speaking at a panel discussion at the National Energy Summit &International Dialogue in Washington, USA, Infosys CEO Kris Gopalakrishnan discussed how Infosys partners with customers to reduce their carbon footprint. Infosys helps energy companies manage smart grids and design turbines to reduce the cost of global supply chains and logistics and minimize their impact on the environment.

3.3.p.Milestones

- 1981 - Infosys was incorporated by N R Narayana Murthy and six engineers in Pune, India with an initial capital of $250. In the same year, the company received an order from its first client Data Basics Corporation of New York.

- 1983 - The company shifts its headquarters from Pune to Bangalore.

- 1987 - The company opens its first international office in Boston, US.

- 1993 - Infosys Introduced Employee Stock Options (ESOP) program. The same year company received ISO 9001/TickIT certification

- 1994 -The company relocated its corporate headquarters to Electronics City, Bangalore. It opened a development center at Fremont.

- 1995 - The company opened its first European office in the UK and Global Development Centers at Toronto and Mangalore. It also established e-Business practice.

- 1996 - The Infosys Foundation was set up.

- 1997 - The software major set up an office in Toronto, Canada. The company was assessed at CMM Level 4.

- 1998 - The company began enterprise solutions (packaged applications) practices.

- 1999 - The company generated revenues of $100 million. In 1999, Infosys was listed in NASDAQ. Later in the year 2006, the company became part of NASDAQ-100; it was first Indian and only the company to be part of any of the major global indices. It achieved a CMM Level 5 certification. The same year the company commissioned various offices in Germany, Sweden, Belgium, Australia, and two development centers in the US. The company launched Infosys Business Consulting Services.

- 2000 - The company's revenues touched $200 million mark. Infosys opened offices in France and Hong Kong, a global development center in Canada and UK, and three development centers in the US. It company re-launched its universal banking solution- Banks 2000 as Finacle.

- 2001 - The company touched $400 million revenues mark. It set up offices in UAE and Argentina, and a development center in Japan. Infosys was rated as the Best Employer by Business World/Hewitt

- 2002 - Infosys touched $ 500 million revenues mark. Nandan M Nilekani takes over as CEO from N R Narayana Murthy, who is appointed Chairman and Chief Mentor. The company opened offices in the Netherlands, Singapore and Switzerland. Infosys collaborated with the Wharton School of the University of Pennsylvania to set up The Wharton Infosys Business Transformation Awards (WIBTA). The same year, company launched Progeon, that offers business process outsourcing services.

- 2003 - The company established subsidiaries in China and Australia. It expanded its operations in Pune and China and established a Development Center in Thiruvananthapuram

- 2004 - The company touched $1 billion revenues mark. Infosys Consulting Inc was launched.

- 2005 - The company records the largest international equity offering of $1 billion from India.

- 2006 - Infosys celebrated 25 years of its existence. The company touches $2 billion revenues mark. The employee strength grew to 50,000+. N R Narayana Murthy retired from the services of the company and board of directors appointed him as an Additional Director. He continues Board of Directors appoints him as an Additional Director.

- 2007 - Infosys crossed revenues of $3 billion. Employees strength grew to over 70,000+. Kris Gopalakrishnan, COO became CEO and Nandan M Nilekani was appointed as Co-Chairman of the board of directors. The company set up a new subsidiary in Latin America.

- 2008 - Infosys crossed revenues of $4.18 billion.

- 2009 - Infosys USA Foundation has provided a grant for the New York City (NYC) Science Education Initiative to spread science literacy among students of underserved communities.

- 2011 - The company bags Rs 700-crore financial services systems integrator contract from the Department of Posts (DoP). This is the second contract from the department for Infosys

3.3.q.Achievements/ recognition:

Certification

The company's certifications include SEI-CMMI Level 5, CMM Level 5, PCMM Level 5, TL 9000 and ISO 9001-2000.

Awards

2011

- Infosys wins Platinum Award in The Asset Corporate 2010 Awards

2010

- Infosys wins the RMMY 'Best in Show' award for the third year in a row
- Infosys among Top 20 Global Companies to win the Most Admired Knowledge Enterprises (MAKE) Award 2010
- Infosys BPO wins 'BPO Organization of the Year' and 'Fun at Work' awards from Stars of the Industry Opens
- Infosys wins American Society for Training & Development (ASTD) award for excellence in inclusivity

2009

- Infosys BPO bags Excellence Award for diversity hiring initiatives

2008

- Infosys BPO wins special award at the 2008 NOA Awards
- Infosys BPO wins the Global Six Sigma award
- Infosys wins two Banker Technology Awards for its exceptional work in wholesale and capital markets
- Infosys wins Eastman Chemical's Supplier Excellence Award for the second consecutive year
- Infosys received the '2007 Vendor of the Year' award from Ameriprise Financial
- Infosys wins Investor Relations Global Rankings 2008 awards in APAC categories

2007

- Infosys becomes the first Indian company to win Nielsen Norman Group's Intranet Design Annual Award
- Infosys wins the 2007 Optimas Award in the 'Global Outlook' category

Infosys was ranked among the top 50 most respected companies in the world by Reputation Institute's Global Reputation Pulse 2009.

Infosys won Sears Holding Corporation's Partners in Progress award for the second consecutive year.

Infosys also won HDS' Diamond Award for 'Best Virtualization Strategy' and Platinum Award for 'Best Green Strategy for a Data Center'.

Infosys was also listed in the Most Admired Knowledge Enterprises (MAKE) 2008 study and Forbes' Asian Fabulous 50 for the fourth consecutive year.

The company was conferred with the NASSCOM gender inclusivity award and the Asset magazine acclaimed their Corporate Governance, acknowledging their corporate policies and practices as amongst the best in the industry

Table :3.2.competitors:

Company	Sales (Rs.Million)	Current Price	Change (%)	P/E Ratio	Market Cap.(Rs.Million)	52-Week High/Low	
TCS	388585.40	1229.15	-0.36	21.96	2410317.66	1295/903	
Infosys	312540.00	2368.00	0.84	16.62	1327533.63	3020/2169	
Wipro	263005.00	407.00	-0.11	21.03	985354.15	453/310	
HCL Tech.	67944.80	487.30	-1.36	20.14	337828.75	524/360	
Oracle Finl. Service	23605.06	2570.00	0.46	23.32	215648.81	2766/1699	
Mahindra Satyam	47761.00	70.10	-2.03	18.96	81552.09	94/62	
Tech Mahindra	49655.00	645.00	-1.85	14.47	81416.89	798/524	
Mphasis	34041.30	388.00	0.35	11.26	81096.55	488/277	
Patni Computer Sys.	21516.66	512.00	-0.04	14.57	69555.97	521/250	
Info Edge	2936.21	697.00	-0.52	31.36	38459.02	800/548	
Hexaware Tech.	6785.80	117.80	-0.72	13.11	35293.56	134/61	
Core Education & Tec	5155.92	287.00	-2.26	17.48	32880.93	324/245	
Financial Technology	3308.89	593.00	-1.51	34.19	26886.83	959/518	
Flextronics Software	6657.43	723.10	0.00	22.11	23914.17	0/0	

Table: 3.3 Product Performance

Product Name	Year	Month	Sales Quantity	Sales Value(Rs.Million)	% of STO		
Income from Software Services and Products	2012	03	0.00	312540.00	0.00		
Income from Software Services and Products	2011	03	0.00	253850.00	100.00		

117

3.4 .WIPRO-Profile

In the year of 1945, in pre–independent India, a vision was born, which would eventually stand out as a brand name synonymous with innovation and integrity. Starting off with consumer products business, Wipro then diversified into newer areas including IT hardware and IT services. Such has been the dynamic power of the organization that over the past 50 years, Wipro has evolved into a leading global IT company, a company which has pioneered many an innovation in the IT services, BPO and R&D services space.

Headquartered at Bangalore, India, Wipro implements the philosophy of 'Applying Thought', thereby helping clients to "Do Business Better". The path breaking innovations and ideas have culminated into the `Wipro Way' – a process which directly impacts customer benefits by improving time-to-market, enhancing predictability and reliability, and cutting costs.

Wipro Global IT Business delivers winning business outcomes through its deep industry experience and a 360 degree view of "Business through Technology" - helping clients create successful and adaptive businesses. A company recognized globally for its comprehensive portfolio of services, a practitioner's approach to delivering innovation and an organization wide commitment to sustainability, Wipro Technologies has over 130,000 employees and clients across 54 countries.

Completing the circle of transformation

Wipro, one of the world's most trusted brands, is a name with a long history that powers itself into new ventures. This trust extends to a series of products, services and solutions that cover diverse businesses - from consumer care to cutting-edge information technology. Over the years, its identity has evolved with our business, adapting to changing global dynamics.

3.4.a. Company History:

Wipro Ltd., the flagship company of the Azim H Premji group was incorporated in the year 1945. The company started off originally as a manufacturer of vegetable ghee/vanaspati, refined edible oils etc. Gradually the company has diversified into various other businesses.

Today Wipro Limited is the first PCMM Level 5 and SEI CMM Level 5 certified IT Services Company globally. Wipro provides comprehensive IT solutions and services, including systems integration, Information Systems outsourcing, package implementation, software application development and maintenance, and research and development services to corporations globally.

In the Indian market, Wipro is a leader in providing IT solutions and services for the corporate segment in India offering system integration, network integration, software solutions and IT services. Wipro also has profitable presence in niche market segments of consumer products and lighting. In the Asia Pacific and Middle East markets, Wipro provides IT solutions and services for global corporations.

Wipro's ADSs are listed on the New York Stock Exchange, and its equity shares are listed in India on the Stock Exchange - Mumbai, and the National Stock Exchange, among others. Wipro is the leading strategic IT partner for companies across India, the Middle East and Asia-Pacific - offering integrated IT solutions. They plan, deploy, sustain and maintain your IT lifecycle through their total outsourcing, consulting services, business solutions and professional services. Wipro InfoTech helps one drive momentum in their organization - no matter what domain they are in.

3.4.b. Core values of Wipro:

At Wipro, they promise to pay more value to customers as individuals, recognize that they have different needs and continually strive towards satisfying those needs to improve the quality of their lives. With utmost respect to human values it promises to serve its customers with integrity through a variety of innovative, value for money products and services which are developed by applying thought day after day.

3.4.c. Quality at Wipro:

Backed by their strong quality processes and rich experience managing global clients across various business verticals, they align IT strategies to your business goals. Along with their best of breed technology partners, Wipro InfoTech also helps you with your hardware and IT infrastructure needs.

The various accreditations that they have achieved for every service they offer reflect their commitment towards quality assurance. Wipro InfoTech was the first global software company to achieve Level 5 SEI-CMM, the world's first IT Company to achieve Six Sigma, as well as the world's first company to attain Level 5 PCMM.

Their continuing success in executing projects is a result of their stringent implementation of quality processes. Deploying quality frameworks to align with your business will give you the benefit of a smooth and transparent transition while providing complete IT lifecycle management. Reliability and perfection are a result of their adherence to these quality benchmarks and this has been their key differentiator while helping drive your business momentum.

The company's experience and expertise are measured against globally recognized standards to ensure their commitment in delivering competitive solutions to their customers. Wipro InfoTech epitomises quality by maintaining high standards in service offerings and products, as well as internal processes and people management. They believe in constantly scaling quality standards by expanding our efficiency in all areas beyond their basic IT offerings.

Different people perceive innovation in various ways. At Wipro InfoTech, their innovative thinking helps them adopt newer business lines and offerings based on your business expectations. They have adapted to the changes brought about by technology and business and this has helped us improve customer experience through service delivery and process optimization.

3.4.d.Performance of Wipro

Consistent with our performance over the last few years, Wipro has grown by 35 percent in revenues and 122 percent in profits after tax. While this kind of growth is impressive, For Wipro it's the thinking behind the performance that is important. It's what helps them protect the interest of our stakeholders notwithstanding slowdowns in the economy, frenetic competition or shrinking global demand. Realising that global economic conditions are not always going to be conducive, They have spread their markets so that they are not excessively dependent on a single geography, diversified its revenue streams, increased business from existing customers and improved the quality of its client profile. It continues to invest in building the global talent pool to ensure that they are best equipped to meet our customers' requirements.

a. Business leadership:

Wipro is among the top 10 information technology services globally and No.1 information technology company in India.

b. Customer leadership:

It has established itself as the NO.1 choice of customers through innovative solutions of sharing wealth in India through Wipro Stock Award Program in 1984. Today, over 6000 Wiproites participate in the shareholder value we create. A key ingredient of vision is in sharing the wealth that they create for their shareholders with their team.

E-culture - for response

The ultimate payoff is in transforming the entire organization to be customer sensitive.

As Wipro increased its size, success in being faster, leaner and quicker. E-culture helps to continually enhancing the speed of response. Our focus on knowledge management, people management and building exciting client relationship using the web is and will be the differentiator in creating value as we grow in size.

3.4 e. Innovation - for customer delight

At Wipro they have launched a new initiative on innovation in IT businesses. The first focus in this initiative is on customer satisfaction and intellectual properties based Products and services. Its endeavour is to harness the technical and domain skills to provide customers with solution that address their latent needs and help them serve their customers. In its global IT services business, they have an aim to create intellectual properties in the technology area.

3.4.f.Different divisions of the company:

Wipro Technologies - Wipro Technologies is the global IT services business division of Wipro Limited. With over 20 offices around the world, Wipro Technologies is the No.1 provider of integrated business, technology and process solutions on a global delivery platform.

Wipro Infotech- Wipro Infotech is the leading strategic IT partner for companies across India, the Middle East and Asia-Pacific - offering integrated IT solutions. We plan, deploy, sustain and maintain your IT lifecycle through our total outsourcing, consulting services, business solutions and professional services.

Wipro Consumer Care and Lighting- Wipro Consumer Care and Lighting, a business unit of Wipro Limited, has a profitable presence in the branded retail market of toilet soaps, hair care soaps, baby care products and lighting products. It is also a leader in institutional lighting in specified segments like software, pharma and retail.

Wipro Infrastructure Engineering - Wipro Infrastructure Engineering was Wipro Limited's first diversification in 1975, which addressed the hydraulic equipment requirements of mobile original equipment manufacturers in India. Over the past 25 years, the Wipro Infrastructure Engineering business unit has become a leader in the Hydraulic Cylinders and Truck Tipping Systems markets in India, and intends growing its business to serve the global manufacturing requirements of Hydraulic Cylinders and Truck Tippers.

Wipro GE Medical Systems - Wipro GE Medical Systems is a joint venture between Wipro and General Electric Company. As a part of GE Medical Systems South Asia, it caters to customer and patient needs with a commitment to uncompromising quality. Wipro GE is India's largest exporter of medical systems, with unmatched distribution and service reach in South Asia. Wipro GE pioneered the manufacture of Ultrasound and Computed Tomography systems in India and is a supplier for all GE Medical Systems products and services in South Asia.

3.4 .g. Products and services offered by the company:

Wipro is having ists presence across various verticals viz;

- Wipro Personal Computing Products
- Enterprise Products
- Software Products and Licences

Wipro Personal Computing Products:-

DesktopsEntry Level:

- Wipro Desktop WSG37205
- Wipro Desktop WSG37555
- Wipro Desktop WSG15C55
- Wipro Desktop WSG15D55

- Wipro Desktop WSG41155.

Mainstream:

- Wipro Desktop WSG53255
- Wipro Desktop WSG37555
- Wipro Desktop WSG15C55
- Wipro Desktop WSG15D55
- Wipro Desktop WSG41155.

Performance:

- Wipro Desktop WSG38105
- Wipro Desktop WSG41155

Gaming PC :

- Intel® Processor based
- AMD Processor based

Palm-Sized PC:

Protos Desktop

Wipro Green Computing:

- Wipro Desktop WSG 15D55V
- Wipro Desktop WSG 37555V.

Note Book:

- Wipro 7B1610
- Wipro EM4700
- Wipro 7B1630
- Wipro 7E1100
- Wipro 7B1100
- Wipro 7B3800
- Wipro 7710P
- Wipro 7B1650.

Server:

- Entry level and dual servers
- Performance Segment
- Blade server
- Enterprise class server.

AMD- performance & Enterprise class Wipro LooKeys.Supercomputing

Services offered by the company:

- System Integration
- Managed Services
- Total Outsourcing
- Application Development and Portals
- Business Transformation Services
- Security Governance
- Data Warehousing and Biz Intelligence
- Availability Services

3.4.h. Milestones

- 2011: Inaugurated its first rural BPO at Manjakkudi village in Tamil Nadu to capitalize on literate talent pool available in the region.

- 2011: Wipro has signed an agreement to acquire majority stake of Brazil based hydraulic cylinder manufacturer R.K.M. EQUIPAMENTOS HIDRAULICOS.

- 2010: Wipro Infotech -- the India, Middle East and Africa, IT Business of Wipro--has been awarded a 5-year IT outsourcing contract by Vasan Eye Care - one of India's largest network of eye care centers and a unit of Vasan Healthcare Group.

- 2010: Wipro Technologies, the global IT services business division of Wipro, has jointly with Citrix Systems entered into an agreement with Microsoft.

- 2008: Launch of Wipro Egypt Development Center

- 2008: Launch of Wipro GSMC in Kuala Laumpur

- 2007: Wipro Arabia Joint Venture found

- 2006: Acquisition of 3D networks

- 2006: Launch of GSMC- Global Service Management Centre for remote service delivery
- 2004: Start of Total Outsourcing business
- 2002: Start of Consulting business unit
- 2001: Launch of Wipro Infotech Middle East & Asia-Pacific operations
- 1998: Mission Quality journey started with focus on Six Sigma
- 2000: Wipro Listed on NYSE
- 1998: Re-launch of Wipro branded PC
- 1995: Wipro-BT joint venture started
- 1995: Joint Venture with Acer started
- 1995: Partnership with Cisco announced
- 1995: Offshoring services started
- 1992: Launch of global R&D services
- 1990: Launch of global software services business
- 1988: Partnership with Sun Microsystems announced
- 1986: Manufacturing tie-up with Epson for printers
- 1986: Start of Wipro PC manufacturing (with India's first surface mounted technology)
- 1984: Start of Wipro Systems - focus on software products (Wipro branded as well as distribution business)
- 1981: Manufacture of mini computers started at the Mysore factory
- 1980: Birth of IT business under banner of Wipro Information Technology Ltd. focused on hardware manufacturing and R&D
- 1945: Manufacturing of edible oils

3.4.i.Achievements/ recognition:

- Best Websphere Partner Award.
- Authorized EMC Signature Partner in South Asia.
- Best TSG Partner of HP.
- Best System Integrator award 2007-08.
- Best Technology Partner for the Year.
- Network Integrator of the Year 2008.

- SAP Pinnacle Award 2008.

- Golden Peacock Innovation Management Award 2007.

- Riverbed Partner of the year 2007 award.

- National Partner of the Year 2007 Award from Microsoft.

- Wipro wins FIVE awards from CISCO.

- India's first ever Microsoft Platinum Partner Award.

- Wipro 3D Networks once again emerged as the most formidable partner for Nortel in FY 2006 bagging all the highest awards in significant categories - Sales, pre sales & post sales

- **Partner of the Year award:--**Over Drive Excellence of the Year award -Sales Champion of the Year award -Pre-Sales Champion of the Year award -Customer Champion of the Year award

KEY EXECUTIVE DIRECTORS

S.No	Name	Designation
1	Azim Premji	Chairman
2	V Ramachandran	Company Secretary
3	B C Prabhakar	Director
4	Suresh C Senapaty	Chief Financial Officer & Director
5	T K Kurien	Chief Executive Officer & Executive Director

Figure : 3.4 COMPETITORS of Wipro

Company	Sales (Rs.Million)	Current Price	Change (%)	P/E Ratio	Market Cap.(Rs.Million)	52-Week High/Low
TCS	388585.40	1229.15	-0.36	21.96	2410317.66	1295/903
Infosys	312540.00	2368.00	0.84	16.62	1327533.63	3020/2169
Wipro	263005.00	407.00	-0.11	21.03	985354.15	453/310
HCL Tech.	67944.80	487.30	-1.36	20.14	337828.75	524/360
Oracle Finl. Service	23605.06	2570.00	0.46	23.32	215648.81	2766/1699
Mahindra Satyam	47761.00	70.10	-2.03	18.96	81552.09	94/62
Tech Mahindra	49655.00	645.00	-1.85	14.47	81416.89	798/524
Mphasis	34041.30	388.00	0.35	11.26	81096.55	488/277
Patni Computer Sys.	21516.66	512.00	-0.04	14.57	69555.97	521/250
Info Edge	2936.21	697.00	-0.52	31.36	38459.02	800/548
Hexaware Tech.	6785.80	117.80	-0.72	13.11	35293.56	134/61
Core Education & Tec	5155.92	287.00	-2.26	17.48	32880.93	324/245
Financial Technology	3308.89	593.00	-1.51	34.19	26886.83	959/518
Flextronics Software	6657.43	723.10	0.00	22.11	23914.17	0/0
Mindtree Ltd	15090.00	590.00	0.95	10.83	23681.55	618/321
KPIT Cummins Infosys	5385.55	110.00	-4.18	26.62	19876.22	121/68
Glodyne Technoserve	9820.75	420.00	0.29	7.61	18708.18	435/191
Infotech Enterprise	6476.67	160.50	-3.28	11.24	17820.87	182/100
Vakrangee Software	8523.38	32.30	-0.77	23.91	16140.47	36/16
NIIT Tech	7292.81	265.00	-1.67	14.09	15939.65	285/166
Persistent Systems	8103.64	361.00	-0.65	10.53	14462.00	407/281
Igate Global Sol	9321.87	404.20	0.00	8.01	12839.47	415/399
Igate Global Sol	9321.87	404.20	0.00	8.01	12839.47	415/399
Polaris Finl. Tech	13759.65	125.10	-2.19	6.73	12350.71	205/113
Rolta India	14487.50	68.80	-2.13	3.16	11276.90	144/50
Zylog Systems	9158.43	628.30	-0.05	7.05	10371.93	664/346

Company						
Zensar Technologies	5669.98	202.00	-1.00	9.30	8792.23	242/113
Tata Elxsi	4110.12	199.00	-0.80	18.27	6202.73	264/167
Onmobile Global	4550.27	50.50	-4.17	11.80	5934.91	118/48
Genesys Intl. Corpn	948.49	185.70	-0.75	10.02	5506.87	291/114
Commex Technology	95.30	29.60	-4.52	119.88	4707.50	32/9
Unisys Software	1330.45	202.00	-0.64	247.22	4657.54	230/56
Geometric	2349.92	62.50	-1.73	9.39	3866.76	81/35
Geodesic	6714.31	40.35	-1.47	2.24	3632.70	85/39
Take Solutions	452.49	28.90	0.87	8.04	3482.28	49/20
Aztecsoft	2737.80	76.20	0.00	45.51	3475.30	76/73
Infinite Computer	2233.91	76.50	-0.65	4.55	3277.12	170/56
Net 4 India	1969.75	161.45	0.00	16.04	3246.43	180/113
Sasken Commn. Tech	3941.96	114.15	-2.64	7.93	3006.93	165/91
Micro Technologies	3742.93	158.50	-1.37	4.62	2573.88	183/99
Mastek	3639.71	93.00	-0.53	0.00	2526.95	136/73
3I Infotech	5502.50	12.52	-1.96	0.00	2403.67	54/12
LGS Global	2986.77	95.45	5.94	6.85	2374.57	141/42
Sonata Software	2503.63	20.20	-3.12	6.23	2118.96	49/18
R Systems Intl.	1916.86	164.05	1.27	22.11	2105.43	170/91
Nucleus Software Exp	1995.50	63.05	-1.64	6.31	2061.21	90/56
Kale Consultants	1702.74	126.50	1.08	10.87	1903.24	153/62
Ramco Systems	1504.02	118.50	-0.59	0.00	1832.67	135/49
Aurionpro Solutions	1172.05	114.50	2.14	10.79	1799.91	179/103
Datamatic Global Ser	1384.49	28.65	0.35	6.69	1697.74	34/20

3.5. Tata Consultancy services

TCS is the leader in the global marketplace and among the top 10 technology firms in the world. Its continued rapid growth is a testament to the certainty our clients experience every day. Building on more than 40 years of experience, we add real value to global organizations through domain expertise plus solutions with proven success in the field and world-class service. It's how it has kept moving forward.

TCS offers a consulting-led integrated portfolio of IT and IT-enabled services delivered through its unique Global Network Delivery Model™ (GNDM™), recognized as the benchmark of excellence in software development.

Lineage: TCS is part of the Tata group, one of India's largest industrial conglomerates and most respected brands.

Workforce: TCS has over 238,583 of the world's best-trained IT consultants in 42 countries.

Financial Information: Revenue of $10.17 billion (fiscal year ending March 31, 2012). For detailed financial information including annual reports and quarterly statements, visit our Investor pages.

Quality Framework: We are the world's first organization to achieve an enterprise-wide Maturity Level 5 on CMMI® and P-CMM® based on SCAMPI^{SM}, the most rigorous assessment methodology.

TCS Integrated Quality Management System (iQMS) integrates processes, people and technology maturity through various established frameworks and practices, including IEEE, ISO 9001: 2000, CMMi, SW-CMM, P-CMM and Six-Sigma.

Alliances: TCS has a strong network of strategic and solution partners with a joint objective of helping its customers become high-performance businesses by maximizing the value of their technology investments.

'Board of Directors: TCS has 12 non-executive and two executive board members.

- **N. chandrashekharan-** CEO& MD
- **S. Mahalingam-** chief financial officer and Executive Director.

The TCS Advantage

TCS provides the insight, support and expertise that will propel any business forward. The key features which differentiates TCS:

3.5.A CUSTOMER-CENTRIC ENGAGEMENT MODEL

Its deep-set commitment to customers defines how they do business, and years of experience working across industries underpin the vast array of services they offer. They focus on building teams around the customer's domain and technology requirements, offering specialized services and solutions that meet the distinct needs of your business.

3.5.B GLOBAL NETWORK DELIVERY MODEL (GNDM™)

Its unique global engagement model allows the customers to choose the sourcing strategy best suited to their

business needs. They take a follow-the-sun approach, meaning that no matter where the business of the customer's business is located, they keep it running 24/7, while providing a seamless experience across all operations..

3.5C. FULL SERVICES PORTFOLIO

Full services portfolio combines traditional IT and Remote Infrastructure services with knowledge-based services such as Consulting and Business Process Outsourcing. This enables it to provide integrated solutions that help you recognize value quickly by reducing costs and improving business agility.

3.5.D. INNOVATION LABS AND CO-INNOVATION NETWORK (COIN™)

TCS Innovation Labs and Co-innovation Network offers research-based solutions in advanced technologies that help support the client's business objectives.

3.6 ACCENTURE

Accenture is one of the largest computer services and software companies on the Fortune Global 500 list. It possesses expertise in consulting, technology and outsourcing. The company divides its practices into five main operating groups based on client industry types and growth platforms -

communications and high technology, financial services, public service, products, and resources. Accenture's clients span the full range of industries around the world and include 94 of the Fortune Global 100 and more than two-thirds of the Fortune Global 500.

In March 2008, Forrester named Accenture a leader in SAP implementation. It has signed a contract with international division of Universal Music Group, the world's largest music company, for providing the next-generation digital supply chain. The company recently completed its acquisition of MAXIM Systems, Inc., an employee-owned defense consulting firm that provides advanced engineering and technical services in the areas of command and control, multi-level security and satellite communications. It has also acquired Corliant, Inc., a privately held technology consulting firm that helps clients deploy and support advanced Internet protocol networks.

At Accenture, employees come from wide range of cultural, educational and geographic backgrounds and work in a dynamic and professional environment that values each person's perspective. They deliver superior business solutions for Accenture and its clients. They are involved in capitalizing on business and technology opportunities that enable higher levels of performance.

Executive Team:

1. William D.Green- Executive chairman
2. Pierre nanteme- Chief executive officer.
3. Pamella.J.craig- Chief financial officer.

Operations

A world map showing the 54 countries where Accenture has operations as of 2012 (coloured in blue)

Accenture organizes its services and people in these three primary cross-functional groupings. Accenture client engagement teams typically consist of a combination of industry experts, capability specialists and professionals with local market knowledge.

3.6 a. Workforces

The four workforces serve clients in the areas of consulting, technology, and outsourcing, as well as the company itself. This is almost always an internal designation as it is commonplace for Accenture employees to work in blended teams for a variety of reasons.

- **Consulting:** Focus on management consulting, process design work and the application of technologies to business. Responsible for sales, delivery, and leadership of most of Accenture's project-based work. Contains Accenture Technology Labs. Levels are Analyst to Senior Executive.

- **Services:** Most focus on outsourcing engagements in the areas of business operations, IT, applications development and maintenance, help desk services, and HR. Can also work on Consulting-led projects. Levels are H through A (reverse alphabetical order, lowest to highest) and Senior Executive.

- **Solutions:** The Accenture Technology Solutions subsidiary focuses on the specific technology skills needed to deliver projects or outsourcing arrangements. Comprises the majority of Accenture's employees in delivery centers in developing countries like Brazil, India, and the Philippines. Levels are Programmer to Senior Executive, with slight regional variations.

- **Enterprise:** Focus on managing and supporting all activities across Accenture's business, including legal, security, facilities, marketing, and client financial management. Levels are Junior Assistant to Senior Executive.

3.6. b. Operating Groups

As most consulting firms, Accenture operates in a matrix structure. The first axis is dedicated to the operating groups, or industries of its clients. The five Operating Groups comprise 19 industry groups which focus on industry evolution, business issues, and applicable technologies.[13]

- **Communications, Media & Technology:** Communications, Electronics and High Tech, Media and Entertainment

- **Financial Services:** Banking, Capital Markets, Insurance

- **Products:** Automotive, Air, Freight & Travel Services, Consumer Goods & Services, Industrial Equipment, Infrastructure & Transportation Services, Life Sciences, Retail

- **Resources:** Chemicals, Energy, Natural Resources, Utilities
- **Health & Public Service:** Health, Public Sector, Non-profit, International Organizations, Non-governmental Organizations (NGOs)

3.6.c.Growth Platforms

The second axis is the growth platforms, which broadly refer to the functional or technical domains in which Accenture's client-facing people specialize their skills, develop and use Accenture's methodology, and create and deliver solutions to clients.

- **Consulting:** This growth platform is focused on business solutions, processes, and change management in the areas of Customer Relationship Management, Finance & Performance Management, Process & Innovation Performance, Risk Management, Strategy, Supply Chain Management, and Talent & Organization Performance.

- **Technology:** This growth platform brings together the full range of systems integration, technology consulting, and IT outsourcing skills. Specialties include enterprise solutions, system integration, technical architecture, business intelligence, infrastructure consulting, and technology research/development. Most people in the Services and Solutions workforces are aligned under the Technology growth platform

3.7 CSC - Computer science corporation

Computer science corporation started in the year 1959, but its India operations started in the year 1991. Since then it has 18 delivery systems across India. Ingenuity has been the driving force in the company. CSC's India operations are the company's second largest globally with a strong team of 24,000 people across its development and delivery centers across seven locations in India.

It is a global consultancy, systems integration and outsourcing company. The solutions offered include, credit services, customer relationship management, enterprise solutions, hosting services, legal solutions, management consulting, outsourcing, risk management and claims, security and supply chain management. It caters to industries including aerospace and defense, banking, chemical, energy and natural resources, communications, media and entertainment, financial services, government, health services, high technology, insurance, manufacturing, retail and travel and transportation. It is seamlessly integrated with global tools and methodologies.

The company bagged contract worth $ 70 million from Pension Benefit Guaranty Corporation (PBGC) to look after their IT infrastructure operations. It inaugurated its new Dallas Technology Center in February 2008. CSC was recognized by American Banker as one of the top 25 enterprise companies in the financial services industry.

The organization provides opportunities to grow and learn. It lays stress on job enrichment, job rotation and lateral and vertical growth plans. It has global e-learning programs and mandatory 90 hours of training for all employees. Through its unique initiatives like innovation @work, it provides its employees, the opportunity to work on latest software and cutting-edge technologies.

It has headquarters in Falls Church, Virginia, USA, and three other major offices in Australia, Asia and Europe, and has over 97,000 professionals serving clients in more than 90 countries.

Mission:

The mission of CSC is to be a global leader in providing technology enabled business solutions and services

3.7.a.CSC values

At CSC, people are deeply committed, consistently inventive and determined to deliver. As a major global delivery player ,excellence in every aspect of their business is what they aim for at the end of any service delivery proposition. For more than 50 years from now, their mission critical systems have resulted in lasting business impact to our clients. The agility and adaptability combined with reputation from going that extra mile to make IT work for its clients have helped in driving customer delight.

CLIENT FOCUSED

CSC's success derives from a deep understanding of its clients, to whom all of CSC is committed to deliver exceptional service and value.

LEADERSHIP

At CSC they lead from the front, displaying integrity and using facts to support straight talk. it create an environment for positive change built on collaboration and trust.

EXECUTION EXCELLENCE

it insists on excellence in all they do for clients and ourselves, striving always for recognition among the leaders in our industry.

ASPIRATION

It aspires individually and collectively to be more tomorrow than what they are today.

RESULTS

They accept individual responsibility for their commitments and are accountable for results.

3.7.b.Diversity Statement

We value the diversity of our employees and the unique perspectives they bring to CSC. Diversity at CSC not only includes age, race, sex, sexual orientation/gender identity, genetic information, disabilities, and ethnicity, but also jobs and functional roles within the company, the markets and clients we serve, our geographic locations, educational background and whether one joined CSC independently or through an acquisition or outsourcing arrangement. By valuing these differences, we demonstrate our commitment to treating everyone with fairness and respect.

Executive team:

CSC's India Executive Profiles are for people wishing to find out about the leadership team spearheading and driving operations for CSC in India.

BRIAN J. MANNING

Brian J. Manning is the President & Managing director of CSC in India. His responsibilities include managing 23,000+ employees based in India, ensuring that the delivery capacity in India continues to expand with CSC's global business requirements and that CSC India's portfolio of services across diverse industry segments continues to enhance CSC's global competitiveness.

SHANKAR VISHWANATHAN

Shankar Vishwanathan is the Head of Application Services for CSC India and the Applications Regional Executive for Asia Pacific.

He provides the key support for new business opportunities and portfolio enablement to all customer engagements in the Applications domain at CSC India and now across Asia. He has successfully managed critical and complex assignments in IT Delivery, including IT Project Management and establishing and managing large outsourcing engagements in global delivery environments at different organizations.

3.7.c.The CSC Difference

A Fortune 200 company, CSC is one of the world's largest and most respected providers of information technology services. Since 1959, the organizations that collaborate with us have benefited from every wave of IT innovation. Here are just a few reasons why:

- **Deeply Committed**

  customer's Mission Is their Mission

- **Partnerships That Span 50 Years**

drive to help clients accomplish more has made CSC one of the world's most enduring IT leaders. When two young computer analysts founded our company in 1959 with $100 and a coffee pot, fewer than 4,000 computers existed in the world. By writing programs that made it much easier to use information technology, we quickly became the world's largest independent IT services firm.

- **The World's Most Complex Jobs**

No job is too large for CSC, or too complex. For example, they are currently modernizing the world's largest supply chain, with a $4.5 billion inventory of 6 million items involving 50,000 vendors. We're also building what will likely be the world's largest health IT program, which means creating the most extensive virtualized data center ever implemented. As projects like these demonstrate, CSC is one of the few IT services providers in the world with the skill to handle intricate technical refinements, one day, and the commitment to help the client efficiently deliver a massive transformation project, the next.

- **Local Expertise, Global Reach**

CSC is a truly global organization. Maintaining a robust presence worldwide helps us get to know your enterprise, wherever you operate. Our culturally savvy professionals speak no fewer than 34 languages and operate out of more than 80 countries. But more important than those numbers is our ability to deliver services globally - from virtually anywhere in the world to virtually anywhere else - via 60 World Sourcing Centers that empower your organization with flexibility and value.

- **Consistently Inventive**

Harnessing New Ideas

- **Innovation You Can Use**

We've had a hand in countless industry firsts, and our solutions consistently incorporate cutting-edge ideas and powerful new technologies. To extend that tradition of innovation, our Leading Edge Forum brings together a global network of thought leaders, CSC experts and alliance partners to help you take advantage of the very latest business and technology trends.

- **Addressing Your Key Challenges**

The CSC culture of innovation powers every advanced capability we deliver - in systems design and integration, information technology and business process outsourcing, applications software development, Web and application hosting, mission support and management consulting. And there are many more: The solutions we design are as varied as the challenges our clients seek to address.

- **The Best Total Solution**

  Regardless of the specific service offering, we continually take steps to tailor every element of our solutions - from hardware and software, to expertise and organizational structure, to contract terms and world-class security - to meet the unique requirements of the organizations we serve. Throughout, maximizing your return on investment remains a central focus. And that means using sophisticated metrics to validate a sound business case, expertly managing change to minimize disruption and risk and providing mechanisms to bring you continuous improvement and ongoing value creation.

- **Determined to Deliver**

  Promises Kept

- **Vendor Independence**

  Unlike our competitors, we give our clients software and hardware choices with objective advice about how well technologies work and what they should cost. And, to keep our clients ahead of the curve with new offerings, we leverage our formal alliances with Microsoft, SAP, Oracle, Cisco, Dell and many other industry leaders.

- **The Best From Every Industry**

  While CSC might be especially well known for our public sector support, we partner with successful organizations in all industries. Ultimately, that experience enables us to harness the best ideas, practices and solutions from both the public and private sectors, for the benefit of every client.

- **The Quality You Expect**

  CSC was the first organization to achieve two Level 5 SEI CMMI certifications, and we've subsequently attained six such recognitions. The result? Our unmatched commitment to quality management brings you efficiency improvements, productivity gains and lower total cost of ownership.

- **"What's most important to you?"**

  It's a question which they never stop asking. The answer might be: improving efficiency and reducing costs. Or making it easier for stakeholders to access the services they need. It might be something as critical as making the warfighter safer, or as strategic as building customer loyalty. While some organizations need to be more agile to capitalize on new markets, others seek a sharper focus on the core mission. Whatever the vision of progress, if your organization can imagine it, the people of CSC stand ready to help you make it happen

3.7.d.Recognitions and awards:

Ranked No. 14 in NASSCOM Top 20 IT-BPO Employers in India FY 2011

Ranked No. 29 in Dataquest's annual 'DQ Top 20' in FY 2011

Winner of the DSCI Excellence Award 2011 for Raising Security Awareness

Named to the 2011 Global Services 100 List Ranked No. 10 in NASSCOM TOP   20 IT software and service exporters list

Ranked No.1 in IT Software - Best Workplaces in Rank Order

Winner of Best Exporter Award from an Indian State Government

Honored with National Women of Color STEM Awards.

Out of 28, 4 CSC in India employees have been acknowledged in Technology Rising Stars category

DQ Top 20 Women across Indian IT Industry has named 3women of CSC in India – Dataquest

- This growth platform focuses on the full range of Business Process Outsourcing (BPO) services to enable high performance, including function-specific services such as procurement, HR and finance and accounting, as well as services geared to the needs of specific industries such as utilities, insurance and health care.

3.8. HCL- Profile

3.8.a.Company overview

HCL technologies is a leading global IT services company ,working with clients in the areas that impact and redefine the core of their businesses. Since its inception into the global landscape after its IPO in 1999, HCL focuses on transformational outsourcing underlined by innovation and value creation and offers integrated portfolio of services including software –led IT solutions ,remote infrastructure.

HCL Technologies is a leading global IT services company, working with clients in the areas that impact and redefine the core of their businesses. Since its inception into the global landscape after its IPO in 1999, HCL focuses on 'transformational outsourcing', underlined by innovation and value creation, and offers integrated portfolio of services including software-led IT solutions, remote infrastructure management, engineering and R&D services and BPO.

HCL Technologies has portfolio of services including software-led IT solutions, remote infrastructure management, engineering and R&D services and BPO. HCL has global partnerships with several leading Fortune 1000 firms, including several IT and technology majors. It provides services to industry sectors including financial services, manufacturing, aerospace & defense, telecom, retail & CPG, life sciences & healthcare, media & entertainment, travel, transportation & logistics, automotive, government and energies & utilities.

HCL leverages its extensive global offshore infrastructure and network of offices in 26 countries to provide holistic, multi-service delivery in key industry verticals including Financial Services,

Manufacturing, Consumer Services, Public Services and Healthcare. HCL Technologies is leader in providing IT services to its clients restructuring the core of their businesses.

HCL takes pride in its philosophy of 'Employees First, Customers Second' which empowers its 77,046 transformers to create a real value for the customers. HCL Technologies, along with its subsidiaries, had consolidated revenues of US$ 3.5 billion (Rs. 16,034 crores), as on 30 June 2011 (on LTM basis).

The acquisition of UK-based Axon for close to 441.1 million ponds, is expected to ramp up HCL Technologies' client base and will have a positive effect on its profit. The company is also on the lookout for more acquisitions in the near future.

3.8.b.Recognition

- HCL Technologies has been named as one of Britain's Top Employers 2010 by the Corporate Research Foundation (CRF) Institute, for the fourth consecutive year.

- HCL Technologies has been conferred with the prestigious 'Golden Peacock Innovation' Award for its MTaaS™ (a Business Service Management centric service delivery platform) offering in the IT Sector category in October, 2009.

- HCL Customer Standard Parking Wins Oracle's 'Empower the Green Enterprise' Award

- HCL Receives 6 HR Congress Awards 2008 – a recognition for having great human resources practices

- India's Most Preferred Personal Computer Brand – CNBC AWAAZ Consumer Award 2007 HCL Technologies (HCL) was named Meritorious Performance Supplier in Sun Microsystems' 2007 Supplier Awards program. The award recognize companies that make outstanding contributions to Sun's record of delivering superior technology, quality service and excellent value to its customers.

Key executive Directors:

No	Name	Designation
1	Shiv Nadar	Chairman
2	Manish Anand	Company Secretary
3	Vineet Nayar	Vice Chairman
4	R Srinivasan	Non Executive Director
5	T S R Subramanian	Non Executive Director
6	Robin Abrams	Non Executive Director
7	Ajai Chowdhry	Non Executive Director
8	Subroto Bhattacharya	Non Executive Director
9	Amal Ganguli	Non Executive Director
10	P C Sen	Non Executive Director

Fig: 3.5. competitors

Company	Sales (Rs.Million)	Current Price	Change (%)	P/E Ratio	Market Cap.(Rs.Million)	52-Week High/Low
TCS	388585.40	1229.15	-0.36	21.96	2410317.66	1295/903
Infosys	312540.00	2368.00	0.84	16.62	1327533.63	3020/2169
Wipro	263005.00	407.00	-0.11	21.03	985354.15	453/310
HCL Tech.	67944.80	487.30	-1.36	20.14	337828.75	524/360
Oracle Finl. Service	23605.06	2570.00	0.46	23.32	215648.81	2766/1699
Mahindra Satyam	47761.00	70.10	-2.03	18.96	81552.09	94/62
Tech Mahindra	49655.00	645.00	-1.85	14.47	81416.89	798/524
Mphasis	34041.30	388.00	0.35	11.26	81096.55	488/277
Patni Computer Sys.	21516.66	512.00	-0.04	14.57	69555.97	521/250
Info Edge	2936.21	697.00	-0.52	31.36	38459.02	800/548
Hexaware Tech.	6785.80	117.80	-0.72	13.11	35293.56	134/61
Core Education & Tec	5155.92	287.00	-2.26	17.48	32880.93	324/245
Financial Technology	3308.89	593.00	-1.51	34.19	26886.83	959/518
Flextronics Software	6657.43	723.10	0.00	22.11	23914.17	0/0
Mindtree Ltd	15090.00	590.00	0.95	10.83	23681.55	618/321
KPIT Cummins Infosys	5385.55	110.00	-4.18	26.62	19876.22	121/68
Glodyne Technoserve	9820.75	420.00	0.29	7.61	18708.18	435/191
Infotech Enterprise	6476.67	160.50	-3.28	11.24	17820.87	182/100
Vakrangee Software	8523.38	32.30	-0.77	23.91	16140.47	36/16
NIIT Tech	7292.81	265.00	-1.67	14.09	15939.65	285/166
Persistent Systems	8103.64	361.00	-0.65	10.53	14462.00	407/281

Igate Global Sol	9321.87	404.20	0.00	8.01	12839.47	415/399
Igate Global Sol	9321.87	404.20	0.00	8.01	12839.47	415/399
Polaris Finl. Tech	13759.65	125.10	-2.19	6.73	12350.71	205/113
Rolta India	14487.50	68.80	-2.13	3.16	11276.90	144/50
Zylog Systems	9158.43	628.30	-0.05	7.05	10371.93	664/346
Zensar Technologies	5669.98	202.00	-1.00	9.30	8792.23	242/113
Tata Elxsi	4110.12	199.00	-0.80	18.27	6202.73	264/167
Onmobile Global	4550.27	50.50	-4.17	11.80	5934.91	118/48
Genesys Intl. Corpn	948.49	185.70	-0.75	10.02	5506.87	291/114
Commex Technology	95.30	29.60	-4.52	119.88	4707.50	32/9
Unisys Software	1330.45	202.00	-0.64	247.22	4657.54	230/56
Geometric	2349.92	62.50	-1.73	9.39	3866.76	81/35
Geodesic	6714.31	40.35	-1.47	2.24	3632.70	85/39
Take Solutions	452.49	28.90	0.87	8.04	3482.28	49/20
Aztecsoft	2737.80	76.20	0.00	45.51	3475.30	76/73
Infinite Computer	2233.91	76.50	-0.65	4.55	3277.12	170/56
Net 4 India	1969.75	161.45	0.00	16.04	3246.43	180/113
Sasken Commn. Tech	3941.96	114.15	-2.64	7.93	3006.93	165/91

Micro Technologies	3742.93	158.50	-1.37	4.62	2573.88	183/99
Mastek	3639.71	93.00	-0.53	0.00	2526.95	136/73
3I Infotech	5502.50	12.52	-1.96	0.00	2403.67	54/12
LGS Global	2986.77	95.45	5.94	6.85	2374.57	141/42
Sonata Software	2503.63	20.20	-3.12	6.23	2118.96	49/18
R Systems Intl.	1916.86	164.05	1.27	22.11	2105.43	170/91
Nucleus Software Exp	1995.50	63.05	-1.64	6.31	2061.21	90/56
Kale Consultants	1702.74	126.50	1.08	10.87	1903.24	153/62
Ramco Systems	1504.02	118.50	-0.59	0.00	1832.67	135/49
Aurionpro Solutions	1172.05	114.50	2.14	10.79	1799.91	179/103
Datamatic Global Ser	1384.49	28.65	0.35	6.69	1697.74	34/20

Fig : 3.6.Products

Product Name	Year	Month	Sales Quantity	Sales Value(Rs.Million)	% of STO
Income from Software Services	2011	06	0.00	66108.00	97.30
Software Licenses (Unlimited Users)	2011	06	0.00	606.90	0.89
Others	2011	06	183666.00	464.00	0.68
Routers	2011	06	943.00	319.50	0.47

141

Switches	2011	06	506.00	193.30	0.28
Servers	2011	06	463.00	145.60	0.21
Storage Devices	2011	06	17.00	107.50	0.16

References:

1. www.dqindia.com June,2009 issue

2. www.dqindia.com Dec ,2010issue

3. www.dqindia.com June ,2012 issue

4. www.infosys.com

5. www.wipro.com

6. www.csc.com

7. www.accenture.com

8. www.hcl.com

9.   Infosys Annual Report,09,10,11

10.   Wipro Annual Report,10,11

CHAPTER-4

- COMPETENCY MAPPING PROCESS IN IT FIRMS
- TALENT MANAGEMENT PRACTICES IN VARIOUS IT FIRMS

4.1 COMPETENCY MAPPING TOOLS AND METHODS IN IT SECTOR:

Competency mapping, the buzz word in any industry is not complicated as it may appear. At the heart of any successful activity lies a competence or skill. In the recent years, various thought leaders in business strategy have emphasized the need to identify what competencies a business needs, in order in a specific environment. Competency mapping is a strategic HR framework for monitoring the performance and development of human resource in organizations .Regardless of whatever happens to the future of software in India, the people who are outstanding in their performance will continue to be in demand and will keep rising and for this the human resource of each organization should develop the competencies which they have in order to compete with the highly competitive market.

A competency is a specific, identifiable, definable and measurable skill or characteristic that is essential for the performance of an activity within a specific business or industry context. Some examples of competencies are safety awareness, critical analytical thinking, problem solving, communication, team work etc.

The first competency model was developed in the early 1970s for the US Department of State by DavidMcClelland and his colleagues of McBer and Company as an alternative selection tool for junior Foreign Service Information Officers. Later McBer and Company developed a methodology that is   useful today in competency model building and comprises of and "focus on outstanding performers, use of behavioral event interviews, and thematic analysis of interview data and distillation of the results into a smaller set of competencies described in behaviorally specific terms". In the last 30   technique has gained importance as an integral practice in human resource management.

Based on the US Department of Labor's (DOL) framework, the competency model can be described as a pyramid consisting of a hierarchical set of tiers.

The pyramid is divided into 3 main blocks of **Foundational competencies**, **Industry Related** and **Occupation related competencies**. Each of these blocks is made up of tiers which consist of a set of competencies that represent the skills, knowledge and abilities essential to be successful in an occupation in the industry the model represents. Starting from the base, the tiers cover competencies that are common to several occupations and industries. As we traverse up the pyramid, the competencies become industry and occupation specific.

It is important to note that the above picture does not suggest that this is a sequential model i.e. one needs to have all the below competencies in order to posses / develop the higher level competencies. The model is constructed in a bottom-up approach using a combination of research, data collection and analysis, focus groups and case study interviews.

- Ideally Competency Mapping allows management to specify what employees must do; combines feedback and goal setting.

144

- Everyone involved needs to recognize that Competency Mapping involves human judgment and information

- System should aim to be easy to operate, easy to explain, easy to maintain, easy to administer
- System should be job related, relevant, sensitive, reliable, acceptable, practical, open, fair, and useful.
- Need to take legal issues into account.
- Yearly performance reviews are critical.
- Organizations are hard pressed to find good reasons why they can't dedicate an hour-long meeting once a year to ensure the mutual needs of the employee and
- Performance reviews help supervisors feel more honest in their relationships with their subordinates and feel better about themselves in their supervisory roles. Subordinates are assured clear understanding of what's expected from them, their own personal strengths and areas for development and a solid sense of their relationship with their supervisor. Avoiding performance issues ultimately decreases morale, decreases credibility of management, decreases the organization's overall effectiveness and wastes more of management's time.

Effective Competency Mapping systems contain two basic systems operating in conjunction: an evaluation system and a feedback system. The main aim of the evaluation system is to identify the performance gap (if any). This gap is the shortfall that occurs when performance does not meet the standard set by the organization as acceptable. The main aim of the feedback system is to inform the employee about the quality of his or her performance.

(However, the information flow is not exclusively one way.the appraisers also receive feedback from the employee about job problems etc.)

One of the best ways to appreciate the purposes of Competency Mapping is to look at it from the different viewpoints of the main stakeholders; the employee andthe organization.

Employee Viewpoint

From the employee viewpoint, the purpose of Competency Mapping is four-fold:

1. Tell me what you want me to do.
2. Tell me how well I have done it.
3. Help me improve my performance.
4. Reward me for doing well.

Organizational Viewpoint

From the organization's viewpoint, one of the most important reasons for having a system of Competency Mapping is to establish and uphold the principle of accountability. For decades it has been known to researchers that one of the chief causes of organizational failure is "non-alignment of responsibility and accountability." Non-alignment occurs where employees are given responsibilities and duties, but are not held accountable for the way in whichthose responsibilities and duties are performed. What typically happens is that several individuals or work units appear to have overlapping roles.

- The overlap allows – actively encourages – each individual or business unit to "pass the buck" to the others. Ultimately, in the severely non-aligned system, no one is accountable for anything. In this event, the principle of accountability breaks down completely. Organizational failure is the only possible outcome. In cases where the non-alignment is not so sever, the organization may continue to function, albeit inefficiently. Like a poorly made or badly tuned engine, the non-aligned organization may run, but it will be sluggish, costly and unreliable. One of the principal aims of Competency Mapping is to make people accountable. The objective is to align responsibility

4.2 Uses of Competency Models

Competency Models benefit a wide array of users – as a standard set of skills that can be used for recruiting, profiling jobs, evaluating employees, designing academic and professional certification Programs. They serve as a bridge between educators, businesses and other stakeholders who invest in preparing students and workers for today's workplace challenges.

Competency Models can be used by employers as a **useful selection and professional development tool**. It can assist HR staff match specific skills and work requirements to different jobs at selection, promotion, career path development and while developing training programs for the organization. It can help to assess performance of individuals in their jobs as well as in their roles of managers, direct reports, customers and team members. It can also be a means for businesses to communicate their performance expectations to their workers.

Competency Models can serve as a **measure of the gap between employer needs and the offerings of the current education and training delivery system**. Contents of existing coursework can be reviewed and mapped against the tier competencies and a crosswalk can be created and "gaps" can be identified. As education/ training providers evaluate existing programs or design new ones, the Competency model can **serve as a benchmark**, resulting in addition of courses that will match workplace requirements and trends.

Training providers can also use competency models to **develop industry-validated certifications**. Acquiring such a certification establishes that the graduate of the particular training program has demonstrated mastery in the competencies as stated in model for that industry or sector8.

Competency models work as a guide for Workforce Investment Boards and One Stop Career Centers to **match job requirements and skill sets determined by employers to potential**

candidates. In this way an even larger group of individuals such as in-school youth, out-of school youth, dislocated workers, current workers, and special needs populations are serviced thus increasing the talent pool of available Workers.

As these key partners work together by sharing assets and resources, the competency model provides a **good guidance for government investments in workforce preparation strategies** within

Best Practices

A great deal of research has been done to design competency models by both the private sector and government agencies to address the skill needs of these entities.

- McMurtrey et al conducted a study that investigated the most critical skills for IT professionals. They created taxonomy of skills that were divided into four areas: Core Knowledge, Technical Proficiency, Business Expertise and Personal Attributes. The conclusion of their study was that both technical and non-technical skills were important for success in this profession particularly in entry-level jobs1.

- The Nevada Department of Education in collaboration with local academic institutions andbusinesses developed the Information Technology skill standards. The report identified sevencareer clusters within the IT field and defined eleven essential core IT skills essential to the job. Thepurpose of this report is to prepare current students to attain the skills needed to meet the futuredemands of the IT industry through secondary and post secondary (9-14) IT programs10.

- The Illinois Occupation Skill Standards guides workforce preparation programs and employers to establish the skills and standards necessary for a job in the IT cluster. The components of the skill standard are: Performance Area, Performance Skill, Skill Standard, Performance Elements and Performance Assessment Criteria. The intent of this program is to promote education and training investment as well as to ensure the supply of a trained workforce.

- Sponsored by the National Science Foundation, the National Workforce Center for Emerging Technologies developed a skill standard report for Information Technology jobs in 1999 and later updated it in 2003. Skill standards were developed for eight main career clusters within IT that represented a broad range of jobs. This report was targeted to be of use to educators, human resource professionals, training certification and assessment developers, students and job seekers as well as workforce researchers.

- In Georgia the competency-based curriculum framework for IT outlines core employability skills for IT occupation in collaboration with businesses and educators. The main objective of this initiative is to ensure that curriculum reflects the demands of the workplace and is well positioned to prepare students to meet these needs for success in their future jobs11.

- The *it*WORKS.OHIO report is the career field technical content standards documents for information technology. It serves as the curriculum framework for Ohio College Tech Prep and Career-Technical Educational programs in IT. Used in collaboration with other programs in thestate, this document forms the basis for enhancing and expanding career-technical education and secondary degree programs in IT.

4.3Competency Mapping procedures followed across IT industries

Most of the IT and ITes firms have their own tailor made competency framework, but the basic framework for all the firms are more or less the same. For example each of these firms have their competencies divided into three levels that is:

- Core competencies- core competencies form the roof of competencies that are relevant for the entire organization. In other words these competencies are action oriented or result driven competencies.
- Behavioral competencies: Behavioral competencies are underlying characteristics having a causal relationship with effective or superior performance.
- Functional competencies: Functional competencies stand for the knowledge and skill components that are specific to jobs.

4.3a.Designing a competency model framework:

This stage required that each of the competencies should be defined in terms of the indicators in which it is to be measured. For example: The competency of conflict management can be described as follows:

Anticipates or seeks to resolve confrontations, disagreements or complaints in a constructive manner.

Behavioral indicators-

- Recognizes the root cause for conflicts ,confrontations or disagreements
- Resolves conflicts ,confrontations or disagreements in a constructive manner
- Addresses formal and informal complaints from employees or from person other than employees.
- Attempts to resolve the employee complaints or from persons other than employees.

Figure: 4.1 Process for competency modeling:

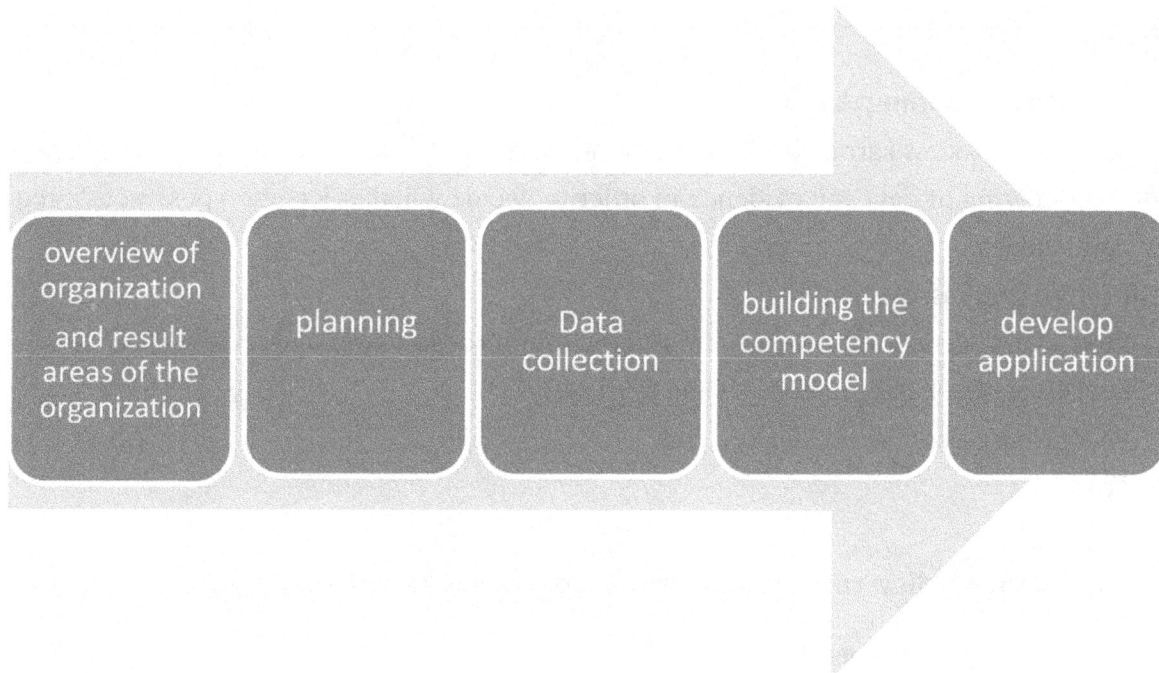

Fig: 4.1competncy model framework

It firms either follow the Global Delivery framework or the PCMM model for designing. But for companies like CSC ,thought they also follow the PCMM model they also have a Lominger card which describes the competencies in detail.

4.3b.Competency profiling:
After creating competency dictionary as per the model and deliverables, each company then creates its own competency profiling. On the basis of thes competency matrix is developed

Figure :4.2Developing a competency matrix

Example of a competency matrix can be as follows:

Competency	Levels			
	Sr.mgr	Manager	Executive	Supervisor
Achievement orientation	5	4	3	3
Relationship building	5	4	3	3
Conceptual thinkinking	5	4	3	3

The numbers indicate the levels of proficiency required for each job position on the basis of the PCMM model.

4.3c. Competency Mapping Assessment:

Assessment is the process carried out by the assessor to determine the level of a person's competency. It involves gathering of data and evidence in order to decide whether a person possesses a required level of competency.

Types of competency assessment:

1. Process assessment and product assessment through observation and review
2. Oral assessment using interviews and third party.
3. Peer group assessments using reviews
4. Tests

Figure: 4.3. Recent studies: correlation of assessment methods with performance

Criterion validity of assessment methods	
Assessment method	r
Assessment centers	.65
BEI	.61
Superior reviews	.54
Tests	.38
Personality tests	.32
Biodata	.23
Non behavioral interview	.05

After establishing the required competency levels (RCL) and measuring the current competency levels (CCL), gap analysis is done by using the following formula:

GAP=RCL-CCL

On completion, each development program is evaluated to measure the competency acquisition that it resulted in.

4.3d. Competency based HRM practices

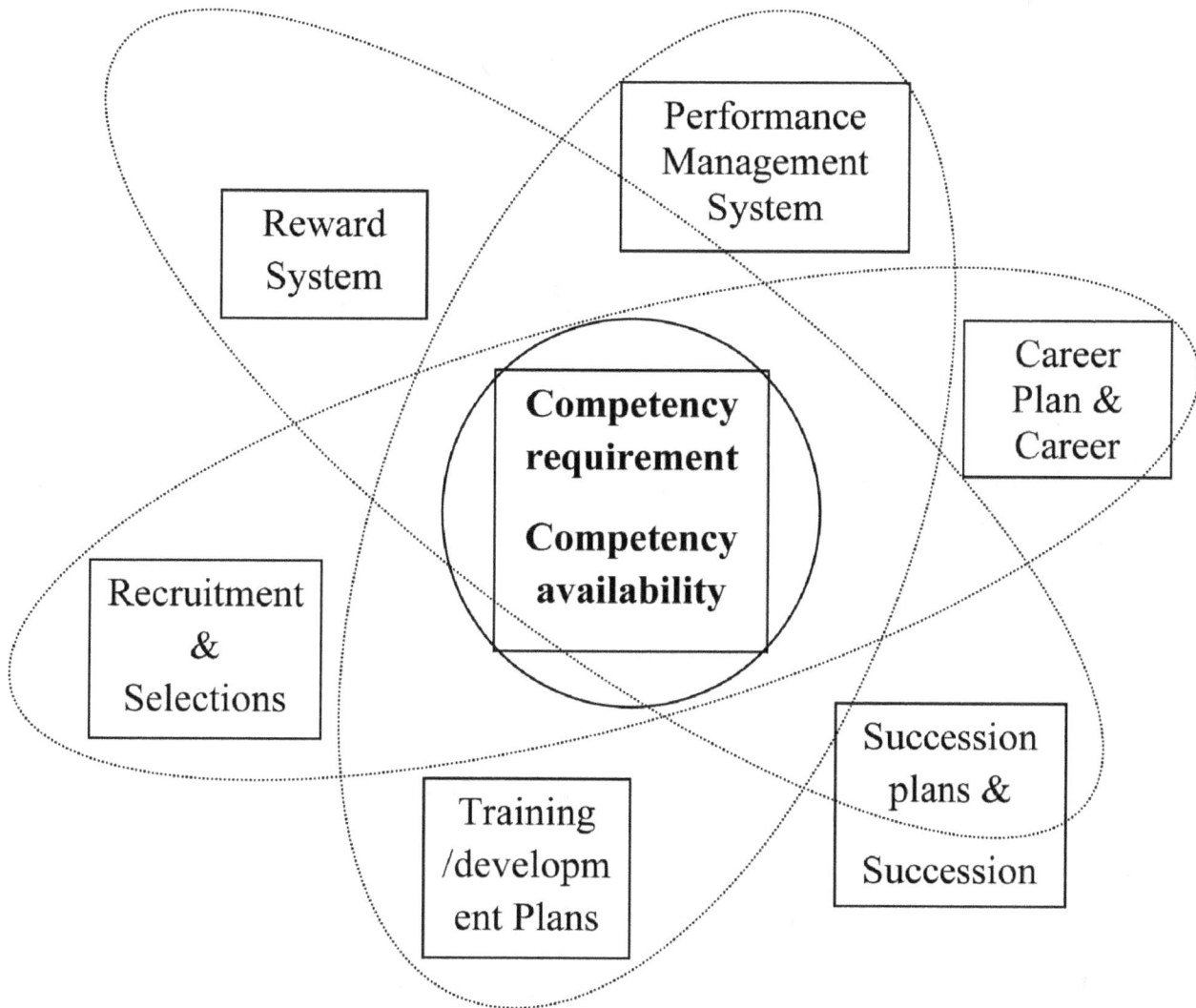

The most important concepts of competency management is the continuous process of managing and developing competency standards which reflect normal good practices of direction setting, monitoring and measuring competencies, providing feedback and taking action accordingly. Feedback is a very important aspect of any competency mapping system, as it this which helps an individual to understand things better and achieve the desired results. Competency based HR practices has shown significant improvement in the productivity of the employees.

4.4. Competency Mapping process at CSC

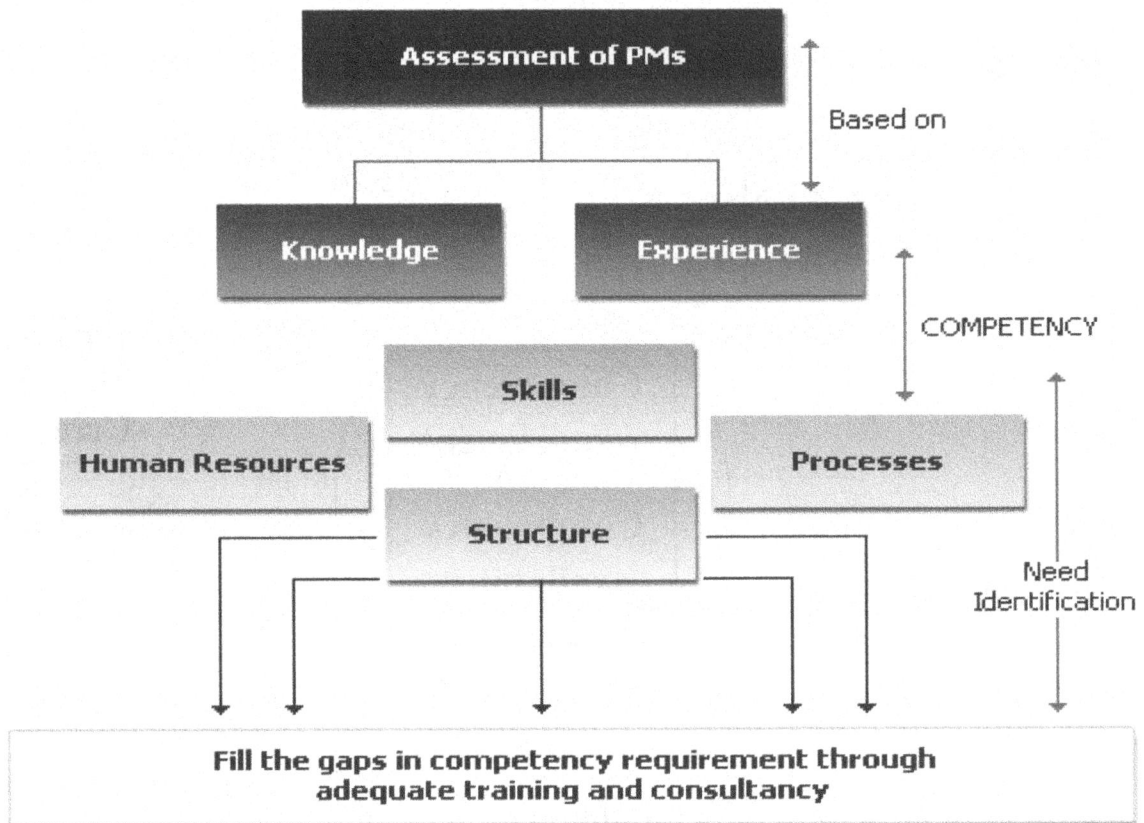

Defining performance effectiveness criterion

The first logical step to development of the competency model at CSC has been to identify the criteria on which to judge superior performance and hence superior performer. Therefore Key result areas are identified for each particular job position of an organization. Each role holder is expected to achieve a minimum 20% of the KRA to qualify of their individual development plan.

Developing competency dictionary:

At CSC they use the Lominger Card to identify the various competency descriptions. Like for example: Action orientation at CSC means:

- A1: managing from within self empowerment
- A2: working for your inner boss: personal accountability
- C1: Emotional intelligence in the workplace
- C2 managing your career: creating a plan
- C3:Managing your career: getting on the right track

Where A refers to action orientation and C refers to change orientation.

- C3:Managing your career: getting on the right track

Where A refers to action orientation and C refers to change orientation.

Lominger Card #	Fit	Related SkillSoft Course Title	SkillSoft Course #	Hours	Proficiency Level
		-			
1	**Action Oriented**				
	A1	Managing from Within: Self-empowerment	pd_05_a02_bs_enus	2	2
	A2	Working for Your Inner Boss: Personal Accountability	pd_05_a01_bs_enus	2	2
			-		
	C1	Emotional Intelligence in the Workplace	comm_09_a02_bs_enus	1.5	1
	C2	Managing Your Career: Creating a Plan	pd_10_a01_bs_enus	1	2
	C3	Managing Your Career: Getting on the Right Track	pd_10_a02_bs_enus	1	2
			-		
2	**Dealing with Ambiguity**				
	B1	Views on Organizational Change	pd_03_a01_bs_enus	2.5	1
	B2	Preparing for Change	pd_03_a02_bs_enus	3	2
	B3	Communication during Organizational Change	pd_03_a03_bs_enus	3.5	2
	B4	Handling Organizational Change	PD003A	0.5	2

		Simulation			
	B5	Managing the Stress of Organizational Change	_pc_bi_mgbi004	0.2	2
	B6	The Importance of Flexibility in the Workplace	_pc_bi_pfbi007	0.2	2
			-		
	C1	Creating a Positive Attitude	pd_05_a04_bs_enus	2	2
	C2	Leadership Essentials: Leading Change	lead_05_a07_bs_enus	1	2
	C3	Managing Change: Understanding Change	mgmt_13_a01_bs_enus	1	2
	C4	Managing Change: Building Positive Support for Change	mgmt_13_a02_bs_enus	1	2
	C5	Managing Change: Dealing with Resistance to Change	mgmt_13_a03_bs_enus	1	2
	C6	Managing Change: Sustaining Organizational Change	mgmt_13_a04_bs_enus	1	2
	C7	Using Change Process to Support Teams Simulation	MGMT006B	0.5	2
			-		
3	**Approachability**				
	A1	Interpersonal Communication: Being Approachable	comm_21_a05_bs_enus	1	2

B1		Listening Basics	comm_03_a01_bs_enus	2	1
B2		Listening to Comprehend	comm_03_a02_bs_enus	4	2
B3		Higher Purpose Listening	comm_03_a03_bs_enus	1.5	2
B4		Enhancing Listening Skills	comm_03_a04_bs_enus	2	2
B5		Effective Listening Simulation	COMM003A	0.5	2
			-		
C1		Emotional Intelligence in the Workplace	comm_09_a02_bs_enus	1.5	2
			-		
4	**Boss Relationships**				
A1		Managing Upward Relationships	mgmt_02_a05_bs_enus	3	2
A2		Obtaining Results from the Boss	comm_13_a06_bs_enus	3	2
			-		
5	**Business Acumen**				
	Thinking Strategically		-		

155

A1		Thinking Strategically	stgy_01_a 01_bs_en us	2	2
A2		Sustaining Competitive Advantage	stgy_01_a 02_bs_en us	3	2
A3		The Imperatives of Innovation and Leadership in Strategy	stgy_01_a 03_bs_en us	2.5	2
A4		Planning and Implementing a Business Strategy	stgy_01_a 04_bs_en us	2.5	2
A5		Moving from an Operational Manager to a Strategic Thinker Simulation	STGY001 A	0.5	2
A6		Leading Outside the Organization	_pc_bi_ls bi005	0.2	2
A7		Effective Critical Analysis of Business Reports	_pc_bi_pf bi004	0.2	2
A8		External Consultants Can Help	_pc_ch_m gch004	0.2	2
Thinking Globally					
A9		Globalization and Our Changing World	STGY035 1	1.5	1
A10		Globalization and Your Company	STGY035 2	4	1
A11		The Process of Globalizing a Product or Service	STGY035 3	3.5	2
A12		Managing from a Global Viewpoint	STGY035 4	4.5	2
A13		The Fundamentals of Globalization	STGY035	0.5	2

		Simulation	0		
A14		Managing Expatriates' Career Development	_pc_bi_m gbi011	0.2	2
A15		The Etiquette of Cross-cultural Gift Giving	_pc_bi_sp bi015	0.2	2
	Finance Fundamentals for Nonfinancial Professionals		_		
A16		The Principles of Financial Management	fin_01_a0 1_bs_enus	2.5	1
A17		The Basics of Budgeting	fin_01_a0 2_bs_enus	2	1
A18		Management of Cash Flows	fin_01_a0 3_bs_enus	2	1
A19		Financial Statements	fin_01_a0 4_bs_enus	2	1
A20		Increasing Cash Flow in Times of Need	_pc_bi_fa bi003	0.2	2
A21		Depreciation Methods	_pc_ch_fa ch002	0.2	2
A22		What's Your Gross Profit Margin Really Saying?	_pc_bi_fa bi006	0.2	2
A23		Recognizing the Value of Intangible Assets	_pc_bi_fa bi007	0.2	2
A24		Recession: How it Affects Business	_pc_bi_fa bi008	0.2	2
A25		Using Financial Analysis for Credit Decisions	_pc_ch_la ch012	0.2	2
	Creating a Business Case		_		

A26	Preparing a Business Case	comm_01_a01_bs_enus	2.5	2
A27	Writing a Business Case	comm_01_a02_bs_enus	2.5	2
A28	Presenting Your Case	comm_01_a03_bs_enus	2.5	2
A29	Preparing an Effective Internal Business Case Simulation	COMM001A	0.5	2
		-		
Industry Overviews		-		
C1	The Automotive Industry Overview: Version 2	indo_01_a01_bs_enus	3	1
C2	The Oil and Gas Industry Overview: Version 2	indo_01_a02_bs_enus	2.5	1
C3	The Pharmaceutical Industry Overview: Version 2	indo_01_a03_bs_enus	2.5	1
C4	The Food and Beverage Industry Overview: Version 2	indo_01_a04_bs_enus	2.5	1
C5	The Health Care Industry Overview: Version 2	indo_01_a05_bs_enus	1.5	1
C6	The Banking Industry Overview: Version 2	indo_01_a06_bs_en	2.5	1

			us		
	C7	The Manufacturing Industry Overview: Version 2	indo_01_a07_bs_enus	2.5	1
	C8	The Retail Industry Overview: Version 2	indo_01_a08_bs_enus	2.5	1
	C9	The Telecommunications Industry Overview: Version 2	indo_01_a09_bs_enus	2.5	1
	C10	The Insurance Industry Overview: Version 2	indo_01_a10_bs_enus	3	1
	C11	Industry Overview: Information Technology	indo_02_a11_bs_enus	2	1
	C12	Industry Overview: Federal Government	indo_02_a12_bs_enus	1.5	1
6					
	A1	Managing Your Career: Creating a Plan	pd_10_a01_bs_enus	1	2
	A2	Managing Your Career: Getting on the Right Track	pd_10_a02_bs_enus	1	2
	A3	Managing Your Career: Professional Networking Essentials	pd_10_a03_bs_enus	1	2
	A4	Managing Your Career: You and Your Boss	pd_10_a04_bs_enus	1	2
	A5	Managing Your Career: Leveraging the	pd_10_a0	1	2

		Performance Appraisal	5_bs_enus		
			-		
7					
		no SkillSoft courses directly related			
8					
	A1	Managing Upward Relationships	mgmt_02 a05_bs_e nus	3	2
9					
	A1	Leadership Essentials: Leading with Emotional Intelligence	lead_05_a 04_bs_en us	1	2
	A2	Leadership Essentials: Leading Business Execution	lead_05_a 05_bs_en us	1	2
	A3	Foundations for Business Execution	LEAD015 1	4	1
	A4	Creating a Business Execution Culture	LEAD015 2	4.5	2
	A5	Business Execution in Action	LEAD015 3	3	2
	A6	Business Execution Simulation	LEAD015 0	0.5	2
	A7	Developing a Business Execution Culture	_pc_ch_la ch001	0.2	2
	A8	Taking Calculated Risks in Leadership	_pc_bi_ls bi006	0.2	2

		Leading Change Process	–		
	C1	Leadership Essentials: Leading Change	lead_05_a 07_bs_cn us	1	2
	C2	Starting the Change Process	mgmt_06 _a01_bs_e nus	3	2
	C3	Managing the Change Process	mgmt_06 _a02_bs_e nus	3	2
	C4	Integrating Change in Your Organization	mgmt_06 _a03_bs_e nus	3	2
	C5	Using Change Process to Support Employees Simulation	MGMT00 6A	0.5	2
	C6	Using Change Process to Support Teams Simulation	MGMT00 6B	0.5	2
	C7	Leading Change	pc_ch_la ch004	0.2	2
	C8	Leading Teams through Change	pc_bi_ls bi003	0.2	2
10					
		no SkillSoft courses directly related			
11					
	A1	What is Emotional Intelligence?	pc_bi_pf bi009	0.2	1
	A2	Defining Emotional Intelligence	comm_09 _a01_bs_e	2	1

			nus		
	A3	Emotional Intelligence in the Workplace	comm_09_a02_bs_enus	1.5	2
	A4	Emotional Intelligence and Teamwork	comm_09_a03_bs_enus	2	2
	A5	Increasing Emotional Intelligence	comm_09_a04_bs_enus	2	2
	A6	Emotionally Intelligent Leadership	comm_09_a05_bs_enus	2	2
	A7	Emotional Intelligence at Work Simulation	COMM009A	0.5	2
			-		
	B1	Experiencing Anger	COMM0701	5	2
	B2	Managing Your Anger	COMM0702	5.5	2
	B3	Managing Anger in the Workplace Simulation	COMM0700	0.5	2
			-		
12					
	A1	Workplace Conflict: Recognizing and Responding to Conflict	comm_22_a01_bs_enus	1	2
	A2	Workplace Conflict: Strategies for Resolving Conflicts	comm_22_a02_bs_enus	1	2

	A4	Conflict in the Workplace Simulation	COMM007A	0.5	2
	A5	Managing Workplace Conflict Simulation	COMM007B	0.5	2
	A6	Coping with Accusations in the Workplace	pc_ch_ls ch003	0.2	2
	A7	Managing Conflict	pc_ch_la ch009	0.2	2
	A8	Confrontation: What's the Best Approach	pc_bi_m gbi009	0.2	2
	A9	Manager to Manager Conflict	pc_ch_m gch003	0.2	2
			-		
13					
	A1	Problem Performance Prevention	mgmt_05 a01_bs_e nus	2.5	2
	A2	Problem Performance Identification	mgmt_05 a02_bs_e nus	2.5	2
	A3	Problem Performance Improvement	mgmt_05 a03_bs_e nus	3	2
	A4	Addressing Problem Performance	mgmt_05 a04_bs_e nus	2.5	2
	A5	Avoiding Problem Performance Simulation	MGMT005A	0.5	2
	A6	Dealing with Problem Performance Simulation	MGMT005B	0.5	2

	A7	Underperforming Employee - Now What?	_pc_bi_hr bi010	0.2	2
	A8	Managing Performance	_pc_ch_la ch002	0.2	2
14					
	A1	Generating Creative and Innovative Ideas: Enhancing Your Creativity	pd_09_a0 1_bs_enus	1	2
	A2	Generating Creative and Innovative Ideas: Maximizing Team Creativity	pd_09_a0 2_bs_enus	1	2
	A3	Generating Creative and Innovative Ideas: Verifying and Building on Ideas	pd_09_a0 3_bs_enus	1	2
	A4	Executing Innovation	_pc_bi_ls bi016	0.2	2
	Leading Innovation		-		
	C1	Leadership Essentials: Leading Innovation	lead_05_a 06_bs_en us	1	2
	C2	Leading Innovation	_pc_ch_la ch010	0.2	2
	C3	Wanted-Innovation Leaders	_pc_bi_ls bi013	0.2	2
			-		
15					
	Customer Focus for Individuals		-		
	A1	The Fundamentals of Exceptional Customer Service	cust_05_a 02_bs_en us	3	2

A2		The Customer's Voice	cust_05_a 03_bs_en us	5	2
A3		Advancing Service Expertise	cust_05_a 04_bs_en us	3.5	2
A4		Customers, Confrontation and Conflict	cust_05_a 05_bs_en us	5	2
A5		Overcoming Difficult Service Situations	cust_05_a 06_bs_en us	4.5	2
A6		The EXCEL Acronym: Instilling Service Excellence	cust_05_a 07_bs_en us	5	2
A7		Service Teams and Service Stars	cust_05_a 08_bs_en us	5	2
A8		Excel at Customer Service Simulation	CUST005 A	0.5	2
A9		Providing Customer Service Simulation	CUST005 B	0.5	2
			-		
	Leading a Customer-Focused Team		-		
B1		Identifying Your Customer's Expectations	CUST017 1	4.5	2
B2		Using Surveys to Measure Customer Satisfaction	CUST017 2	3	2

	B3	Bridge The Expectations Gap	CUST0173	4.5	2
	B4	Leading A Customer-Focused Team	CUST0174	4	2
	B5	Managing a Customer-focused Department Simulation	CUST0170	0.5	2
	B6	Creating a Customer-focused Organization	_pc_ch_la_ch020	0.2	2
	B7	Aligning Performance to Key Indicators	_pc_bi_ct_bi007	0.2	2
16					
	A1	The Fundamentals of Effective Thinking	pd_04_a01_bs_enus	3	1
	A2	Making Decisions Dynamically	pd_04_a04_bs_enus	2.5	2
	A3	Decision Making: Implementation and Evaluation	pd_04_a05_bs_enus	2.5	2
	A4	Playing the Devil's Advocate in Decision Making	_pc_bi_pf_bi005	0.2	2
			-		
	C1	Basic Business Skills to Get You on the Fast Track	PD0132	2.5	2
	C2	Decisions and Risk	PD0243	2	2
	C3	Taking Calculated Risks in Leadership	_pc_bi_ls_bi006	0.2	2
			-		
17					
	A1	Developing Fundamental Critical Thinking Skills	PD0252	3	2

	A2	Strategies for Facilitating Critical Thinking	PD0253	4.5	2
	A3	Critical Thinking Skills for Managing	PD0254	3.5	2
	A4	Making Decisions Dynamically	pd_04_a04_bs_enus	2.5	2
	A5	Decision Making: Implementation and Evaluation	pd_04_a05_bs_enus	2.5	2
	A6	Rational Decision-making and Problem Solving Simulation	PD004B	0.5	2
	A7	Playing the Devil's Advocate in Decision Making	pc_bi_pfbi005	0.2	2
	C1	Risk Basics	PD0241	2	1
	C2	Approaches to Risk Management	PD0242	2	2
	C3	Decisions and Risk	PD0243	2	2
	C4	Strategic Planning and Risk Management	PD0244	2.5	2
	C5	Risk Strategies: The Cutting Edge	PD0245	2.5	2
	C6	Working without a Net: Decisions Simulation	PD0240	0.5	2
	C7	Taking Calculated Risks in Leadership	pc_bi_lsbi006	0.2	2
18					
	A1	The Basics of Delegation	mgmt_07a01_bs_enus	1.5	1
	A2	Delegation: the Personal Approach	mgmt_07a02_bs_enus	2	2

167

	A3	Managing Delegation	mgmt_07_a03_bs_enus	3	2
	A4	Delegating Effectively Simulation	MGMT007A	0.5	2
	A5	Delegating Appropriate Tasks	pc_bi_mgbi007	0.2	2
	A6	Developing Employees through Delegation	pc_ch_lach017	0.2	2
			-		
	C1	Basic Business Skills to Get You on the Fast Track	PD0132	2.5	2
	C2	A Primer for Ensuring Accountability	mgmt_04_a05_bs_enus	4.5	2
19					
	A1	Tomorrow's Managers' Development Tools	mgmt_04_a02_bs_enus	3.5	2
	A2	Managing as Project Champion	mgmt_04_a04_bs_enus	3.5	2
	A3	Assessing Performance Continuously	mgmt_11_a01_bs_enus	3	2
	A4	Performance Reviews	mgmt_11_a02_bs_enus	3.5	2
	A5	Appraising Performance Simulation	MGMT01	0.5	2

			1A		
A6		Developing Adaptable Managers	_pc_bi_m gbi013	0.2	2
B1		Managing and Rewarding Top Performers	mgmt_01 _a01_bs_e nus	2.5	2
B2		Managing Managers	mgmt_02 _a04_bs_e nus	3.5	2
Coaching			-		
C1		Business Coaching: Getting Ready to Coach	mgmt_14 _a01_bs_e nus	1	2
C2		Business Coaching: Conducting Coaching Sessions	mgmt_14 _a02_bs_e nus	1	2
C3		Business Coaching: Building the Coaching Relationship	mgmt_14 _a03_bs_e nus	1	2
C4		Business Coaching: Using Different Coaching Styles	mgmt_14 _a04_bs_e nus	1	2
C5		Coaching with Confidence Simulation	MGMT00 9A	0.5	2
C6		Coaching Teams and Personalities Simulation	MGMT00 9B	0.5	2
Mentoring			-		

	C7	Mentoring Effectively	mgmt_10_a01_bs_enus	2	1
	C8	Mentoring as a Manager	mgmt_10_a02_bs_enus	2	2
	C9	Implementing a Mentoring Program for the Organization	mgmt_10_a03_bs_enus	2.5	2
	C10	Mentoring Strategies for the 21st Century	mgmt_10_a04_bs_enus	2.5	2
	360-Degree Performance Appraisal				
	C11	About 360-Degree Performance Feedback	MGMT0151	2.5	1
	C12	Elements of a 360-degree Performance Review	MGMT0152	2	2
	C13	Delivering 360-Degree Performance Feedback	MGMT0153	5	2
	C14	360-Degree Performance Appraisal Simulation	MGMT0150	0.5	2
			-		
	Succession Planning		-		
	C15	Succession Planning Overview	LEAD0301	2	1
	C16	Succession Planning Strategies	LEAD0302	4.5	2
	C17	Succession Planning and Human Resources	LEAD0303	5	2

	C18	Succession Planning Management	LEAD0304	2.5	2
	C19	Initiating a Succession Plan Simulation	LEAD0300	0.5	2
	C20	Implementing a Succession Plan Simulation	LEAD030S	0.5	2
	C21	Succession Planning	_pc_bi_ls bi002	0.2	2
	C22	Succession Planning and Management Programs	_pc_ch_ls ch004	0.2	2
20					
	A1	Taking on a Management Role	mgmt_03 _a01_bs_e nus	3.5	1
	A2	Becoming a Manager: Responsibilities and Fears	mgmt_03 _a02_bs_e nus	3.5	2
	A3	Becoming a Manager: Leading and Communicating	mgmt_03 _a03_bs_e nus	4	2
	A4	A New Manager and the Company's Future	mgmt_03 _a04_bs_e nus	3.5	2
	A5	Moving into a Management Role Simulation	MGMT003A	0.5	2
	A6	Leadership and Management Simulation	MGMT003B	0.5	2
	A7	Tomorrow's Managers' Competencies	mgmt_04 _a01_bs_e	3	1

			nus		
	A8	Tomorrow's Managers' Development Tools	mgmt_04_a02_bs_e nus	3.5	1
	A9	Managing as Project Champion	mgmt_04_a04_bs_e nus	3.5	2
	A10	A Primer for Ensuring Accountability	mgmt_04_a05_bs_e nus	4.5	2
	A11	Crucial Skills for Tomorrow's Managers Simulation	MGMT00 4A	0.5	2
	A12	Adopting the Appropriate Management Style	_pc_ch_m gch005	0.2	2
	A13	Employee Engagement	_pc_ch_m gch006	0.2	2
			-		
	B1	Managing in a Global Business Environment	mgmt_02_a01_bs_e nus	3	2
	B2	Managing Cross-Functions	mgmt_02_a02_bs_e nus	3	2
	B3	Managing for High Performance	mgmt_02_a03_bs_e nus	4	2
	B4	Managing Managers	mgmt_02_a04_bs_e nus	3.5	2
	B5	Managing Upward Relationships	mgmt_02	3	2

			a05_bs_e nus		
	B6	Advanced Management Skills Simulation	MGMT00 2A	0.5	2
	B7	Managing and Rewarding Top Performers	mgmt_01 _a01_bs_e nus	2.5	2
	B8	Assessing Employees for Cultural Adaptability	_pc_ch_pf ch001	0.2	2
			-		
	C1	Leadership Essentials: Leading with Emotional Intelligence	lead_05_a 04_bs_en us	1	2
	C2	The Emotionally Intelligent Leader	_pc_ch_la ch014	0.2	2
	C3	Leadership Essentials: Leading Business Execution	lead_05_a 05_bs_en us	1	2
	C4	Developing a Business Execution Culture	_pc_ch_la ch001	0.2	2
	C5	Foundations for Business Execution	LEAD015 1	4	1
	C6	Creating a Business Execution Culture	LEAD015 2	4.5	2
	C7	Business Execution in Action	LEAD015 3	3	2
	C8	Business Execution Simulation	LEAD015 0	0.5	2
	C9	Taking Calculated Risks in Leadership	_pc_bi_ls bi006	0.2	2

21					
	A1	Diversity on the Job: The Importance of Diversity and the Changing Workplace	pd_07_a01_bs_enus	1	2
	A2	Diversity on the Job: Diversity and You	pd_07_a02_bs_enus	1	2
	A5	Managing Diversity in the Workplace Simulation	HR002A	0.5	2
	A6	Managing Diversity	_pc_ch_la ch015	0.2	2
	A7	Understanding Workplace Diversity	_pc_bi_hr bi002	0.2	2
	A8	Instituting a Dress Code	_pc_bi_hr bi011	0.2	2
22					
	A1	Making Decisions Ethically	pd_02_a01_bs_enus	2.5	1
	A2	Business Ethics for Managers	pd_02_a02_bs_enus	1.5	2
	A3	Understanding Organizational Ethics	pd_02_a03_bs_enus	3	2
	A4	Social Responsibility in Corporations	pd_02_a04_bs_enus	3	2
	A5	Business Ethics Simulation	PD002A	0.5	2
	A6	Ethics, Integrity, and Trust	_pc_ch_la ch005	0.2	2
	B1	Office Politics - What Will You Do?	_pc_ch_pf	0.2	2

174

			ch004		
	B2	Ethical Self-promotion	_pc_ch_pf ch005	0.2	2
	B3	Ethics and Risks: Why They Matter in Project Success	_pc_ch_p mch003	0.2	2
			-		
23					
		no SkillSoft courses directly related			
24					
	Marketing Professional				
	A1	Elements of Marketing Strategy	MKT0201	3	1
	A2	Analyzing the Market	MKT0202	2.5	1
	A3	Competitive Factors in Strategic Marketing	MKT0203	2.5	1
	A4	Writing a Marketing Plan: Phase 1	MKT0204	3	1
	A5	Writing the Marketing Plan: Creative Strategy	MKT0205	2.5	1
	A6	Creating a Marketing Campaign	MKT0206	4	1
	A7	Marketing Management	MKT0207	4	1
	A8	Financial Analysis for Successful Marketing	MKT0208	4.5	1
	A9	Advertising Costs, PR Pays	_pc_bi_sp bi008	0.2	2
	A10	Sales and Marketing: Two Sides of the Same Coin?	_pc_bi_sp bi011	0.2	2
	A11	Trade Show Marketing - Planning Ahead	_pc_bi_sp bi013	0.2	2
	A12	Competitive Strategies for a New	MKT0231	2.5	1

		Marketplace			
	A13	Surpassing the Competition	MKT0232	3	1
	A14	Increasing Competitiveness through Collaboration	pc_ch_ls ch006	0.2	2
	A15	Introduction to Product Management	MKT0241	2	1
	A16	Developing a New-product Strategy	MKT0242	2	2
	A17	Pricing and Profitability for Product Managers	MKT0243	3	2
	A18	Introduction to Brand Management	MKT0211	3.5	1
			-		
	A19	Building Brand Equity	MKT0212	3.5	2
	A20	Managing the Creative Elements of Brand	MKT0213	3.5	2
	A21	Promoting Your Brand to Consumers	MKT0214	3	2
	A22	Evaluating Brand Effectiveness	MKT0215	6	2
	A23	Managing and Maintaining Brand Equity	MKT0216	4.5	2
			-		
	A24	Introduction to Online Branding	MKT0221	3.5	1
	A25	The Online Branding Environment	MKT0222	3	2
	A26	Strategies for Building an Online Brand	MKT0223	7	2
	Finance / Accounting Professional				
	A1	Accounting Fundamentals	FIN0121	3.5	1
	A2	Accrual Accounting Procedures	FIN0122	2	2
	A3	Accounting Systems and Closing Activities	FIN0123	2.5	2
	A4	Accounting for Cash Control	FIN0124	3	2
	A5	Accounting for Merchandising	FIN0125	2.5	2

		Businesses			
	A6	Final Exam: Accounting 101	FE0004_eng		2
	A7	Accounting for Sales Returns	_pc_bi_fa bi005	0.2	2
	A8	Accounting for Partnerships	FIN0221	3.5	2
	A9	Accounting for Corporations	FIN0222	2.5	2
	A10	Analyzing Cash Flow Statements	FIN0223	2	2
	A11	Master Budgets	FIN0224	4	2
	A12	Final Exam: Accounting 102	FE0006_eng		2
			-		
	A13	Introduction to Auditing	FIN0231	3	1
	A14	Introduction to Internal Auditing	FIN0232	4.5	2
	A15	Principles of Internal Auditing	FIN0233	3	2
	A16	Introduction to External Auditing	FIN0234	3.5	2
	A17	Principles of External Auditing	FIN0235	4	2
	A18	Using Audits to Help Prevent Business Fraud	_pc_bi_fa bi002	0.2	2
	A19	Establishing the Role of the Audit Department	_pc_ch_fa ch001	0.2	2
	A20	Overview of Managerial Accounting	FIN0241	5	1
	A21	Managerial Decisions and Capital Budgeting	FIN0242	5	2
	A22	Managing for Asset Control	FIN0243	5.5	2
	A23	Cost Accounting Decisions	FIN0244	4	2
			-		
	A24	Introduction to Advanced Finance	FIN0211	3	1

A25	Investment Project Analysis and Selection	FIN0212	2	2
A26	Raising Capital and Financing Decisions	FIN0213	3	2
A27	Managing Working Capital	FIN0214	4	2
A28	Corporate Restructuring	FIN0215	2.5	2
A29	Financial Risk Management	FIN0216	1.5	2
A30	International Finance	FIN0217	2	2
A31	Final Exam: Advanced Business Finance	FE0005_eng		2
A32	Outsourcing Financial Activities	_pc_bi_fa bi001	0.2	2
Administrative Professional				
A1	Administrative Professionals: Representing Your Boss	ad_01_a01_bs_enus	1	2
A2	Administrative Professionals: Common Administrative Support Tasks	ad_01_a02_bs_enus	1	2
A3	Administrative Professionals: Maximizing Your Relationship with Your Boss	ad_01_a03_bs_enus	1	2
A4	Administrative Professionals: Interacting with Others	ad_01_a04_bs_enus	1	2
A5	Administrative Professionals: Putting Your Best Foot Forward	ad_01_a05_bs_enus	1	2
HR Professional				
A1	Human Resources Fundamentals (HRCI/PHR - 2007-aligned)	HR0261	2	3
A2	Strategic Management (HRCI/PHR -	HR0262	2.5	3

		2007-aligned)			
	A3	Affirmative Action and the EEO (HRCI/PHR - 2007-aligned)	HR0263	2.5	3
	A4	Employment Management (HRCI/PHR - 2007-aligned)	HR0264	2.5	3
	A5	Recruiting and Selecting Candidates (HRCI/PHR - 2007-aligned)	HR0265	2	3
	A6	Offers, Contracts, and Exit from the Organization (HRCI/PHR - 2007-aligned)	HR0266	3	3
	A7	Developing Employees (HRCI/PHR - 2007-aligned)	HR0267	1.5	3
	A8	Developing Human Resources (HRCI/PHR - 2007-aligned)	HR0268	1.5	3
	A9	Compensating Employees (HRCI/PHR - 2007-aligned)	HR0269	3	3
	A10	Programs to Benefit Employees (HRCI/PHR - 2007-aligned)	HR0271	1.5	3
	A11	Employment Relations (HRCI/PHR - 2007-aligned)	HR0272	1.5	3
	A12	Sexual Harassment at Work (HRCI/PHR - 2007-aligned)	HR0273	1.5	3
	A13	Non-Unionized Workplaces (HRCI/PHR - 2007-aligned)	HR0274	1.5	3
	A14	Unionized Workplaces (HRCI/PHR - 2007-aligned)	HR0275	1.5	3
	A15	Health and Safety in the Workplace (HRCI/PHR - 2007-aligned)	HR0276	1.5	3
	A16	Risk Assessment and Prevention (HRCI/PHR - 2007-aligned)	HR0277	2.5	3

			-		
B1		HR's Strategic Role in the Organization (HRCI/SPHR - 2007-aligned)	hr_04_a01 bs_enus	1	4
B2		Management of the HR Process (HRCI/SPHR - 2007-aligned)	hr_04_a02 bs_enus	2	4
B3		Strategic Approaches to Workforce Planning and Employment (HRCI/SPHR - 2007-aligned)	hr_04_a03 bs_enus	3	4
B4		Strategic Approaches to Human Resource Development (HRCI/SPHR - 2007-aligned)	hr_04_a04 bs_enus	2.5	4
B5		Strategic Approaches to Total Rewards (HRCI/SPHR - 2007-aligned)	hr_04_a05 bs_enus	2	4
B6		Strategic Approaches to Labor Relations (HRCI/SPHR - 2007-aligned)	hr_04_a06 bs_enus	4.5	4
B7		Strategic Approaches to Risk Management (HRCI/SPHR - 2007-aligned)	hr_04_a07 bs_enus	2	4
B8		Final Exam: HRCI/SPHR (Senior Professional Human Resource)	FE0028_e ng		4
Business Analyst Professional					
A1		Introduction to Business Analysis and Essential Competencies	ib_buap_a 01_it_enu s	2	3
A2		Introduction to Business Analysis Planning	ib_buap_a 02_it_enu s	2	3
A3		Planning Business Analysis Communication and Monitoring	ib_buap_a 03_it_enu	2	3

180

		s		
A4	Business Analysis Requirements Elicitation	ib_buap_a 04_it_enu s	1.5	3
A5	Business Analysis Requirements Management and Communication	ib_buap_a 05_it_enu s	1.5	3
A6	Business Analysis: Enterprise Analysis	ib_buap_a 06_it_enu s	2	3
A7	Business Analysis: Introduction to Requirements Analysis	ib_buap_a 07_it_enu s	1.5	3
A8	Business Analysis: Verify and Validate Requirements	ib_buap_a 08_it_enu s	1	3
A9	Business Analysis: Solution Assessment and Validation	ib_buap_a 09_it_enu s	2	3
Sales Professional - Field				
A1	Field Sales Foundations	SALE010 1	3.5	2
A2	Planning Your Field Sales Approach	SALE010 2	4.5	2
A3	Applying Your Field Sales Approach	SALE010 3	4	2
A4	Completing Your Field Sales Approach	SALE010 4	3.5	2
A5	Field Sales Skills Simulation	SALE010	0.5	2

			0		
A6	Don't Only Go for the Big Fish	_pc_bi_sp bi009	0.2	2	
A7	The Territorial Account Sales Approach	SALE011 1	3	2	
A8	Understanding Your Target Customer's Business	SALE011 2	3.5	2	
A9	Effectively Using Customer-focused Research Meetings	SALE011 3	3.5	2	
A10	Gaining Access to Key Personnel at Your Target Accounts	SALE011 4	3.5	2	
A11	Delivering High-impact Territorial Account Sales (TAS) Presentations	SALE011 5	5	2	
A12	Territorial Account Sales Skills Simulation	SALE011 0	0.5	2	
A13	Listening to your Customers	_pc_bi_sp bi002	0.2	2	
A14	The Strategic Account Sales Approach	SALE013 1	3	2	
A15	Understanding Your Customer	SALE013 2	3.5	2	
A16	Conducting Effective Sales Research Meetings	SALE013 3	3.5	2	
A17	Working with Your Customer's Key Players	SALE013 4	3.5	2	
A18	Delivering High-Impact Sales Presentations	SALE013 5	6	2	
A19	Strategic Account Sales Skills	SALE013	0.5	2	

		Simulation	0		
A20		Selling to Key Players	_pc_bi_sp bi001	0.2	2
A21		Planning for Effective Selling	_pc_bi_sp bi004	0.2	2
A22		Crafting Sales Strategies	_pc_ch_sp ch002	0.2	2
A23		Pricing Strategy	_pc_ch_sp ch003	0.2	2
A24		Performance Payout Plans	_pc_ch_sp ch004	0.2	2
A25		Prepare for Success	SALE022 1	3	2
A26		Strategic Planning	SALE022 2	3.5	2
A27		Progressing through the Complex Sale	SALE022 3	4	2
A28		Presenting Your Proposition	SALE022 4	4	2
A29		Negotiating to Mutual Benefit	SALE022 5	4	2
A30	From Executive-level Sale to Strategic Partnership	SALE022 6	4	2
A31	Preparing for the Executive-level Sale Simulation	SALE022 0	0.5	2
A32	Progressing through the Complex Sale Simulation	SALE022 S	0.5	2
A33	Closing Executive-level Sales Simulation	SALE022 T	0.5	2

	Sales Professional - Inside				
	A1	Preparing for Outbound Sales Calls	SALE012 1	6	2
	A2	Initiating Outbound Sales Calls	SALE012 2	3.5	2
	A3	Completing Outbound Sales Calls	SALE012 3	5	2
	A4	Preparing for Inbound Sales Calls	SALE012 4	5	2
	A5	Completing Inbound Sales Calls	SALE012 5	5	2
	A6	Inside Sales Skills Simulation	SALE012 0	0.5	2
	Sales Management Professional				
	A1	Building a Winning Sales Team	SALE015 1	5.5	2
	A2	Using Business Tools to Manage Sales Teams	SALE015 2	3	2
	A3	Motivating a Winning Sales Team	SALE015 3	4.5	2
	A4	Communicating in Sales Teams	SALE015 4	2.5	2
	A5	Sales Team Management Simulation	SALE015 0	0.5	2
	A6	Storming: Developing and Leading Your Sales Team	_pc_bi_sp bi003	0.2	2
	A7	Planning Direct Mail to Generate Leads for Complex Sales	_pc_bi_sp bi006	0.2	2

	A8	Sales Support Roles for Better Customer Interaction	_pc_bi_sp bi007	0.2	2
	A9	The Ethics of Gift Giving	_pc_bi_sp bi014	0.2	2
Customer Support Professional					
	A1	The Customer Service Representative (CSR)	cust_06_a 01_bs_en us	3.5	2
	A2	Support Center Services and Work Environment |n	cust_06_a 02_bs_en us	3	2
	A3	Team and Customer Relationships	cust_06_a 03_bs_en us	3	2
	A4	Customer Interactions	cust_07_a 01_bs_en us	3.5	2
	A5	Communication Skills	cust_07_a 02_bs_en us	3.5	2
	A6	Conflict, Stress, and Time Management	cust_07_a 03_bs_en us	3.5	2
	A7	Customer Service Processes and Procedures	cust_08_a 01_bs_en us	3	2
	A8	Quality in a Support Center	cust_08_a 02_bs_en us	3.5	2

A9	Support Center Tools, Technologies and Metrics	cust_08_a 03_bs_en us	3	2
A10	Dealing with Irrational Customers and Escalating Complaints	cust_08_a 04_bs_en us	2	2
		-		
Technical Support Professional				
A1	The Contact Center and Technical Support Agent	CUST016 1	4.5	2
A2	Technical Support Essentials	CUST016 2	5	2
A3	Assessing Customer Behavior	CUST016 3	4.5	2
A4	Technical Support Agent Survival Skills	CUST016 4	3.5	2
A5	Technical Support Agent Skills Simulation	CUST016 0	0.5	2
Call Center Management Professional				
A1	The Inbound Call Center	CUST021 1	2.5	2
A2	Inbound Call Center Management: Leadership	CUST021 2	3	2
A3	Inbound Call Centers: People Management	CUST021 3	3	2
A4	Inbound Call Center Technology	CUST021 4	4	2
A5	Performance Metrics for an Inbound Call Center	CUST021 5	2.5	2

A6	Converting a Call Center to a Profit Center	_pc_bi_ct bi001	0.2	2
A7	Managing Your Call Center More Efficiently	_pc_bi_ct bi002	0.2	2
A8	Customer Service Training - The Interview and Beyond	_pc_bi_ct bi004	0.2	2
A9	Disaster Recovery - Keeping the Lines Open	_pc_bi_ct bi005	0.2	2
A10	Preventing Agent Absenteeism through Better Working Conditions	_pc_bi_ct bi006	0.2	2
A11	Workforce Management Software - Is It Worth It?	_pc_bi_ct bi009	0.2	2
A12	Prioritizing Rewards and Recognition in Call Centers	_pc_bi_ct bi011	0.2	2
		-		
Consulting Professional - External Clients				
A1	Essentials of External Consulting	CONS011 1	5	2
A2	The Client-Consultant Relationship	CONS011 2	5	2
A3	Diagnosing and Planning	CONS011 3	4	2
A4	Managing Delivery	CONS011 4	3.5	2
A5	Evaluation and Review	CONS011 5	4	2
A6	Consulting with the External Client Simulation	CONS011 0	0.5	2
Consulting Professional - Internal Clients				

	A1	Essentials of Internal Consulting	CONS012 1	4	2
	A2	Internal Consulting Skills	CONS012 2	3.5	2
	A3	Establishing a Relationship with Internal Clients	CONS012 3	4	2
	A4	A Workable Solution for Internal Clients	CONS012 4	4	2
	A5	Evaluating Internal Assignments	CONS012 5	4.5	2
	A6	Consulting with the Internal Client Simulation	CONS012 0	0.5	2
	Consulting Professional - Internal Clients for IT Projects				
	A1	The Technical Professional as Internal Consultant	CONS013 1	4	2
	A2	Creating Effective Contracts	CONS013 2	3	2
	A3	Using Data as a Technical Professional Consultant	CONS013 3	4	2
	A4	Resistance and Technical Professional Consultants	CONS013 4	2.5	2
25					
	A1	What to Consider When Hiring	hr_03_a01 _bs_enus	2	2
	A2	Interviewing Effectively	hr_03_a02 _bs_enus	2.5	2
	A3	Choosing the Best Applicant	hr_03_a03 _bs_enus	1.5	2

A4		Effective Hiring and Interviewing Simulation	HR003A	0.5	2
A5		Screening Applicants for Emotional Intelligence	pc_bi_hr bi012	0.2	2
A6		Hiring Strategic Thinkers	pc_ch_la ch011	0.2	2
A7		Guarding against Interviewing Biases	pc_bi_hr bi003	0.2	2
A8		Recruiting Talent	hr_05_a01 bs_enus	2	2
A9		Retaining Your Talent Pool	hr_05_a02 bs_enus	2	2
A10		Creating a High-Retention Organizational Culture Simulation	HR005A	0.5	2
A11		Surviving the Talent Crunch	pc_ch_ls ch007	0.2	2
A12		Aligning Recruitment to Job Requirements	pc_bi_hr bi001	0.2	2
A13		Understanding Employment Attrition in High Performing Teams	pc_ch_hr ch001	0.2	2
A14		Preventing High Turnover Rates: How to Keep the Best	pc_bi_m gbi008	0.2	2
A15		Fringe Benefits: Maintaining a Competitive Hiring Advantage	pc_bi_hr bi004	0.2	2
A16		Employer Branding	pc_bi_hr bi007	0.2	2
A17		Devising an Effective Corporate Wellness Program	pc_bi_hr bi009	0.2	2
			-		

		Behavioral Interviewing	-		
	B1	Building a Firm Foundation	HR0211	3	2
	B2	Screening Applicants	HR0212	3	2
	B3	Preparing for the Behavioral Interview	HR0213	3	2
	B4	Conducting the Behavioral-based Interview	HR0214	2.5	2
	B5	Preparing as the Interviewee	HR0215	2.5	2
	B6	Experiencing the Behavioral-based Interview	HR0216	2.5	2
	B7	Behavioral Interviewing Simulation	HR0210	0.5	2
		Using Contractors and Temporary Workers	-		
	C1	Doing Business with Independent Contractors	MGMT0701	4.5	2
	C2	Hiring Temporary (Contingent) Employees	MGMT0702	5	2
	C3	Managing Contingent Employees	MGMT0703	4.5	2
	C4	Legal Pitfalls Regarding Independent Contractors	MGMT0704	3	2
	C5	Working with Temporary Agencies	MGMT0705	5.5	2
	C6	Hiring and Managing Contractors Simulation	MGMT0700	0.5	2
	C7	Final Exam: Managing Contractors and Temporary Employees	FE0009_eng		2
26					
		no SkillSoft courses directly related			

190

27					
	B1	Interpersonal Communication: Communicating with Confidence	comm_21 _a01_bs_e nus	2	2
	B2	Interpersonal Communication: Targeting Your Message	comm_21 _a02_bs_e nus	2	2
	B3	Interpersonal Communication: Communicating Assertively	comm_21 _a04_bs_e nus	2	2
			-		
	C1	An Essential Guide to Giving Feedback	COMM05 21	2.5	1
	C2	Coping with Criticism and Feedback	COMM05 22	5	2
	C3	Giving Feedback to Colleagues	COMM05 23	4.5	2
	C4	Team Feedback: A guide	COMM05 24	4	2
	C5	Giving Feedback: A Manager's Guide	COMM05 25	4	2
	C6	Effective Feedback for Employees and Colleagues Simulation	COMM05 20	0.5	2
	C7	Effective Use of Feedback for Teams Simulation	COMM05 2S	0.5	2
	C8	Criticism in Context	_pc_bi_pf bi016	0.2	2
	C9	Giving Appropriate Feedback	_pc_ch_la ch006	0.2	2

28					
	A1	Leadership Essentials: Leading Innovation	lead_05_a 06_bs_en us	1	2
	A2	Leading Innovation	_pc_ch_la ch010	0.2	2
	A3	Executing Innovation	_pc_bi_ls bi016	0.2	2
	A4	Generating Creative and Innovative Ideas: Enhancing Your Creativity	pd_09_a0 1_bs_enus	1	2
	A5	Generating Creative and Innovative Ideas: Maximizing Team Creativity	pd_09_a0 2_bs_enus	1	2
	A6	Generating Creative and Innovative Ideas: Verifying and Building on Ideas	pd_09_a0 3_bs_enus	1	2
			-		
29					
	A1	Making Decisions Ethically	pd_02_a0 1_bs_enus	2.5	1
	A2	Business Ethics for Managers	pd_02_a0 2_bs_enus	1.5	2
	A3	Understanding Organizational Ethics	pd_02_a0 3_bs_enus	3	2
	A4	Social Responsibility in Corporations	pd_02_a0 4_bs_enus	3	2
	A5	Business Ethics Simulation	PD002A	0.5	2
	A6	Ethics, Integrity, and Trust	_pc_ch_la ch005	0.2	2
	B1	Office Politics - What Will You Do?	_pc_ch_pf	0.2	2

			ch004		
	B2	Ethical Self-promotion	_pc_ch_pf ch005	0.2	2
	B3	Ethics and Risks: Why They Matter in Project Success	_pc_ch_p mch003	0.2	2
			-		
	C1	An Essential Guide to Giving Feedback	COMM05 21	2.5	1
	C2	Coping with Criticism and Feedback	COMM05 22	5	2
	C3	Giving Feedback to Colleagues	COMM05 23	4.5	2
	C4	Team Feedback: A guide	COMM05 24	4	2
	C5	Giving Feedback: A Manager's Guide	COMM05 25	4	2
	C6	Effective Feedback for Employees and Colleagues Simulation	COMM05 20	0.5	2
	C7	Effective Use of Feedback for Teams Simulation	COMM05 2S	0.5	2
30					
		no SkillSoft courses directly related	-		
			-		
31					
	A1	Interpersonal Communication: Communicating with Confidence	comm_21 _a01_bs_e nus	1	2
	A2	Interpersonal Communication: Targeting Your Message	comm_21 _a02_bs_e	1	2

			nus		
	A3	Interpersonal Communication: Listening Essentials	comm_21 _a03_bs_e nus	1	2
	A4	Interpersonal Communication: Communicating Assertively	comm_21 _a04_bs_e nus	1	2
	A5	Interpersonal Communication: Being Approachable	comm_21 _a05_bs_e nus	1	2
	A6	Business Interpersonal Communication Skills Simulation	COMM00 2A	0.5	2
	A7	Team Interpersonal Communication Skills Simulation	COMM00 2B	0.5	2
			-		
	A8	Effective Interfunctional Relationships	comm_12 _a01_bs_e nus	2.5	2
	A9	Effective Intercultural Relationships	comm_12 _a02_bs_e nus	2	2
	A10	Effective Intergender Relationships	comm_12 _a03_bs_e nus	2	2
	A11	Effective Relationships with Customers	comm_12 _a04_bs_e nus	2	2
	A12	Effective Relationships with Business Partners	comm_12 _a05_bs_e nus	3	2

		Building Improved Work Relationships Simulation	COMM01 2A	0.5	2
A13					
	Working with Difficult People		-		
	C1	Difficult People in the Workplace Environment	comm_04 _a01_bs_e nus	3	1
	C2	How to Work with Aggressive People	comm_04 _a02_bs_e nus	3	2
	C3	How to Work with Negative People and Procrastinators	comm_04 _a03_bs_e nus	3	2
	C4	How to Work with Arrogant and Duplicitous People	comm_04 _a04_bs_e nus	2	2
	C5	Working with and Managing Difficult People Simulation	COMM00 4A	0.5	2
	C6	Effective Communication with Difficult Coworkers Simulation	COMM00 4B	0.5	2
	C7	Reacting to Co-workers Who Try Taking Advantage	pc_ch_pf ch003	0.2	2
	C8	Blame Backfires--Conquer Negative Thinking	pc_bi_pf bi003	0.2	2
	Emotional Intelligence		-		
	C9	Defining Emotional Intelligence	comm_09 _a01_bs_e nus	2	1
	C10	Emotional Intelligence in the	comm_09	1.5	2

		Workplace	a02_bs_e nus		
	C11	Emotional Intelligence and Teamwork	comm_09 _a03_bs_e nus	2	2
	C12	Increasing Emotional Intelligence	comm_09 _a04_bs_e nus	2	2
	C13	Emotionally Intelligent Leadership	comm_09 _a05_bs_e nus	2	2
	C14	Emotional Intelligence at Work Simulation	COMM00 9A	0.5	2
	C15	What is Emotional Intelligence?	_pc_bi_pf bi009	0.2	2
			-		
Assertiveness			-		
	C16	Asserting Yourself Professionally	comm_10 _a01_bs_e nus	2.5	2
	C17	Assertiveness from Inside to Outside	comm_10 _a02_bs_e nus	2.5	2
	C18	Communicating Assertively Simulation	COMM01 0A	0.5	2
Communicating Globally			-		
	C19	The Impact of Culture on Communication	COMM00 21	2.5	1
	C20	The Art of Global Communication	COMM00	3.5	2

			22		
	C21	Improving Your Cross-cultural Communications	COMM00 23	3	2
	C22	International Communications Simulation	COMM00 20	0.5	2
	C23	Cross-cultural Communications Simulation	COMM00 2S	0.5	2
			-		
32					
		no SkillSoft courses directly related	-		
			-		
33					
	A1	Listening Basics	comm_03 _a01_bs_e nus	2	1
	A2	Listening to Comprehend	comm_03 _a02_bs_e nus	4	2
	A3	Higher Purpose Listening	comm_03 _a03_bs_e nus	1.5	2
	A4	Enhancing Listening Skills	comm_03 _a04_bs_e nus	2	2
	A5	Effective Listening Simulation	COMM00 3A	0.5	2
34					
	B1	An Essential Guide to Giving Feedback	COMM05 21	2.5	1

	B2	Giving Feedback to Colleagues	COMM05 23	4.5	2
	B3	Team Feedback: A guide	COMM05 24	4	2
	B4	Giving Feedback: A Manager's Guide	COMM05 25	4	2
	B5	Effective Feedback for Employees and Colleagues Simulation	COMM05 20	0.5	2
	B6	Effective Use of Feedback for Teams Simulation	COMM05 2S	0.5	2
	B7	Asserting Yourself Professionally	comm_10 _a01_bs_e nus	2	2
	B8	Assertiveness from Inside to Outside	comm_10 _a02_bs_e nus	2	2
	B9	Communicating Assertively Simulation	COMM01 0A	2	2
35					
	Budget Management				
	B1	Creating and Analyzing an Operating Budget	FIN0161	3.5	2
	B2	The Ins and Outs of Capital Budgeting	FIN0162	3.5	2
	B3	Effective Budget Management	FIN0163	3	2
36					
	A1	Leadership Essentials: Motivating Employees	lead_05_a 01_bs_en	1	2

198

			us		
	A2	Leadership Essentials: Communicating Vision	lead_05_a 02_bs_en us	1	2
	A3	Leadership Essentials: Building Your Influence as a Leader	lead_05_a 03_bs_en us	1	2
	A4	Leadership Essentials: Leading with Emotional Intelligence	lead_05_a 04_bs_en us	1	2
	A5	Leadership Essentials: Leading Business Execution	lead_05_a 05_bs_en us	1	2
	A6	Leadership Essentials: Leading Innovation	lead_05_a 06_bs_en us	1	2
	A7	Leadership Essentials: Leading Change	lead_05_a 07_bs_en us	1	2
	A8	Leader as Motivator	_pc_ch_la ch008	0.2	2
	A9	Communicating a Shared Vision	_pc_bi_ls bi001	0.2	2
	A10	Motivating Human Behavior	_pc_ch_ls ch002	0.2	2
	B1	Developing a Business Execution Culture	_pc_ch_la ch001	0.2	2
	B2	Leading Change	_pc_ch_la ch004	0.2	2

	B3	Leading Innovation	_pc_ch_la ch010	0.2	2
	B4	Leading Teams through Change	_pc_bi_ls bi003	0.2	2
	B5	Taking Calculated Risks in Leadership	_pc_bi_ls bi006	0.2	2
	B6	Wanted-Innovation Leaders	_pc_bi_ls bi013	0.2	2
			-		
	C1	Managing and Rewarding Top Performers	mgmt_01 _a01_bs_e nus	2.5	2
	C2	Attracting, Motivating, and Retaining Technical Professionals	MGMT02 92	3.5	2
	C3	Recognizing Natural Leaders	_pc_ch_ls ch001	0.2	2
	C4	Managing Top Performers Is Always Easy...Right?	_pc_bi_hr bi013	0.2	2
37					
	A1	Crafting Deals	comm_08 _a01_bs_e nus	2.5	1
	A2	Connecting and Communicating	comm_08 _a02_bs_e nus	2	2
	A3	The Process of Negotiation	comm_08 _a03_bs_e nus	2	2
	A4	The Dynamics of Interacting	comm_08	2	2

			_a04_bs_e nus		
	A5	Negotiating Inclusively	comm_08 _a05_bs_e nus	2	2
	A6	What to Do When the Going Gets Tough	comm_08 _a06_bs_e nus	2	2
	A7	Mastering Negotiation	comm_08 _a07_bs_e nus	1.5	2
	A8	Winning Negotiation Simulation	COMM00 8A	0.5	2
	A9	Effective Body Language in Negotiations	_pc_bi_pf bi013	0.2	2
	A10	Location Does Matter	_pc_ch_pf ch002	0.2	2
	B1	Getting Results by Building Relationships	comm_13 _a01_bs_e nus	2	2
	B2	Results and Teamwork without Authority	comm_13 _a02_bs_e nus	2.5	2
	B3	Leading without Authority	comm_13 _a03_bs_e nus	3	2
	B4	Creating Change, Gaining Allies	comm_13 _a04_bs_e nus	2.5	2

	B5	Communicating to Get Results	comm_13_a05_bs_enus	2.5	2
	B6	Obtaining Results from the Boss	comm_13_a06_bs_enus	3	2
	B7	Getting Results with No Authority Simulation	COMM013A	0.5	2
	B8	Influencing Key Decision Makers	_pc_bi_ls_bi015	0.2	2
			-		
38					
	A1	Managing Cross-Functions	mgmt_02_a02_bs_enus	3	2
	A2	Managing Upward Relationships	mgmt_02_a05_bs_enus	3	2
	A3	Managing in a Global Business Environment	mgmt_02_a01_bs_enus	3	2
	B1	Leadership Essentials: Leading Business Execution	lead_05_a05_bs_enus	1	2
	B2	Creating a Business Execution Culture	LEAD0152	4.5	2
	B3	Business Execution in Action	LEAD0153	3	2
	B4	Business Execution Simulation	LEAD015	0.5	2

			0		
B5		Developing a Business Execution Culture	_pc_ch_la ch001	0.2	2
B6		Taking Calculated Risks in Leadership	_pc_bi_ls bi006	0.2	2
	Crisis Management		-		
C1		Preparing for Business Crises	MGMT01 71	2	2
C2		Responding to Business Crises	MGMT01 72	3	2
C3		Recovering from Business Crises	MGMT01 73	2	2
C4		The Fundamentals of Business Crises Management Simulation	MGMT01 70	0.5	2
C5		Is Your Company Prepared for a Crisis?	_pc_bi_m gbi006	0.2	2
C6		Demonstrating Accountability in a Crisis Situation	_pc_ch_la ch007	0.2	2
39					
A1		Time Management: Analyzing Your Use of Time	pd_11_a0 1_bs_enus	1	2
A2		Time Management: Planning and Prioritizing Your Time	pd_11_a0 2_bs_enus	1	2
A3		Time Management: Avoiding Time Stealers	pd_11_a0 3_bs_enus	1	2
A4		Taking Control of Your Time Simulation	PD001A	0.5	2
A5		Planning for Interruptions Helps with	_pc_bi_pf	0.2	2

		Procrastination	bi014		
	A6	Prioritizing Personal and Professional Responsibilities	_pc_bi_m gbi003	0.2	2
	A7	Coping with Information Overload	_pc_bi_pf bi002	0.2	2
	B1	Basic Business Skills to Get You on the Fast Track	PD0132	2.5	2
Business Meetings			-		
	C1	Planning an Effective Business Meeting	comm_06 _a01_bs_e nus	2.5	2
	C2	Leading an Effective Business Meeting	comm_06 _a02_bs_e nus	2.5	2
	C3	Participating Effectively in a Business Meeting	comm_06 _a03_bs_e nus	2.5	2
	C4	The Effective Business Meeting Simulation	COMM00 6A	0.5	2
	C5	When Too Many Meetings Are Just Too Much	_pc_bi_pf bi008	0.2	2
	C6	Making Meetings Work	_pc_bi_pf bi018	0.2	2
			-		
Working As A Remote/Telecommuting Employee			-		
	C7	Telecommuting Basics: Maximizing Productivity as a Remote Employee	pd_08_a0 1_bs_enus	1	2
	C8	Telecommuting	pd_08_a0	1	2

		Basics: Communication Strategies for the Remote Employee	2_bs_enus		
			-		
40					
		no SkillSoft courses directly related	-		
			-		
41					
	C1	Defining Emotional Intelligence	comm_09 a01_bs_e nus	2	1
	C2	Emotional Intelligence in the Workplace	comm_09 a02_bs_e nus	1.5	2
	C3	Emotional Intelligence and Teamwork	comm_09 a03_bs_e nus	2	2
	C4	Increasing Emotional Intelligence	comm_09 a04_bs_e nus	2	2
	C5	Emotionally Intelligent Leadership	comm_09 a05_bs_e nus	2	2
	C6	Emotional Intelligence at Work Simulation	COMM00 9A	0.5	2
	C7	What is Emotional Intelligence?	_pc_bi_pf bi009	0.2	2
42					
	A1	Effective Interfunctional Relationships	comm_12 a01_bs_e	2.5	2

205

			nus		
A2		Effective Intercultural Relationships	comm_12_a02_bs_e nus	2	2
A3		Effective Intergender Relationships	comm_12_a03_bs_e nus	2	2
A4		Effective Relationships with Customers	comm_12_a04_bs_e nus	2	2
A5		Effective Relationships with Business Partners	comm_12_a05_bs_e nus	3	2
A6		Building Improved Work Relationships Simulation	COMM012A	0.5	2
B1		Asserting Yourself Professionally	comm_10_a01_bs_e nus	2.5	2
B2		Assertiveness from Inside to Outside	comm_10_a02_bs_e nus	2.5	2
B3		Communicating Assertively Simulation	COMM010A	0.5	2
	Understanding Age Generations in the Workforce		-		
C1		Introduction to Work Force Generations	LEAD0231	2.5	1
C2		Attracting, Developing, and Retaining Generations	LEAD0232	3	2

	C3	Leading Silent Generation and Baby Boom Workers	LEAD0233	3	2
	C4	Leading Generations X and Next	LEAD0234	3.5	2
	C5	Making Cross-generational Teams Work	LEAD0235	3	2
	C6	Cross-generational Workers in the 21st Century	LEAD0236	3	2
	C7	Leading the Workforce Generations Simulation	LEAD0230	0.5	2
	C8	Managing an Aging Workforce	_pc_bi_mgbi005	0.2	2
	C9	Understanding the Motives of Millennials	_pc_bi_mgbi014	0.2	2
	C10	Developing the Next Generation	_pc_bi_lsbi007	0.2	2
Cross-Cultural Communication			-		
	C11	The Impact of Culture on Communication	COMM0021	2.5	1
	C12	The Art of Global Communication	COMM0022	3.5	2
	C13	Improving Your Cross-cultural Communications	COMM0023	3	2
	C14	International Communications Simulation	COMM0020	0.5	2
	C15	Cross-cultural Communications Simulation	COMM002S	0.5	2
43					

207

	B1	The Importance of Flexibility in the Workplace	_pc_bi_pf bi007	0.2	2
44					
		no SkillSoft courses directly related			
45					
	A1	Pursuing Successful Lifelong Learning	pd_05_a0 5_bs_enus	2	1
			-		
46					
	A1	Thinking Strategically	stgy_01_a 01_bs_en us	2	1
	A2	Sustaining Competitive Advantage	stgy_01_a 02_bs_en us	3	2
	A3	The Imperatives of Innovation and Leadership in Strategy	stgy_01_a 03_bs_en us	2.5	2
	A4	Planning and Implementing a Business Strategy	stgy_01_a 04_bs_en us	2.5	2
	A5	Moving from an Operational Manager to a Strategic Thinker Simulation	STGY001 A	0.5	2
	A6	Leading Outside the Organization	_pc_bi_ls bi005	0.2	2
	A7	Effective Critical Analysis of Business Reports	_pc_bi_pf bi004	0.2	2
	A8	External Consultants Can Help	_pc_ch_m	0.2	2

			gch004		
			-		
	Critical Thinking		-		
	B1	The Role of Critical Thinking in Organizations	PD0251	4	1
	B2	Developing Fundamental Critical Thinking Skills	PD0252	3	2
	B3	Strategies for Facilitating Critical Thinking	PD0253	4.5	2
	B4	Critical Thinking Skills for Managing	PD0254	3.5	2
	B5	Organizational Scope of Critical Thinking	PD0255	3.5	2
	B6	Critical Thinking Strategies Simulation	PD0250	0.5	2
			-		
	Global Perspective		-		
	B7	Globalization and Our Changing World	STGY0351	1.5	1
	B8	Globalization and Your Company	STGY0352	4	1
	B9	The Process of Globalizing a Product or Service	STGY0353	3.5	2
	B10	Managing from a Global Viewpoint	STGY0354	4.5	2
	B11	The Fundamentals of Globalization Simulation	STGY0350	0.5	2
	B12	Evaluating Globalization Opportunities	_pc_ch_la ch019	0.2	2
	B13	Dispute Resolution in International Contracts	_pc_ch_ls ch005	0.2	2

	A1	Integrated Initiation and Planning	proj_06_a 01_bs_en us	2	1
	A2	Scope Definition Tools and Techniques	_pc_ch_p mch002	0.2	2
	A3	Integrated Project Execution, Monitoring, and Control	proj_06_a 02_bs_en us	1.5	2
	A4	Integrated Project Change Control and Close	proj_06_a 03_bs_en us	1	2
	A5	Project Requirements and Defining Scope	proj_07_a 01_bs_en us	2	2
	A6	Create Work Breakdown Structure	proj_07_a 02_bs_en us	1.5	2
	A7	Defining and Sequencing Project Activities	proj_08_a 01_bs_en us	2	2
	A8	Estimating Activity Resources and Durations	proj_08_a 02_bs_en us	2	2
	A9	Estimating and Budgeting Project Costs	proj_09_a 01_bs_en us	2	2
	A10	Project Quality Planning	proj_10_a 01_bs_en us	2	2

	A11	Planning Project Human Resources	proj_11_a 01_bs_en us	2	2
	A12	Stakeholders and the Communication Management Plan	proj_12_a 01_bs_en us	2	2
	A13	Risk Management Planning	proj_13_a 01_bs_en us	1.5	2
	A14	Performing Risk Analysis	proj_13_a 02_bs_en us	2	2
	A15	Planning Project Procurement	proj_14_a 01_bs_en us	2	2
	A16	Anticipating and Solving Problems as a Project Champion	_pc_bi_p mbi007	0.2	2
			-		
	C1	Risk Basics	PD0241	2	1
	C2	Approaches to Risk Management	PD0242	2	2
	C3	Decisions and Risk	PD0243	2	2
	C4	Strategic Planning and Risk Management	PD0244	2.5	2
	C5	Risk Strategies: The Cutting Edge	PD0245	2.5	2
	C6	Working without a Net: Decisions Simulation	PD0240	0.5	2
	C7	Mitigating Risks when Improving Processes	_pc_bi_p mbi011	0.2	2
	C8	Ethics and Risks: Why They Matter in Project Success	_pc_ch_p mch003	0.2	2

48			-		
A1	Managing Cross-Functions	mgmt_02_a02_bs_enus	3	2
A2	Managing Upward Relationships	mgmt_02_a05_bs_enus	3	2
A3	Managing in a Global Business Environment	mgmt_02_a01_bs_enus	3	2
			-		
B1	Office Politics - What Will You Do?	_pc_ch_pf_ch004	0.2	2
Influencing Others			-		
B1	Getting Results by Building Relationships	comm_13_a01_bs_enus	2	2
B2	Results and Teamwork without Authority	comm_13_a02_bs_enus	2.5	2
B3	Leading without Authority	comm_13_a03_bs_enus	3	2
B4	Creating Change, Gaining Allies	comm_13_a04_bs_enus	2.5	2
B5	Communicating to Get Results	comm_13_a05_bs_enus	2.5	2

		nus		
B6	Obtaining Results from the Boss	comm_13_a06_bs_enus	3	2
B7	Getting Results with No Authority Simulation	COMM013A	0.5	2
B8	Influence and Persuasion	_pc_ch_lach016	0.2	2
B9	Influencing Key Decision Makers	_pc_bi_lsbi015	0.2	2
B10	Leadership Essentials: Building Your Influence as a Leader	lead_05_a03_bs_enus	1	2
		-		
Emotional Intelligence				
B10	Defining Emotional Intelligence	comm_09_a01_bs_enus	2	1
B11	Emotional Intelligence in the Workplace	comm_09_a02_bs_enus	1.5	2
B12	Emotional Intelligence and Teamwork	comm_09_a03_bs_enus	2	2
B13	Increasing Emotional Intelligence	comm_09_a04_bs_enus	2	2
B14	Emotional Intelligence at Work Simulation	COMM009A	0.5	2
B15	Leadership Essentials: Leading with	lead_05_a	1	2

		Emotional Intelligence	04_bs_en us		
	B16	What is Emotional Intelligence?	_pc_bi_pf bi009	0.2	2
49					
	A1	Presenting Successfully	comm_05 _a01_bs_e nus	3	2
	A2	Delivering the Message	comm_05 _a02_bs_e nus	3	2
	A3	Available Presentation Resources	comm_05 _a03_bs_e nus	3.5	2
	A4	Giving Successful Presentations Simulation	COMM00 5A	0.5	2
	Presenting a Business Case		-		
	B1	Presenting Your Case	comm_01 _a03_bs_e nus	2.5	2
			-		
	Investor Presentations		-		
	C1	Attracting New Investors - Keeping Presentations Focused	_pc_bi_fa bi004	0.2	2
			-		
50					
	A1	Goals and Setting Goals	pd_05_a0 3_bs_enus	2	2

	A2	Prioritizing Personal and Professional Responsibilities	_pc_bi_m gbi003	0.2	2
			-		
	B1	Time Management: Analyzing Your Use of Time	pd_11_a0 1_bs_enus	1	2
	B2	Time Management: Planning and Prioritizing Your Time	pd_11_a0 2_bs_enus	1	2
	B3	Time Management: Avoiding Time Stealers	pd_11_a0 3_bs_enus	1	2
	B4	Taking Control of Your Time Simulation	PD001A	0.5	2
	B5	Planning for Interruptions Helps with Procrastination	_pc_bi_pf bi014	0.2	2
	B6	Coping with Information Overload	_pc_bi_pf bi002	0.2	2
			-		
51					
	A1	Problem Solving: The Fundamentals	pd_12_a0 1_bs_enus	1	2
	A2	Problem Solving: Determining and Building Your Strengths	pd_12_a0 2_bs_enus	1	2
	A3	Problem Solving: Digging Deeper	pd_12_a0 3_bs_enus	1	2
	A5	Effective Thinking and Creative Problem Solving Simulation	PD004A	0.5	2
	A6	Rational Decision-making and Problem Solving Simulation	PD004B	0.5	2
	A7	Turning Problems Around with Reverse Brainstorming	_pc_bi_ls bi017	0.2	2
	A8	Uncovering the Root Problem	_pc_ch_la	0.2	2

			ch003		
			-		
	B1	The Role of Critical Thinking in Organizations	PD0251	4	1
	B2	Developing Fundamental Critical Thinking Skills	PD0252	3	2
	B3	Strategies for Facilitating Critical Thinking	PD0253	4.5	2
	B4	Critical Thinking Strategies SIMULATION	PD0250	0.5	2
			-		
	C1	What is Systems Thinking?	STGY0401	2.5	1
	C2	Systems-thinking Models and Thinking Skills	STGY0403	2.5	2
52					
	Project Management Foundations for Business Professionals		-		
	A1	Project Management Fundamentals	proj_01_a01_bs_en us	2.5	1
	A2	Transitioning into a Project Management Role	proj_01_a02_bs_en us	3	2
	A3	Initiating and Planning a Project	proj_01_a03_bs_en us	2	2
	A4	Managing a Project	proj_01_a04_bs_en	2.5	2

			us		
	A5	Troubleshooting and Closing the Project	proj_01_a 05_bs_en us	2	2
	A6	Project Management for Non-Project Managers Simulation	PROJ001 A	0.5	2
	A7	Managing Projects without Direct Authority	_pc_bi_p mbi001	0.2	2
	A8	Ensuring Management Buy-In on a Project	_pc_bi_p mbi002	0.2	2
	A9	Managing Conflict in Project Teams	_pc_bi_p mbi003	0.2	2
	A10	Implementing a Scope Change Control System	_pc_bi_p mbi004	0.2	2
	A11	Weighing the Costs of Project Change	_pc_bi_p mbi005	0.2	2
	A12	Managing Vendor Relationships	_pc_bi_p mbi006	0.2	2
	A13	Anticipating and Solving Problems as a Project Champion	_pc_bi_p mbi007	0.2	2
	A14	Addressing Stakeholder Conflicts	_pc_bi_p mbi008	0.2	2
	A15	Portfolios, Programs, and Projects: What's the Difference?	_pc_bi_p mbi009	0.2	2
	A16	Controlling Project Cost	_pc_bi_p mbi010	0.2	2
	A17	Mitigating Risks when Improving Processes	_pc_bi_p mbi011	0.2	2
	A18	Handling a Change Request	_pc_ch_p mch001	0.2	2

	A19	Scope Definition Tools and Techniques	_pc_ch_p mch002	0.2	2
	A20	Ethics and Risks: Why They Matter in Project Success	_pc_ch_p mch003	0.2	2
			-		
	Project Management Certification for Project Management Professionals (PMI PMP & CAPM Certification				
	A1	Managing Projects within Organizations	proj_05_a 01_bs_en us	2	3
	A2	Project Management Overview	proj_05_a 02_bs_en us	1.5	3
	A3	Project Management Process Groups	proj_05_a 03_bs_en us	2	3
	A4	Integrated Initiation and Planning	proj_06_a 01_bs_en us	2	3
	A5	Integrated Project Execution, Monitoring, and Control	proj_06_a 02_bs_en us	1.5	3
	A6	Integrated Project Change Control and Close	proj_06_a 03_bs_en us	1	3
	A7	Project Requirements and Defining Scope	proj_07_a 01_bs_en us	2	3
	A8	Create Work Breakdown Structure	proj_07_a 02_bs_en	1.5	3

			us		
	A9	Monitoring and Controlling Project Scope	proj_07_a 03_bs_en us	1.5	3
	A10	Defining and Sequencing Project Activities	proj_08_a 01_bs_en us	2	3
	A11	Estimating Activity Resources and Durations	proj_08_a 02_bs_en us	2	3
	A12	Developing and Controlling the Project Schedule	proj_08_a 03_bs_en us	2	3
	A13	Estimating and Budgeting Project Costs	proj_09_a 01_bs_en us	2	3
	A14	Controlling Costs	proj_09_a 02_bs_en us	1.5	3
	A15	Project Quality Planning	proj_10_a 01_bs_en us	2	3
	A16	Quality Assurance and Quality Control	proj_10_a 02_bs_en us	2	3
	A17	Planning Project Human Resources	proj_11_a 01_bs_en us	2	3
	A18	Managing Project Human Resources	proj_11_a 02_bs_en us	2	3

A19		Planning and Managing Project Human Resources Simulation	PROJ011A	0.5	3
A20		Stakeholders and the Communication Management Plan	proj_12_a 01_bs_en us	2	3
A21		Processes for Managing Project Communications	proj_12_a 02_bs_en us	2	3
A22		Risk Management Planning	proj_13_a 01_bs_en us	1.5	3
A23		Performing Risk Analysis	proj_13_a 02_bs_en us	2	3
A24		Risk Response, Monitor, and Control	proj_13_a 03_bs_en us	2	3
A25		Identifying Project Risks	proj_13_a 04_bs_en us	2	3
A26		Planning Project Procurement	proj_14_a 01_bs_en us	2	3
A27		Managing Procurements	proj_14_a 02_bs_en us	2	3
A28		The Role of Ethics in Project Management	proj_15_a 01_bs_en us	1.5	3
A29		Core PMI® Values and Ethical Standards	proj_15_a 02_bs_en	2	3

			us		
	Project Management Certification for Project Management Professionals (aligned with PRINCE2 Foundation Certification objectives)				
A1		Overview of Project Managing a PRINCE2-aligned Project	proj_04_a 01_bs_en us	1	3
A2		Project Planning and Controlling a PRINCE2-aligned Project	proj_04_a 02_bs_en us	2	3
A3		Managing Quality and Risk in a PRINCE2-aligned Project	proj_04_a 03_bs_en us	2	3
A4		Initial and Ongoing Processes in a PRINCE2-aligned Project	proj_04_a 04_bs_en us	2	3
A5		Controlling, Managing and Closing a PRINCE2-aligned Project	proj_04_a 05_bs_en us	2	3
A6		Techniques for Managing a PRINCE2-aligned Project	proj_04_a 06_bs_en us	1.5	3
IT Project Management			-		
A1		Introduction to IT Project Management	PROJ035 1	4	1
A2		Functions of IT Project Management	PROJ035 2	4.5	2
A3		The Life Cycle of an IT Project	PROJ035 3	5	2

A4		Managing the Execution and Control of IT Projects	PROJ035 4	5.5	2
A5		Managing Efficiencies of IT Projects	PROJ035 5	4.5	2
A6		Project IT Management Simulation - The Early Stages	PROJ035 0	0.5	2
A7		Project IT Management Simulation - Design to Rollout	PROJ035 S	0.5	2
A8		Final Exam: Project Management for IT Professionals	FE0013_e ng		2
A9		Strategic Planning and Positioning for IT Projects	PROJ036 1	5	2
A10		Strategic Approaches to Managing IT Projects	PROJ036 2	5	2
A11		Estimating the IT Project Work Effort	PROJ036 3	5.5	2
A12		IT Project Leadership, Authority & Accountability	PROJ036 4	6	2
A13		Managing Multiple IT Projects	PROJ036 5	5.5	2
A14		Cost Management and IT Project Trade-offs	PROJ036 6	4.5	2
A15		Strategic Project Management for IT Projects Simulation	PROJ036 0	0.5	2
A16		Final Exam: Strategic Project Management for IT Projects	FE0014_e ng		2
	Program Management		-		
B1		Introduction to Program Management	proj_02_a 01_bs_en	2	2

222

			us		
B2		Program Life Cycle and Organization	proj_02_a 02_bs_en us	2.5	2
B3		Program Management Processes and the Initiating Process Group	proj_02_a 03_bs_en us	1.5	2
B4		Program Planning	proj_02_a 04_bs_en us	2.5	2
B5		The Executing Process Group	proj_02_a 05_bs_en us	1.5	2
B6		Monitoring, Controlling, and Closing Programs	proj_02_a 06_bs_en us	2	2
	Portfolio Management		-		
B7		Introduction to Portfolio Management	proj_03_a 01_bs_en us	2	2
B8		Portfolio Management Processes and the Organization	proj_03_a 02_bs_en us	2	2
B9		Portfolio Management Process Groups	proj_03_a 03_bs_en us	2	2
	Customer-Driven Process Improvement		-		
C1		Why Customer Driven?	OPER012	2.5	1

			1		
	C2	Identifying What the Customer Wants	OPER012 2	3	2
	C3	Translating Requirements into Process Goals	OPER012 3	3.5	2
	C4	Understanding Processes	OPER012 4	2.5	2
	C5	Implementing Improvements	OPER012 5	2.5	2
	C6	Managing Process Improvements	OPER012 6	3	2
	C7	Managing Customer-Driven Process Improvement Simulation	OPER012 0	0.5	2
			-		
53					
	A1	Working for Your Inner Boss: Personal Accountability	pd_05_a0 1_bs_enus	2	2
	A2	Goals and Setting Goals	pd_05_a0 3_bs_enus	2	2
54					
	A1	Pursuing Successful Lifelong Learning	pd_05_a0 5_bs_enus	2	2
			-		
	B1	Achieving Success: the Help of a Mentor	mgmt_10 _a05_bs_e nus	3	2
	B2	Disciplines of Organizational Learning: Personal Mastery	_pc_bi_pf bi011	0.2	2

55					
	B1	Managing Your Career: Getting on the Right Track	pd_10_a0 2_bs_enus	1	2
	B2	Coping with Criticism and Feedback	COMM05 22	5.0 0	**2**
	Emotional Intelligence				
	C1	Defining Emotional Intelligence	comm_09 _a01_bs_e nus	2	1
	C2	Emotional Intelligence in the Workplace	comm_09 _a02_bs_e nus	1.5	2
	C3	Emotional Intelligence and Teamwork	comm_09 _a03_bs_e nus	2	2
	C4	Increasing Emotional Intelligence	comm_09 _a04_bs_e nus	2	2
	C5	Emotionally Intelligent Leadership	comm_09 _a05_bs_e nus	2	2
	C6	Emotional Intelligence at Work Simulation	COMM00 9A	0.5	2
	C7	What is Emotional Intelligence?	_pc_bi_pf bi009	0.2	2
			-		
56					
	Understanding the Age Generations				

	C1	Introduction to Work Force Generations	LEAD023 1	2.5	1
	C2	Attracting, Developing, and Retaining Generations	LEAD023 2	3	2
	C3	Leading Silent Generation and Baby Boom Workers	LEAD023 3	3	2
	C4	Leading Generations X and Next	LEAD023 4	3.5	2
	C5	Making Cross-generational Teams Work	LEAD023 5	3	2
	C6	Cross-generational Workers in the 21st Century	LEAD023 6	3	2
	C7	Leading the Workforce Generations Simulation	LEAD023 0	0.5	2
	C8	Managing an Aging Workforce	pc_bi_m gbi005	0.2	2
	C9	Understanding the Motives of Millennials	pc_bi_m gbi014	0.2	2
	C10	Developing the Next Generation	pc_bi_ls bi007	0.2	2
			-		
Working with Difficult People			-		
	C11	Difficult People in the Workplace Environment	comm_04 a01_bs_e nus	3	1
	C12	How to Work with Aggressive People	comm_04 a02_bs_e nus	3	2
	C13	How to Work with Negative People and Procrastinators	comm_04 a03_bs_e	3	2

			nus		
	C14	How to Work with Arrogant and Duplicitous People	comm_04_a04_bs_enus	2	2
	C15	Working with and Managing Difficult People Simulation	COMM004A	0.5	2
	C16	Effective Communication with Difficult Coworkers Simulation	COMM004B	0.5	2
	C17	Blame Backfires--Conquer Negative Thinking	_pc_bi_pf bi003	0.2	2
	C18	Reacting to Co-workers Who Try Taking Advantage	_pc_ch_pf ch003	0.2	2
57					
		no SkillSoft courses directly related	-		
			-		
58					
	A1	Thinking Strategically	stgy_01_a01_bs_enus	2	2
	A2	Sustaining Competitive Advantage	stgy_01_a02_bs_enus	3	2
	A3	The Imperatives of Innovation and Leadership in Strategy	stgy_01_a03_bs_enus	2.5	2
	A4	Planning and Implementing a Business Strategy	stgy_01_a04_bs_enus	2.5	2
	A5	Moving from an Operational Manager	STGY001	0.5	2

		to a Strategic Thinker Simulation	A		
A6		Leading Outside the Organization	_pc_bi_ls bi005	0.2	2
A7		Effective Critical Analysis of Business Reports	_pc_bi_pf bi004	0.2	2
A8		Returning to Core Competencies	_pc_bi_ls bi014	0.2	2
A9		External Consultants Can Help	_pc_ch_m gch004	0.2	2
			-		
Information Technology Strategic Thinking			-		
C1		Setting the Stage for IT Success	STGY022 1	2.5	2
C2		Strategic Decision Making	STGY022 2	1.5	2
C3		IT Challenges: Present and Future	STGY022 3	2.5	2
C4		Strategic IT Planning Simulation	STGY022 0	0.5	2
			-		
Crisis Management			-		
C5		Preparing for Business Crises	MGMT01 71	2	2
C6		Responding to Business Crises	MGMT01 72	3	2
C7		Recovering from Business Crises	MGMT01 73	2	2
C8		The Fundamentals of Business Crises	MGMT01	0.5	2

		Management Simulation	70		
	C9	Is Your Company Prepared for a Crisis?	pc_bi_m gbi006	0.2	2
	C10	Demonstrating Accountability in a Crisis Situation	pc_ch_la ch007	0.2	2
			-		
	Green/Sustainable Business Strategy				
	C11	Introduction to Green Business and Sustainability	stgy_04_a 01_bs_en us	2	1
	C12	Green Business: Planning Sustainability Strategies	stgy_04_a 02_bs_en us	2	2
	C13	Green Business: Implementing Sustainability Strategies	stgy_04_a 03_bs_en us	2	2
59					
	A1	What is Systems Thinking?	STGY040 1	2.5	1
	A2	Building a Healthy System	STGY040 2	2.5	2
	A3	Systems-thinking Models and Thinking Skills	STGY040 3	2.5	2
	A4	System Archetypes	STGY040 4	3	2
	A5	Redesigning Your Organization: Part 1	STGY040 5	3	2
	A6	Redesigning Your Organization: Part II	STGY040 6	3	2

			-		
60					
	A1	Leading Teams: Launching a Successful Team	team_03_a01_bs_en us	1	2
	A2	Leading Teams: Establishing Goals, Roles, and Guidelines	team_03_a02_bs_en us	1	2
	A3	Leading Teams: Developing the Team and its Culture	team_03_a03_bs_en us	1	2
	A4	Leading Teams: Building Trust and Commitment	team_03_a04_bs_en us	1	2
	A5	Leading Teams: Fostering Effective Communication and Collaboration	team_03_a05_bs_en us	1	2
	A6	Leading Teams: Motivating and Optimizing Performance	team_03_a06_bs_en us	1	2
	A7	Leading Teams: Dealing with Conflict	team_03_a07_bs_en us	1	2
	A8	Leading Teams: Managing Virtual Teams	team_03_a08_bs_en us	1	2
	A9	Building Trust Incrementally	_pc_bi_ls bi004	0.2	2
	A10	Inspiring your Team	_pc_bi_ls bi010	0.2	2

			pc_bi_pf		
A11		Support Your Leader	bi010	0.2	2
A12		Choosing the Right Team Culture	pc_ch_pf ch006	0.2	2
A13		Managing Communications in a Virtual Team	pc_bi_m gbi001	0.2	2
A14		Developing Self-Sufficient Teams	pc_ch_m gch001	0.2	2
			-		
61					
		Hundreds of SkillSoft courses available covering technical skills			
62					
A1		Time Management: Analyzing Your Use of Time	pd_11_a0 1_bs_enus	1	2
A2		Time Management: Planning and Prioritizing Your Time	pd_11_a0 2_bs_enus	1	2
A3		Time Management: Avoiding Time Stealers	pd_11_a0 3_bs_enus	1	2
A4		Taking Control of Your Time Simulation	PD001A	0.5	2
A5		Planning for Interruptions Helps with Procrastination	pc_bi_pf bi014	0.2	2
A6		Prioritizing Personal and Professional Responsibilities	pc_bi_m gbi003	0.2	2
A7		Coping with Information Overload	pc_bi_pf bi002	0.2	2
63					

		ITIL		-		
	A1	ITIL V3 Foundation Syllabus v4.2: ITIL and the Service Lifecycle	ib_itlu_a0 1_it_enus	1.5	3	
	A2	ITIL V3 Foundation Syllabus V4.2: Service Strategy Fundamentals	ib_itlu_a0 2_it_enus	2.4	3	
	A3	ITIL V3 Foundation Syllabus v4.2: Service Strategy Processes	ib_itlu_a0 3_it_enus	1.1	3	
	A4	ITIL V3 Foundation Syllabus v4.2: Service Design Fundamentals	ib_itlu_a0 4_it_enus	2	3	
	A5	ITIL V3 Foundation Syllabus v4.2: Service Design Processes	ib_itlu_a0 5_it_enus	2.5	3	
	A6	ITIL V3 Foundation Syllabus v4.2: Service Transition Processes and Principles	ib_itlu_a0 6_it_enus	2.5	3	
	A7	ITIL V3 Foundation Syllabus v4.2: Service Operation Principles and Functions	ib_itlu_a0 7_it_enus	2	3	
	A8	ITIL V3 Foundation Syllabus v4.2: Service Operation Processes	ib_itlu_a0 8_it_enus	1.5	3	
	A9	ITIL V3 Foundation Syllabus v4.2: Continual Service Improvement Fundamentals	ib_itlu_a0 9_it_enus	1.5	3	
				-		
		Quality Management		-		
	A1	Leadership	oper_04_a 01_bs_en us	2.5	3	
	A2	Team Dynamics	oper_04_a 02_bs_en us	2	3	

A3	Developing and Deploying Strategic Plans	oper_04_a_03_bs_en_us	2.5	3
A4	Managerial Skills and Abilities	oper_04_a_04_bs_en_us	2.5	3
A5	Communication Skills and Project Management	oper_04_a_05_bs_en_us	2	3
A6	Quality Systems, Models, and Theories	oper_04_a_06_bs_en_us	2	3
A7	Problem-Solving and Process Management Tools	oper_04_a_07_bs_en_us	2.5	3
A8	Measurement: Assessment and Metrics	oper_04_a_08_bs_en_us	1.5	3
A9	Customer-Focused Management	oper_04_a_09_bs_en_us	2	3
A10	Supply Chain Management	oper_04_a_10_bs_en_us	1.5	3
A11	Training and Development	oper_04_a_11_bs_en_us	2	3
Six Sigma Quality		-		
A1	Introduction to Six Sigma	oper_10_a	2	1

			01_bs_en us		
	A2	Are you listening to your customers (Role of VOC in Six Sigma)	_pc_bi_ss bi001		
	A3	Quick Wins in Six Sigma Implementation	_pc_bi_ss bi002		
	A4	Six Sigma Versus TQM	_pc_bi_ss bi003		
	A5	Lean Inbound Transportation	_pc_bi_ss bi004		
	A6	Promoting Six Sigma in the Workplace	_pc_bi_ss bi005		
	A7	A Critical-to-quality Tree – What's That?	_pc_bi_ss bi006		
	A8	Basic Measurement Concepts in Six Sigma	_pc_bi_ss bi007		
	A9	Does your Business Really Need Six Sigma?	_pc_ch_ss ch001		
	A10	Identifying Candidates for Key Six Sigma Roles	_pc_ch_ss ch002		
			-		
	A11	Six Sigma and Lean in the Organization	oper_05_a 01_bs_en us	2.5	3
	A12	Design for Six Sigma in the Organization	oper_05_a 02_bs_en us	2	3
	A13	Processes and Customer Analysis in Six Sigma Projects	oper_06_a 01_bs_en us	2.5	3

	A14	Basics of Six Sigma Projects and Teams	oper_06_a 02_bs_en us	2.5	3
	A15	Tools for Planning and Managing Six Sigma Project Opportunities	oper_06_a 03_bs_en us	2.5	3
	A16	Using Six Sigma Analysis Tools and Metrics for Project Decisions	oper_06_a 04_bs_en us	1.5	3
	A17	Modeling and Analyzing Processes in Six Sigma	oper_07_a 01_bs_en us	2	3
	A18	Statistics and Probability in Six Sigma	oper_07_a 02_bs_en us	2	3
	A19	Data Classification and Collection in Six Sigma	oper_07_a 03_bs_en us	1.5	3
	A20	Summarizing and Presenting Data in Six Sigma	oper_07_a 04_bs_en us	1.5	3
	A21	Probability Distributions and Measurement Systems Analysis in Six Sigma	oper_07_a 05_bs_en us	2	3
	A22	Measuring Process Capability and Performance in Six Sigma	oper_07_a 06_bs_en us	2	3
	A23	Exploratory Data Analysis in Six Sigma	oper_08_a 01_bs_en us	1.5	3
	A24	Introduction to Hypothesis Testing and	oper_08_a	2	3

		Testing for Means in Six Sigma	02_bs_en us		
	A25	Hypothesis Tests for Variances, Proportions, ANOVA, and Chi-Square in Six Sigma	oper_08_a 03_bs_en us	1.5	3
	A26	Design of Experiments and Validation of Solutions in Six Sigma	oper_09_a 01_bs_en us	1.5	3
	A27	Statistical Process Control and Control Plans in Six Sigma	oper_09_a 02_bs_en us	1.5	3
	A28	Using Basic Control Charts in Six Sigma	oper_09_a 03_bs_en us	2.5	3
			-		
	A29	Lean and Six Sigma	oper_11_a 01_bs_en us	2	4
	A30	Six Sigma Projects and the Black Belt Role	oper_11_a 02_bs_en us	2	4
	A31	Six Sigma Leadership and Change Management	oper_11_a 03_bs_en us	2	4
	A32	Critical Requirements and Benchmarking for Six Sigma	oper_12_a 01_bs_en us	2	4
	A33	Business Performance and Financial Measures in Six Sigma	oper_12_a 02_bs_en us	2	4

	A34	Forming Project Teams for Six Sigma	oper_13_a 01_bs_en us	2	4
	A35	Motivation and Communication in Six Sigma Teams	oper_13_a 02_bs_en us	2	4
	A36	Managing Six Sigma Team Performance	oper_13_a 03_bs_en us	2	4
	A37	Using Voice of the Customer in Six Sigma	oper_14_a 01_bs_en us	2	4
	A38	Developing Project Charters and Tracking Six Sigma Projects	oper_14_a 02_bs_en us	1.5	4
	A39	Process Characteristics for Six Sigma	oper_15_a 01_bs_en us	2	4
	A40	Data Collection and Measurement in Six Sigma	oper_15_a 02_bs_en us	2	4
	A41	Six Sigma Measurement Systems	oper_15_a 03_bs_en us	2	4
	A42	Basic Statistics and Graphical Methods for Six Sigma	oper_15_a 04_bs_en us	2	4
	A43	Probability for Six Sigma	oper_15_a 05_bs_en us	2	4
	A44	Process Capability for Six Sigma	oper_15_a	2	4

			06_bs_en us		
	A45	Correlation and Regression Analysis in Six Sigma	oper_16_a 01_bs_en us	1.5	4
	A46	Multivariate Analysis and Attribute Data Analysis in Six Sigma	oper_16_a 02_bs_en us	1.5	4
	A47	Hypothesis Testing Concepts and Tests for Means in Six Sigma	oper_16_a 03_bs_en us	2	4
	A48	Tests for Variances and Proportions, ANOVA, and Chi-square Tests in Six Sigma	oper_16_a 04_bs_en us	2	4
	A49	Nonparametric Tests in Six Sigma Analysis	oper_16_a 05_bs_en us	2	4
	A50	Non-Statistical Analysis Methods in Six Sigma	oper_16_a 06_bs_en us	2	4
	A51	Designing and Planning Experiments in Six Sigma	oper_17_a 01_bs_en us	2	4
	A52	Conducting Experiments and Analyzing Results in Six Sigma	oper_17_a 02_bs_en us	2	4
	A53	Improvement Methods and Implementation Issues in Six Sigma	oper_17_a 03_bs_en us	2	4
	A54	Statistical Process Control (SPC) in Six Sigma	oper_18_a 01_bs_en	2	4

			us		
	A55	Non-Statistical Control Tools and Maintaining Controls in Six Sigma	oper_18_a 02_bs_en us	2	4
	A56	Sustaining Improvements and Gains from Six Sigma Projects	oper_18_a 03_bs_en us	2	4
	A57	Common Design for Six Sigma Methodologies, Design for X, and Robust Design	oper_19_a 01_bs_en us	2	4
	A58	Special Design Tools in Design for Six Sigma	oper_19_a 02_bs_en us	2	4
	A59	Introduction to Six Sigma for Champions	oper_03_a 01_bs_en us	3	3
	A60	Six Sigma Process Improvement	oper_03_a 02_bs_en us	3	3
	A61	Six Sigma Projects and Project Teams	oper_03_a 03_bs_en us	2.5	3
	A62	Managing and Deploying Six Sigma	oper_03_a 04_bs_en us	3.5	3
	ISO 9000		-		
	A1	The Who, What & Why of ISO 9000:2000	OPER040 1	3	1

	A2	Building a Quality Management System	OPER040 2	2	2
	A3	Quality-minded Management	OPER040 3	2.5	2
	A4	Customer Satisfaction Through Resource Management	OPER040 4	2.5	2
	A5	Processes for Quality Products and Services	OPER040 5	4	2
	A6	Continual Quality Improvement	OPER040 6	4	2
	A7	Steps for Successful ISO Registration	OPER040 7	3	2
	A8	Transitioning from ISO 9000:1994 to ISO 9001:2000	OPER040 8	2.5	2
64					
	Understanding the Age Generations				
	C1	Introduction to Work Force Generations	LEAD023 1	2.5	1
	C2	Attracting, Developing, and Retaining Generations	LEAD023 2	3	2
	C3	Leading Silent Generation and Baby Boom Workers	LEAD023 3	3	2
	C4	Leading Generations X and Next	LEAD023 4	3.5	2
	C5	Making Cross-generational Teams Work	LEAD023 5	3	2
	C6	Cross-generational Workers in the 21st Century	LEAD023 6	3	2

C7	Leading the Workforce Generations Simulation	LEAD0230	0.5	2
C8	Managing an Aging Workforce	_pc_bi_mgbi005	0.2	2
C9	Understanding the Motives of Millennials	_pc_bi_mgbi014	0.2	2
C10	Developing the Next Generation	_pc_bi_lsbi007	0.2	2
		-		
Working with Difficult People		-		
C11	Difficult People in the Workplace Environment	comm_04_a01_bs_enus	3	1
C12	How to Work with Aggressive People	comm_04_a02_bs_enus	3	2
C13	How to Work with Negative People and Procrastinators	comm_04_a03_bs_enus	3	2
C14	How to Work with Arrogant and Duplicitous People	comm_04_a04_bs_enus	2	2
C15	Working with and Managing Difficult People Simulation	COMM004A	0.5	2
C16	Effective Communication with Difficult Coworkers Simulation	COMM004B	0.5	2
C17	Blame Backfires--Conquer Negative Thinking	_pc_bi_pfbi003	0.2	2
C18	Reacting to Co-workers Who Try Taking Advantage	_pc_ch_pfch003	0.2	2

	Cross-Cultural Communication		-		
	C14	The Impact of Culture on Communication	COMM0021	2.5	1
	C15	The Art of Global Communication	COMM0022	3.5	2
	C16	Improving Your Cross-cultural Communications	COMM0023	3	2
	C17	International Communications Simulation	COMM0020	0.5	2
	C18	Cross-cultural Communications Simulation	COMM002S	0.5	2
65					
	A1	Leadership Essentials: Communicating Vision	lead_05_a02_bs_en us	1	2
	A2	Communicating a Shared Vision	_pc_bi_ls bi001	0.2	2
	B1	Leading Innovation	_pc_ch_la ch010	0.2	2
	B2	Wanted-Innovation Leaders	_pc_bi_ls bi013	0.2	2
	Leading Business Execution		-		
	C1	Foundations for Business Execution	LEAD0151	4	1
	C2	Creating a Business Execution Culture	LEAD0152	4.5	2

C3		Business Execution in Action	LEAD0153	3	2
C4		Business Execution Simulation	LEAD0150	0.5	2
C5		Fostering a Business Execution Culture	_pc_bi_ls bi008	0.2	2
C6		Pave Your Own Path	_pc_bi_ls bi009	0.2	2
C7		Performance Dashboard or Scorecard?	_pc_bi_m gbi012	0.2	2
	Managing Organizational Change		-		
C1		Leadership Essentials: Leading Change	lead_05_a 07_bs_en us	1	2
C2		Leading Change	_pc_ch_la ch004	0.2	2
C3		Leading Teams through Change	_pc_bi_ls bi003	0.2	2
C4		Managing Change: Understanding Change	mgmt_13 a01_bs_e nus	1	2
C5		Managing Change: Building Positive Support for Change	mgmt_13 a02_bs_e nus	1	2
C6		Managing Change: Dealing with Resistance to Change	mgmt_13 a03_bs_e nus	1	2
C7		Managing Change: Sustaining Organizational Change	mgmt_13 a04_bs_e	1	2

			nus		
	C8	Using Change Process to Support Employees Simulation	MGMT00 6A	0.5	2
	C9	Using Change Process to Support Teams Simulation	MGMT00 6B	0.5	2
			-		
66					
	A1	Optimizing Your Work/Life Balance: Analyzing Your Life Balance	pd_06_a0 1_bs_enus	1	2
	A2	Optimizing Your Work/Life Balance: Maintaining Your Life Balance	pd_06_a0 2_bs_enus	1	2
	A3	Optimizing Your Work/Life Balance: Taking Control of Your Stress	pd_06_a0 3_bs_enus	1	2
	A4	Living a Balanced Life Simulation	PD0180	0.5	2
	A5	Employee Exhaustion: Managing a Well-balanced Workload	_pc_bi_m gbi010	0.2	2
	A6	Managing Workplace Stress	_pc_bi_hr bi006	0.2	2
67					
	A1	Business Writing: Know Your Readers and Your Purpose	comm_19 _a01_bs_e nus	1	2
	A2	Business Writing: How to Write Clearly and Concisely	comm_19 _a02_bs_e nus	1	2
	A3	Business Writing: Editing and Proofreading	comm_19 _a03_bs_e nus	1	2
			-		

	Business Grammar Basics		-		
B1	Business Grammar: Parts of Speech	comm_20 _a01_bs_e nus	1	2
B2	Business Grammar: Working with Words	comm_20 _a02_bs_e nus	1	22
B3	Business Grammar: The Mechanics of Writing	comm_20 _a03_bs_e nus	1	2
B4	Business Grammar: Punctuation	comm_20 _a04_bs_e nus	1	2
B5	Business Grammar: Sentence Construction	comm_20 _a05_bs_e nus	1	2
B6	Business Grammar: Common Usage Errors	comm_20 _a06_bs_e nus	1	2
			-		
	Email Communication		-		
C1	Using E-mail and Instant Messaging Effectively	comm_17 _a01_bs_e nus	1	2
C2	Addressing and Redistributing E-mail	comm_17 _a02_bs_e nus	1	2
C3	Managing Your E-mail	comm_17	1	2

			a03_bs_e nus		

Developing questionnaire for measuring competencies

After defining such competency clusters, CSC develops a questionnaire which is based on these competency clusters.

LIST OF GALLUP QUESTIONS MAPPED TO LOMINGER COMPETENCIES. LIST OF COMPETENCIES MAPPED TO SKILLSOFT COURSES										
Attached here is a list of CSC Learning Place courses that CSC and SkillSoft has determined may be relevant to the Gallup 12 Questions.										

Instructions

1. Review your Gallup 12 results and determine which question you would like to focus your development.

2. Locate the appropriate question on the *'Question Mapped to Competency'* tab and review the associated competencies.

3. Narrow you development focus by selecting the competencies for which you would like to develop.

4. Click on the competency name to be directed to the *'Competency Mapped to Courses'* tab to review a list of associated SkillSoft courses.

"Fit"indicates the degree of fit between the recommended course and the Lominger Competency.

"A" indicates very close fit between the SkillSoft course and the Lominger competency

"B" indicates a close fit, but not quite as direct a fit as for the courses marked as "A"

"C" is used to indicate courses that are somewhat related to the Lominger competency, and may be of interest to some

individuals seeking to further their skills and perspectives in the corresponding competency.

The numeric part of each "Fit" code is the recommended sequence for taking the recommended courses. In cases where the you already possess some understanding of the subject, the courses can be taken in the order that interests you.

The "Proficiency" column indicates the level of proficiency with the competency. Proficiency levels are intended as a guide to help you determine whether the course is appropriate for your interest and experience.

Lominger competency) the course helps the learner accomplish. These proficiency levels are defined by SkillSoft, and not by Lominger.

They are intended as a guide to help individuals determine whether the course is likely to be appropriate to their interests and previous

experience.

Proficiency Level		Description
1	Awareness	Has a basic understanding of the competency and can speak to its nature and importance
2	Basic Application	Can apply the competencies in their basic form but needs coaching/supervision
3	Skillful Application	Can consistently apply the competencies regularly in work behavior
4	Mastery	Excels in applying the competencies and is a role model

247

5	Expert	Leads the way internally and helps influence external market best practices/thinking; goes										
		beyond application.										

Last Updated: February 2010

Questions mapped to Job positions:

Each job holder and their senior manager needs to identify which are the competencies which are required for each job position and how each individual employee performs in the human synergistic strategies which are required for superior performance of the job.

Gallup Question Number		Manager	Individual Contributer	Human Synergistic Strategies
1				Achievement
I know what is expected of me at work.	Competency Mapped to Courses'!A822	Managing and Measuring Work	Personal Learning	
		Delegation	Listening	
		Written Communications	-	
		Managing Vision		

		and Purpose		
		Informing		
		Priority Setting		
2				Achievement
I have the materials and equipment I need to do my work right.				
		Planning	Planning	
		Process Management	Process Management	
		Organizational Agility		
		Functional/Technical Skills		
				Self Actualized
3				
At work, I have the opportunity to do what I do best				
		Priority Setting	Career Ambition	

every day.			
	Self Development	Priority Setting	
	Self Knowledge	Self Development	
	Motivating Others	Self Knowledge	
	Understanding Others	-	
4			Humanistic Encouraging
In the last seven days, I have received recognition or praise for doing good work.	Motivating Others	Approachability	
	Understanding Others	Listening	
	Managing and Measuring Work	Boss Relationships	
	Written Communications		
	Conflict	-	

250

		Management		
		Caring about Direct Report		
5				Affiliative
My supervisor, or someone at work, seems to care about me as a person.		Developing Direct Reports/Others Compassion	Compassion	
			Listening	
		Caring about Direct Reports		
		Confronting Direct Reports	Boss Relationships	
			Peer Relationships	
		Listening	Approachability	
		Fairness to Direct Reports		
6				Humanistic Encouraging
There is someone at work		Developing Direct Reports/Others	Peer Relationships	

who encourages my development.			
		Managing and Measuring Work	Boss Relationships
		Motivating Others	
7			Humanistic Encouraging, Supervisor/Self Actualized Result
		Informing	Informing
		Drive for Results	Comfort Around Higher Management
		Command Skills	-
		Decision Quality	
8			Self Actualized
The mission or purpose of my company makes me feel my job is importa		Managing Vision and Purpose	Business Acumen

nt.				
		Customer Focus	Perspective	
		Perspective		
9	-	-	-	Achievement
My associates or fellow employees are committed to doing quality work.		Managing and Measuring Work	Integrity and Trust	
		Informing		
		Integrity and Trust		
10				Affiliative
I have a very good friend at work.		Compassion	Humor	
		Humor	Peer Relationships	
		Peer Relationships	Compassion	
		Listening	Listening	
		Conflict Management	Personal Disclosure	

	Personal Disclosure	Sizing Up People	
	Sizing Up People	Understanding Others	
	Understanding Others	Work/Life Balance	
	Work/Life Balance	Interpersonal Savvy	
11			Humanistic Encouraging
In the last six months, someone at work has talked to me about my progress.	Developing Direct Reports/Others	Boss Relationships	
	Managing and Measuring Work	Informing	
	Informing		
	Conflict Management		
	Confronting Direct Reports		
	Managerial Courage		
12			Humanistic Encouraging

This last year, I have had opportunities at work to learn and grow.		Learning on the Fly	Learning on the Fly	
		Self Knowledge	Self Development	
		Self Development	Self Knowledge	
		Developing Direct Reports/Others	Technical Learning	

Assessment of individual employees to competency clusters:

On the basis of these competency clusters an individual is assessed and an Individual development plan is prepared. With the assessment, the proficiency levels of each individual are identified and Gap analysis is done. By doing this an individual is able to get a clear picture of the proficiency levels which is expected of him and what needs to be done to improve on these skills. Accordingly various Training programme is designed by the HR department using the Skill soft courses which are mapped in line with each competencies. If it is a deficiency in the functional competency, then the respective department heads recommend the persons who needs to be given the training will be decided by the senior manager of the organization.

▼ Competency Mapping

S.N.	Main Tasks	Definition	Level
1	Budgeting and Forecasting	Prepares the budget and does forecasting	
2	Change Management	Establishes methods to track and report on change requests, defines out-of-scope conditions and measures requests against definition, develops change of scope authorization process, analyses change impact on budget, schedule and baselines	
3	Configuration Management (CM)	Maintaining versions of project artifacts, ensuring proper change control mechanism with or without CM tools. Thorough knowledge of Configuration Management (CFM) and change management procedures and understanding about various CFM tools. Complete knowledge of version control, base lining etc.	
4	Customer Management	Dedicated to meet the expectations and requirements of customers, establishes and maintains effective relationships with customers and gains their trust and respect. Is able to understand expectations and also express his point of view. Managing accounts and looking for new opportunity in the respective domains. Ensuring smooth and two-way communication between the project team and the customer. Activities that includes regular progress reporting and effective resolution of queries on technical front, available resource, various domains and project schedules . Link with internal or external customers or departments for hardware, software and other resources.	

Select Keywords [X]

Keywords

1
2
3
NA

OK

Cancel

#		Definition	Level
		documents related to domain.	
4	Networking / Distributed computing/ communication (COM, DCOM, CORBA, RPC, J2EE, .NeT, XML...)	Technologies used for development and deployment of distributed applications / networking applications and online transaction processing	
5	Operational Languages (JCL, CL400,Assembly, Shell, DOS commands and batch programs...)	Languages used to execute programs/applications etc	
6	OS (Windows NT, MVS, OS/2, VSE, Unix, Linux, MF-DOS, OS/400, OS/390, MVS, VM)	Operating System is a set of programs used to manage computer's resources	
7	Product Knowledge (Cyberlife, Vantage, POINT, PMHS, EXCEED, SII, SIII etc)	Able to combine technical design and application design to recommend appropriate product-based solutions, understands integration issues, entry and exit points between application modules	
8	SDLC	Knowledge of various software development models and ability to effectively implement appropriate methodology for a project (development, maintenance & conversion).	

	Attitudes / Soft skills	Definition	Level
1	Communication skills	Communication skills is the competency of conveying requirements and ideas in an effective manner using verbal and written medium. Presentation skills is the competency of communicating to a target audience in an effective manner using verbal communication and presentation aids	
2	Initiative	Volunteer to take additional responsibilities in areas of his/her competence within project or organization. Suggesting improvement in existing processes and takes up responsibilities of implementing them.	
3	IP Skills/ Team skills	Relates well to all kinds of people, up, down, and	

Example of identifying gaps and suggesting for improvement:

Asset(title)	Audience(LF,SLF,E xec forum	Lominger Leadership competencies mapped to competencies	Relevant as learning asset if the manager wants to develop where the	Leadership success profile	Region or entity	Asset owner

257

			manager has low scores in question no. (see Gallup Questions)			
Accolades (reward and recognition, includes ceritficate of appreciation and gift vouchers	all		Motivating others Developing direct reports and others Sizing of people Driving results	4	Motivating others Developing direct reports and others sizing of people	ELT D	MALATI/NE HA

B. Competency Mapping at Wipro

The models which were practiced mostly by Wipro and Infosys were the Be spoke model and the Mc Ber model. The McBer model which is well illustrated in a book 'Competency at work' written by William Spencer. The McBer model originated from McLaren who talked about achievement motivation which came close to what we refer as competency mapping. According to him some generic competencies are achievement, managerial, influencing, personal effectiveness and cognitive. Based on these models, they developed the behavioral dictionary broadly Wipro defined 24 competencies which can describe all the behavioral competencies that were differentiating and relevant. Then the HR team took care to drop some competencies which are differentiating but not relevant and vice versa. Then they made a Functional Dictionary relevant to HR, finance, software, etc. Wipro's HR team strongly advocated making a full functional dictionary since each role tries to become the next role and the previous role must map into this role. But it is not necessary to have all the 24 competencies and depending on the job, each role may have 5 or 6 competencies.

Bespoke computer software, also known as custom-software, is a piece of software specifically developed to meet an organisation exact requirement and need. For example, after completing a needs assessment you become aware of the need for a few certain features on a new customer database. You search for an 'off the shelf' solution and you can't find a solution that fits this design. Therefore, you turn to a solution that is custom designed for you and your business. This is known as a bespoke computer software solution.

Benefits of Be spoke computer software

In the past, bespoke software was limited to the large companies, but with new technology comes new opportunities. Nowadays this once out of reach solution is now within reach of the SME, helping them to gain the benefits of bespoke solutions, such as a competitive advantage and increased efficiency without paying over the odds.

1. Bespoke software exactly matches your requirement

'Off the shelf' solutions include a wide variety of features to appeal to the mass market. With these solutions you will often find that you have many features you will not use, and in some cases you don't have access to the features you need the most. You may also have to adapt how you do business to 'fit in' with the software. This can be a tough compromise as it can increase costs and lower efficiency. However, with a bespoke solution this can be avoided. The solution is developed to fit into your current business process with the features you need to help you do what you do best, that little bit better.

2. Competitive Advantage

Your own software differentiates you from the competition as much as your unique products and services. Through a bespoke software solution, you are ensuring that your competitor is unable to purchase the same solution and gain the benefits that you are receiving, such as increased efficiency

3. Software that works for you.

Ease of use is an important factor when implementing any new software solution. Through the process of developing a bespoke solution you have a close relationship with your software developers. This ensures you get a solution that works for you, and does not over complicate or confuse the users.

4. Increase user adoption

Employees will usually find it easier to use and more efficient as it does not contain unused features and facilities. Combine this with the results of your need assessment where users have a say in the solution and how it works, employees will be more likely to adapt to the new solution.

5. Support

Consider if an 'off the shelf' solution failed, what do you do? When you contact their support they may not fully understand your business and how you use the software, that is development for the masses, and may not be able to give you the best advice or be able to change or 'update' the solution. By working with a development company you gain that direct contact and build a relationship with the company as they begin to understand your business and needs. Therefore, if an issue does arise they will have an understanding of how you use the software, allowing them to quickly make the necessary changes.

6. Reduce the number of mistakes and increase efficiency.

By automating manual tasks you can avoid vital mistake and increase efficiency. Building on the previous benefit, the close working partnerships ensures that the developers can even point out further ways to increase your efficiency and potential your productivity.

7. Incorporate your brand image

with bespoke solutions you can easily incorporate your unique look and feel into the software. Anything from the colours used, to the place of your logo can be altered to meet your exact requirements. This can strengthen your brand image to customers, investors as well as employees.

8. Flexible and Customisable

After your brand image is incorporated into the development, bespoke solutions are renowned for been much more flexible and have a higher level of customisation built into them. This ensures that the solution is always ready and easily modified or changed as your business evolves.

9. Avoid DIY

In some cases the cost can seem a lot lower than a bespoke solution. However, with an off the shelf solution you are required to do it yourself, from installation and set-up to importing important business data. This is not only a time cost but it can result in important information been deleted or imported incorrectly. Allow the experts to complete and transfer all your important data to ensure minimise delays and errors

One of the problems in Be spoke model was that it did it role by role and then the interrelations became astronomically complicated. In a company a person needs to know if he is selected for this role and what will he do in the next role. All the development and training should take the person to the next role. Another problem was that not every role is the same as the job.

In earlier days there was a rigid pattern of job analysis, description, evaluation and job specification. But in today's rapidly changing world, the role gets changed and merged and sometimes even the person defines the role. For instance, if they find a person is interested in both marketing and training, they will create a role like that. Wipro Technologies though it has a huge staff strength, there the number of roles are very few in contrast to Wipro Infotech where there are diverse roles. Therefore, it is better to have a dictionary which maps out the role rather than have a rigid framework.

One can use various methods to measure competency. Simplest among them is a Self-appraisal telling person to rate themselves. Then there is the 360 degree feedback where we take feedback from that person, his peers, seniors, juniors and then take out a pattern to identify competency. Or one can have certain technical tests to grade them as masters or novices. Among these the 360 degree feedback seems to be the most accurate in evaluating people.

That organization which wants to implement PCMM (People Capability Maturity Model) in their organization, they have to get into competency mapping from Level 3. Wipro got a further push for competency, since around the time it defined the dictionaries, PCMM assessment came in and one thing reinforced the other. Once Wipro implemented PCMM they were forced to do competency based recruitment, performance management, compensation, training & development.

Similarly, Wipro has a competency based compensation based on the competency a person has achieved apart from criteria like criticality and potential. Finally it has competency based training where we grade training programs for various competency levels. For instance, if it had communication skills program, it will indicate that this is level 2, so people with higher scores like level 3, need not bother. PCMM Level 3 requires employee competency database to be verified by both its internal and external auditors. Since, ultimately, competency will decide y salary, promotion, perks and everything in the organization, there could be some interference by vested interests.

Capability maturity Model (CMM)

In November ,1986,the software Engineering Institute (SEI) of Carnegie Mellon University of Pittsburg with assistance from the MITRE corporation began developing a process maturity framework to help organizations to improve their software process. After four years of experience with the software process maturity framework and the 1987 maturity questionnaire, SEI evolved the maturity framework into the capability maturity model for software. The CMM is based on the actual practices and reflects the needs of the individuals performing software process improvement and software process appraisals. It is a documented process.

A process is a sequence of steps performed for a given purpose. The process integrates people, tools and procedures. Process is what people do using procedures, methods, tools and equipments, to transform raw material (inputs) into a product (output) that is value to the customers. The CMM focuses on process as a way to empower the people doing the work. An effective process ties together people, tools and methods into an integrated whole. Process capability describes the range of expected results that can be achieved by following a process. Thus, process performance focuses on the results achieved while process capability focuses on results expected. Process maturity is the extent to which a specific process is explicitly defined, managed, measured controlled and affected. Maturity implies a potential for growth in capability indicates both the richness of an organization's software process and the consistency with which it is applied in projects throughout the organization. Process maturity implies that the process capability must have grown. Improvement requires strong management support and a consistent long term focus .As an organization matures It needs an infrastructure and culture to support its methods , practices and procedures so that they endure after those who originally defined them have gone .organizational culture can be summed up as the way things are done .It is seen in people's expectations for how they are to work together . One of the determinants of organizational culture is its infrastructure, which is underlying framework of an organization or system, including organizational structures, policies and standards, training, facilitates and tools that support its ongoing performance.

Istitutionalism is the building of infrastructure and culture to support the methods, practices ,and procedures so that they are the ongoing way of doing business The result of institutionalization is the deployment of processes that are effective ,usable and consistently applied across the organization.

People capability Maturity Model:

Maturity Levels

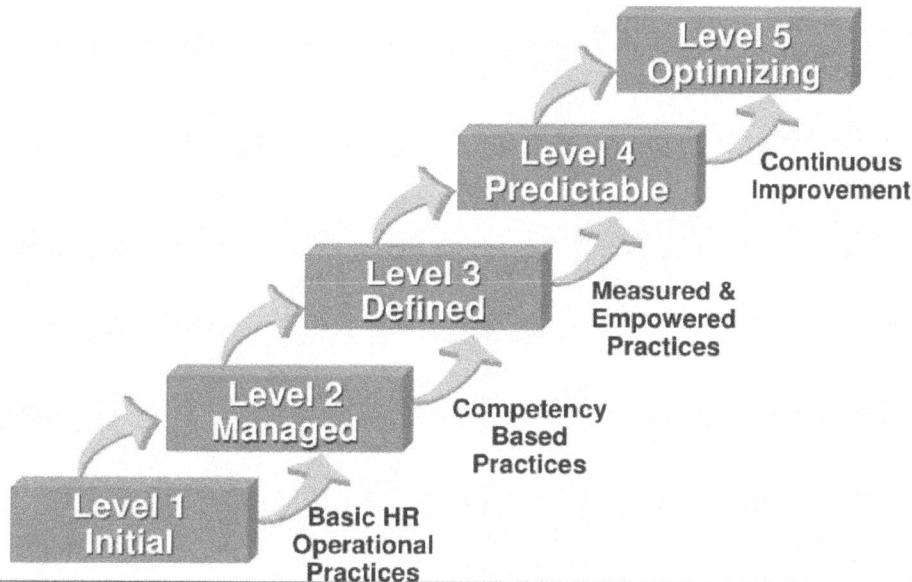

© Software Engineering Institute

18

P-CMM adopts the maturity framework of the CMM for software to managing and developing the organization's work force. To attract, develop and motivate organize and retain talent to continuously improve capability of an organization. PCMM is now widely used by organizations to characterize the maturity of their human resources practices, guides a program of continuous manpower development with process improvement and establish a culture of software engineering excellence. It describes an evolutionary improvement path from ad hoc, inconsistently performed practices to a mature, disciplined development of the knowledge ,skills and motivation of the human resources.

The P-CMM consists of five maturity levels that lay successful foundations for continuously improving talent , developing effective teams and successfully managing the people's assets of the organization. Each maturity levels is a well defined evolutionary plateu that institutionalizes a level capability for developing the talent within the organization.

Except for level 1 , each maturity level is developed into several key process areas that an organization should focus on to improve its human resources capability. Each process area is described in terms of the key practices that contribute to satisfying its goals. The key practices describe the infrastructure and activities that contribute most to the effective implementation and institutionalization of the key process area.

The five maturity levels of the PCMM are:

Initial: workforce practices are applied without analysis.

Repeatable: The key process areas at level 2 focuses on installing basic discipline into workforce activities .They are:

263

- Work environment
- Communication
- Staffing
- Performance management
- Training
- Compensation

Defined: The key process areas at level 3 address issues surrounding the identification of the organization's primary competencies and aligning its people management activities with them . they are:

- Knowledge and skill analysis
- Workforce planning
- Competency development
- Career development
- Competency based practices
- Participatory culture

Managed : the key process areas at level 4 focusses on quantitatively managing organizational growth in people management capabilities and in establishing competency-based teams. They are:

- Mentoring
- Team building
- Team based practices
- Organizational competency management
- Organizational performance management

Optimising: The key process areas at level 5 cover the issues that address continuous improvement methods for developing competency ,at both the organizational and the individual level. They are:

- Personal competency development
- Coaching
- Continuous workforce innovation
- Human Capital return on investment

Two ROI systems widely in use are utitlity analysis and performance value . Nine step Human capital worksheet of Gordon (2000) allows us to accurately estimate the monetary returns both before and after most training programs.

Step-1 calculate all direct costs associated with the training programs

Step-2 calculate all lost productivity while trainers are in the program

Step 3 calculate the total cost of the program

Step 4 Estimate expected hourly,weekly or monthly productivity benefits per trainee. Methods may range from establishing control groups to using standard linear regression formula.

Step 5 Estimate the actual quality benefit from the training.

Step-6: Using a standard discount rate formula ,estimate the time length of the training's effect

Step 7 calculate profit per trainee

Step 8 calculate benefits of the total training program

Step 9 calculate return on investment

Process Areas

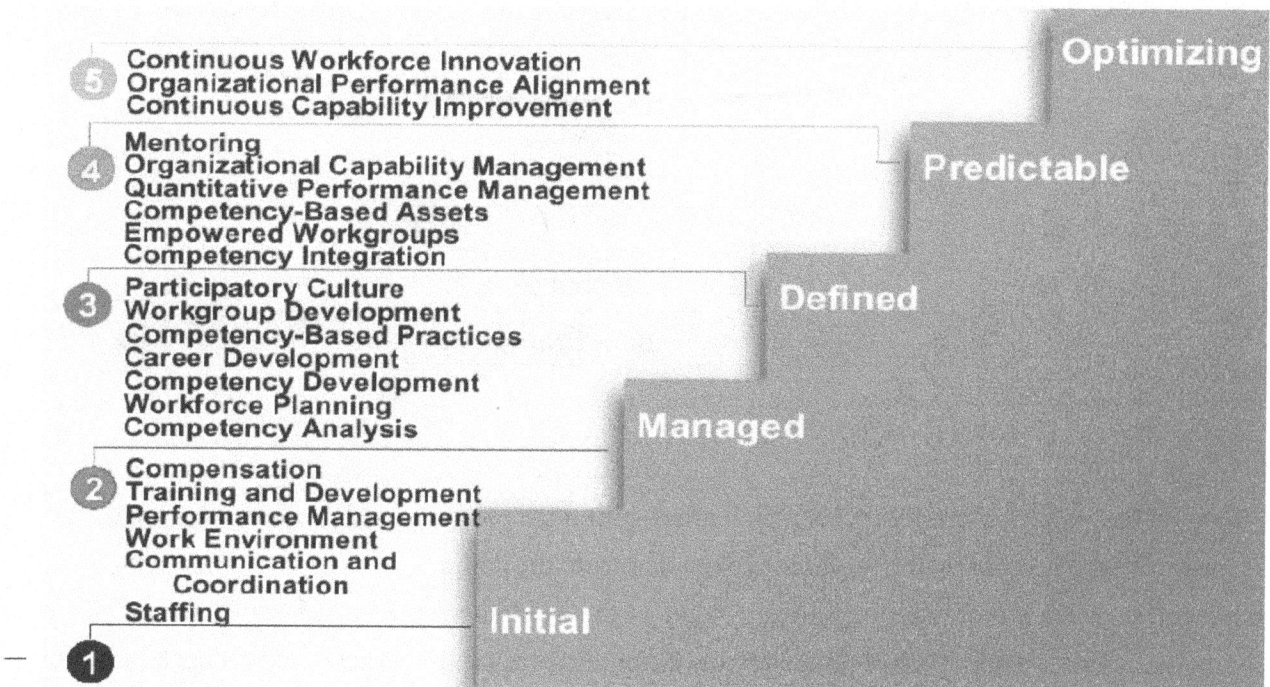

Optimizing

5 — Continuous Workforce Innovation
Organizational Performance Alignment
Continuous Capability Improvement

Predictable

4 — Mentoring
Organizational Capability Management
Quantitative Performance Management
Competency-Based Assets
Empowered Workgroups
Competency Integration

Defined

3 — Participatory Culture
Workgroup Development
Competency-Based Practices
Career Development
Competency Development
Workforce Planning
Competency Analysis

Managed

2 — Compensation
Training and Development
Performance Management
Work Environment
Communication and
Coordination
Staffing

Initial

1

4.4C .Competency mapping at Infosys

On the basis of the PCMM model competencies are defined for each role positions and job clusters.

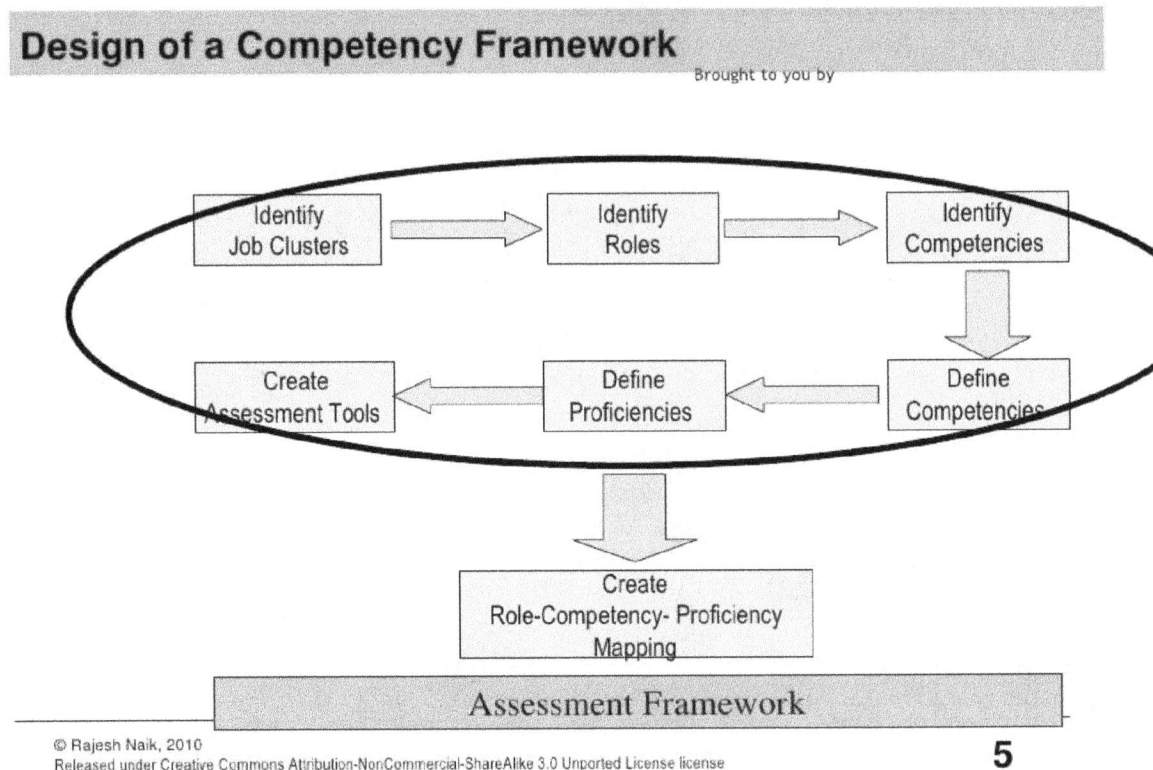

Design of a Competency Framework

From the job clusters, roles are defined and competencies are identified on the basis of the role profiles, basing on the various maturity levels which are required for each role and proficiencies are defined on the basis of each level of maturity which is expected from the people.

Assessment tools are created to find out what is the competency level of each individual on the competency framework. Then competency development programme is designed for each individual to fill in the gaps of the competency requirement.

HRD CDP (Competency Dev Program).
Key principles of the CDP 3.0 framework

- The objective to ensure that competencies across multiple competency dimensions applicable for a role are acquired during the time a person spends in a role
- Competency Development Program requirement completion is:
    - Mandated for promotion
    - Mandated for progression
    - Not linked to appraisals and CRR
- Number of attempts per certification is limited to 2 for every six months, with a minimum

gap of 15 days between two successive attempts

- Maximum number of credit points that can be attempted in every 6 months of a certification cycle is 40

How does it work?

- Employee would need to accumulate a minimum of 60 credit points during his / her tenure in the role
- Employee can choose to obtain the credit points anytime during his/her tenure in the role and there is no restriction with respect to a minimum credit point to be earned every six months. However, every employee will have to plan for a minimum of 15 credit points every year
- At the time of promotion / progression, employee has to have the minimum credit point requirement as outlined in the transition slide
- Credit points can be accumulated through:
    - Means of Assessment (Certification)- Min 45 credit points
    - Means of Non – Assessment (Publishing journals, course material development, Conducting Training, Presenting in conferences, attending training) - Max 15 credit points

Onboarding Plan

Time period	Credit points required for Promotion	Credit points required for Progression
October 2014	60	15
April 2014	50	15
October 2013	40	15
April 2013	30	15
Oct 2012	20	15
April 2012	10	10

- Credit points mentioned for Certifications are Min Credit points required to be taken against Certifications
- This plan is for the first set of promotions only
- Once an employee is promoted in the new role the credit point requirement would be set to 60

Plan for Laterals

To have a provision for laterals joining HRD since they may not have enough time to accrue required credits before being considered for Progression/ Promotion

Credit requirement for laterals to be based on the number of years s/he has spent in Infosys in the same role as on the cut-off date for the cycle

Duration spent in Infosys(years) as on the cut-off date	Credit point requirement
>= 3.0	60
>=2.5 and 3	50
>=2.0 and <2.5	40
>= 1.5 and < 2.0	30
>= 1.0 and <1.5	20
>= 0.5 and <1	10
<0.5	0

Incentives for Higher scores and Timely Completion

%Score	Grade Point	Weightage	Assigned Credit Points
80% and above	A	1.2	12

70%-79%	B	1	10
60%-69%	C	0.8	8

- Applicable only for internal Certifications

- Employees who fail to qualify or those who get a C grade will have an option to take another attempt and improve the score upto grade B in the second attempt

*Illustration for a 10 point Certification

Timely Completion

Certification Plan	Year of Completion			
	Year 1	Year 2	Year 3	Year 4
Certification Plan Year 1	2	0	0	0
Certification Plan Year 2	2	2	0	0
Certification Plan Year 3	2	2	2	0

Applicable for both external/internal Certifications

Credit Point Accumulation – Assessment

- A standard certification (recommended) of 45 hour prescribed (design) learning effort to give 15 credit points
- All our Certifications would offer 5/10 Credit points to HRDians
- External Certifications (for ex. GPHR) will lead to accrual of credit points

Prescribed Design Duration	Assessment Credit Point
15 Hours	5
30 Hours	10
45 Hours	15
60 Hours	20

CDP 3.0 Framework

Agenda

- Competency Task Force recommendations
- Key Policy Objectives
- Key Principles retained from CDP 2.0 Policy
- Credit Point Mechanism
    - Credit Point Requirement – Organization Perspective
    - Credit Point Accumulation
    - Incentives for Higher Scores and Timely completion
- Plan for Laterals
- HES alignment `Infosys_patter_fade.jpg`

Competency Task Force Recommendations

- Focus on Holistic Competency Development versus only certifications
- Based on competency definitions for the role, divide certifications into two categories –
    - Core (generic concepts for the role), and
    - Specific (Tools `Infosys_patter_fade.jpg` ed for the job)
- Establish Unit Competency Councils to facilitate decisions on relevant learning interventions and certifications at unit level.
- Reduce number of certifications from CDP 2.0 policy of two per year to a defined number for each role - based on role competency requirements.
- Introduce Learning Credit point mechanism, with credits for certifications and other competency building assignments such as evaluated courses, teaching and publications

Key Policy Objectives

- Address key employees concerns by implementing Competency Task Force recommendations
- Balance between relevance and flexibility
- Clarity of decision areas between Corporate Competency Council and Unit Competency Council
- Reducing # of certifications from two per year to around four per role
- Transparency and fairness
- Simplicity

Key Principles retained from CDP 2.0 Policy

- The objective to ensure that competencies across multiple competency dimensions applicable for a role are acquired during the time a person spends in a role
- Competency Development Program requirement completion is:
    - Mandated for promotion
    - Mandated for progression*
    - Not linked to appraisals and CRR
- Number of attempts per certification is limited to 2 for every six months, with a minimum gap of 15 days between two successive attempts
- Concept of Competency Level associated with all Certifications
- Training will remain optional

*Mandated by units

Credit Point Requirement – Organization Perspective

For Promotion
- 60 Total Credit Points (TCP) per role – from all mechanism
- 45 Assessment Credit Points (ACP) - from Certifications
- 15 Core Competency Assessment Credit Points (CACP) - from Core Certifications

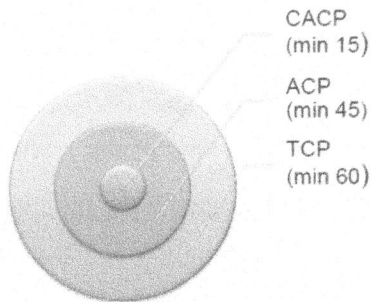

For Progression
- 15 Assessment Credit Points (ACP) - from Certifications

CACP (min 15)

ACP (min 45)

TCP (min 60)

Infosys_patter_fade.jpg

Credit Point Accumulation – Non-Assessment

- Participating in Training
- Delivering Training
- Publications
- Patents

Category	Credit Point
Publication – Course Material (45 Hour)	15
Publication – Conference / Trade Journals	15-30
Publication – Academic Journals	30-60
Defensive Publication	30
Patent	90

Duration (Days)	0.5	1	2	3	4	5	6
CP for participating in training	0	1	1	2	2	3	3
CP for delivering training	1	2	3	5	6	8	9

For employees doing a joint training delivery / publishing / patent, accumulated credits will be distributed equally amongst contributors

Plan for Laterals

- We need to have a provision for laterals joining Infosys, since they may not have enough time to accrue required credits before being considered for a promotion

- Credit Point requirement for a lateral will be based on number of years s/he has spent in Infosys in the CDP journey (in the same role) as on the cut-off date for the cycle

# of years spent in Infosys in the CDP journey as on cut-off date	Total Credit Point Requirement (TCP) for promotion
>= 3.0	60
>= 2.5 and < 3.0	50
>= 2.0 and < 2.5	40
>= 1.5 and < 2.0	30
>= 1.0 and < 1.5	20
>= 0.5 and < 1.0	10
< 0.5	0

Higher Education Scheme (HES) Alignment

- Programs identified by HES, with a duration of one year or more, will accrue credit points
- Programs with a total duration of one year or more will accrue 15 credits for each year, with a cap of 30 credits per program. Accordingly, here are some scenarios:
  - Program of 6 months duration – 0 credits
  - Program of 1 year duration – 15 credits
  - Program of 2 year duration – 30 credits
  - Program of 3 year duration – 30 credits
- Credit points may accrue in stages, across multiple planning cycles, as and when employees complete the programs, and provides sufficient proof for the same

Source: screen prints of the intranet screen of Infosys

4.4 D. Competency Mapping at HCL

The study on competency mapping in few departments such as IT, Customer Care and Business of HCL would act as a concrete base for taking the concept to Top Management to undertake this project for whole organization. Initially, the findings

are given to **Recruitment & selection and Training functions** of Human Resource Department of HCL. Later on, these will help making an effective **Performance Management System**, which will be both goal and competency based. Thesewill aid the training department to improve Return on Investment**(ROI) on training.** The study has helped in **training need analysis** (TNA) of these departments and added the behavioral

dimension to all elements of training and development which willhelp in **designing modules** and selecting **events and activities**for the same. For recruitment & selection function, it will be usedin making **selection criteria** for various designations, to **assess**

eligible pool of candidates in interviews and for giving**assessment feedback** to candidates. It will also explore theworking of various departments to be helpful to HR department in a number of ways. In short, it will act as a new relevant and well informed knowledge base. .

Activities of Commercial Department are the following --

New order

Client Solutions

Billing

Consumer care center

Recovery

HCL is committed to be the leading provider of value added services. It is fully geared to fulfil or exceed the customer expectations by continuously improving the quality of all services.

Findings mentioned are developed on the basis of interview conducted and observation with six business managers as Sample.

- **CADRES & DESIGNATIONS**
- **Officers** are in the Grade ranging from A-1 to A-10. Officers have
- been classified as follows:
- Top Management - CMD, Directors
- Senior Management - A-7 to A-10
- Middle Management - A-4 to A-6
- Junior Management - A-1 to A-3

Grades and Designations of the officers are as follows:

S No	Grade	Designation
1	A-1	Officer/Engineer
2	A-2	Sr. Officer/Sr. Engineer/Asst. Manager
3	A-3	Dy. Manager
4	A-4	Additional manager
5	A-5	Manager /Business Manager
6	A-6	Sr. Manager
7	A-7	Chief Engineer/Chief Controller of Finance & A/Cs Chief Personnel Manager/ Chief of Management Training and Development/Chief Manager
8	A-8	Dy. General Manager*/Addl. vice President
9	A-9	General Manager/ Vice President
10	A-10	Executive Director/Group General Manager/ Senior Vice President/ Chief General Manager
11	A-11	Board of Directors/CEO
12.	A-12	Vice Chairman
13.	A-13	Chairman

WORK PROFILE OF BUSINESS MANAGERS

- Department Head of District / Division Office (Grade-A5)
- Responsible for various functions—
- · Internal administration of staff and all other infrastructure facilities in
- Office eg. Furniture.
- · Material Management (cables quantity, meters with seals, blank
- bills, PC's , infrastructure etc.) and also complaint handling related
- to same.
- · Recovery of pending dues from consumers.
- · Bring new customers into net.
- · Quality upgrading of services etc.

Performance Measures in terms of

- · Increase in revenue collection and recovery from clients.
- · Increase in number of new clients

Competencies for business manager

Behavioural / generic competency set

1. PatiencE :

To remain cool and poised with every type of client in any condition. To have composure, maturity and self control in dealing with all types of customers-external as well as internal. To remain ready to hear any absurd word from disturbed consumers.

2. COPING WITH CHANGE-

The power to overcome difficulties or problems in any modifications in past scenario of system or way of working and acclimatize in new system. To be non-resistant for any reengineering process in system. To be accustomed to a new situation or climate variations in shortest time frame. To learn new upcoming technology and make it a part of system.

3. WORKAHOLIC –

The behaviour of compulsive work with no constraints of time and effort devotion. To remain ready for dedicated work with no time limitations. To be enthusiastic to work in all relevant activities of job profile. To give the job utmost importance and priority.

CUSTOMER SERVICE ORIENTATION –

The ability to anticipate, recognize and meet customer needs by understanding their perspective. To provide best service to customers by taking active interest in their concerns. To satisfy customer needs in present applicable guidelines of system.

To grasp customer's perspective, acting as a trusted advisor. To resolve customer problems by empathizing with him and taking quick initiatives.

COACHING AND DEVELOPING SUBORDINATES-

The ability to sense subordinates developmental needs, bolstering their abilities and instructs, direct or train them for high performance. To identify people's needs for further growth and give pertinent training in this regard To offer timely and correct feedback to subordinates for improvement. To acknowledge people's strengths and coach them to concentrate on same.

TECHNICAL COMPETENCY SET

1. UNDERSTANDING OF BUSINESS-

The sound knowledge of commercial aspects of business to deliver improved results and solving consumer problems. To possess in-depth knowledge of IT business in whole.

2. ATTENTION TO DETAILS-

The ability to focus on all minute details and aspects of any issues of assigned job.

To be meticulous in finding and using relevant intricacies of problem or task.

- Use of clear-cut guidelines for department reference in all scenarios.
- Develop plan of action to get things done quickly.
- To meet all deadly requirements of work assigned under commercial aspect.

3. PROBLEM SOLVING-

The ability to find knowledgeable, workable and fast solution or explanation for any consumer grievances.

- To fix or resolve any type of consumer query in shortest possible time.
- To work out justified reasons for the issue cropped up.
- To hit upon a solution to consumer questions within novel and updated technology framework.
- As Business Manager is responsible for each and every penny calculated
- from consumer and overall revenue efficiency for his division, he should Posses above-mentioned skill set. The business of HCL is related to tangible commodity of use for everyone .Business manager should be knowledgeable and possess maturity and patience to deal with consumers of all profiles and solve their problems as consumer's problem is escalated to him it was not resolved at other levels..

IT DEPARTMENT

The Information Technology (IT) Department at HCL is involved in modernizing the present computing infrastructure and providing assistance to the other department employees to use advanced techniques and emerging technologies in a secure and reliable environment. Software related to Database maintenance & monitoring, Data collection for billing, Consumer billing and attending to online consumer grievances are successfully developed and implemented in all circles and districts.

The functional divisions under IT are –

1. IT Support/Helpdesk
2. Monitoring / Networking
3. Execution
4. Software
5. Training

HEAD IT

- **WORK PROFILE**

Department head of Information Technology Department Monitoring of all projects and activities in terms of time of completion (daily, weekly and monthly) as per activity times defined, cost limited. Undertaken by IT dept. Approvals for different new projects/technology and annual budget decision for dept.Negotiation with vendors for discounts and extra facilities for unlisted items .Understand software or automation requirement by all other HCL ltd.

- Careful scrutiny of all ongoing projects.
- Responsible for providing better IT service to whole organization with optimization of all costs.
- Pre and post release testing of all IT modules.
- Enhance improvement in all ongoing projects and pushing ahead.
- Technology is same for whole organization as per corporate planning, Resource planning. Requirement is to review the planning, give new ideas and discuss the relevance of all projects in present scenario. Role of Head IT is of a facilitator and not inspector so that no havoc is created.

REPORTING

- Dual reporting –
- Administration wise: In NOIDA office
- Technically: To Corporate office in NOIDA

COMPETENCIES REQUIREMENT FOR IT HEAD

BEHAVIORAL COMPETENCY SET

1. LEADERSHIP- It is the ability to lead, give direction, motivatewithin team context for goal attainment by doing right things within policy framework.

- Monitors boundaries and defines limits for working.
- Provides direction and inspiration to all team members.
- Finds a sense of purpose in larger mission.
- Guide the performance of others while holding them accountable.
- Operates openly and is accessible to others.

2. TEAM BUILDING –

It is the art of building a foundation to bind members harmoniously using their capabilities for the achievementof shared goal.

- Creating team synergy in attainment of collective goal.
- Model team capabilities of collaboration, respect and cooperation.
- Work cohesively in team, unleashing every member's energies and abilities to give best output.
- Build effective team spirit with people of diverse abilities, perspectives and talents.

3LEVERAGING DIVERSITY –

It is the ability to cultivate opportunities through different kinds of people and
their skill set.

- Respect and relate well with people possessing different technical skills.
- See diversity as opportunity and blend well to get best out of people Understand every member as crucial and give due importance.

4. NEGOTIATION –

It is the art to confer with another to reach at a solution via mutual agreement.

- Magnanimous spirit will be winning strategy in longrun.
- Compromising with other party more or less equally.
- Reaching a consensus based on mutualunderstanding of each other's needs.
- Listens attentively to second party and using variedstyles to put point.

FUNCTIONAL COMPETENCIES

IT INRASTRUCTURE AND SUPPORT KNOWLEDGE- Sound understanding of all networks, interfaces, software's and technologies blending.Knowledge of connectivity, LAN, WAN, typologies, leased lines, wireless etc.

- Understanding of various connectivity protocols.
- Full information on Lotus Notes 6.5 and it's working
- Exposure to all modules in use under SAP e.g. payroll,
- finance etc.

2. PLANNING- It is the art of setting plans and agreeing for

- **department to complete goals in calculated time and**
- **resources.**
- Ensures all plans are achievable in constraints.
- Sense risks and manage them in time and least effort
- Plans well so that system will not stop working in any scenario. Scheduling of all activities and working according to priority.

3. UNDERSTANDING OF SOFTWARE DEVELOPMENT LIFE CYCLE- It is the ability to use all steps of SDLC in all software projects for optimization of costs.

- Developing Information systems through a multi-step process from information requirement through analysis, design, implementation and maintenance. Use of rational unified process for each critical software development activity. Appropriate model combined into hybrid methodology to make best fit for every project.

4. PROJECT MANAGEMENT SKILLS – It is the ability to planand manage temporary endeavor undertaken to createunique product / service in time and resource constraints.

- Proper planning and scheduling of all activities to accomplish aim of project.
- Taking calculated risk to maximize project output.
- Monitor the progress of project activities as per plan.
- Management of all aspects related to project e.g. costs, time, manpower etc.
- Head IT is responsible for system integration at TECH MAHINDRA, development of consumer support model and satisfying software needs of all departments at and of all offices. At such designation, technical vision and encompassing technology in phases viz knowledge of system integration, IT infrastructure, support and monitoring are critical for high performance. On the other hand, behavioural competencies of team building and leadership are essential to get work done from collaborative teams and task forces. Negotiation skills are add-ons resulting in win-win situations for dealing with outside vendors.

HEAD SYSTEMS

- **WORK PROFILE**
- Responsible for -
- Software development in commercial areas of business.
- SDLC requirement fulfillment of whole Delhi region.
- Development, testing, implementation of various software . And later on providing support for similar modules. Imparting of training to end users of software created.
- Successful Business Process Reengineering (BPR).
- Bridges the gap between user of new system and software developer through interactions.
- Revenue Cycle Generation module in billing by 20 lakh customers.
- Deals with finance, administration, legal, enforcement and customer care department for any software requirement.
- Understand internal customer needs and acts as an interface with software programmer.
- Building different cross functional teams of diverse talents and capabilities according to quantum of work.
- Monitoring the progress of projects undertaken to complete them in least possible time and resources.

COMPETENCIES REQUIREMENT

BEHAVIORAL COMPETENCY SET

1. UNDERSTANDING OF BUSINESS- It is the ability to grasp the working and knowing the gaps of all aspects of power sector.

- Knowing business capabilities and growth parameters.
- Improving the business performance with every decision taken.
- Focus on consumer support model with system integration and automation.

2. ANALYTICAL SKILLS- It is the art of weighing the pros and

- **cons in very uncertain and ambiguous situation and developing Optimal and creative solution.**

  Judging any situation with proper analysis.
- All perspectives should be considered before making any decision.
- Business relevance and all post effects are taken care of.
- Logical understanding of any issue crop up.

3. TIME MANAGEMENT SKILLS- It is the art of utilizing the

- **available time to its optimum, thus making it the greatest available resource.**
- Using every minute available in useful work.
- Scheduling all the activities with strict time frames.
- Execution of all projects by sticking to planned schedul

4. COMMUNICATION- It is the technique of providing andreceiving verbal or written messages in precise manner to ensure proper understanding by receiver.

- Articulate the ideas in a manner that is properly understood by receiver.
- Effective utilization of different channels to provide full information to everyone.
- Delivery of message to receiver in time and taking acknowledgement.

5. SELF-CONFIDENCE- It is the art of sensing self worth and capabilities to enhance performance.

- Presenting oneself with self-assurance.
- Take a stand on what is right.
- Decisive despite uncertainties and pressures of different constraints.
- Make one's presence felt in any business scenario.

6. PERSEVERANCE- It is the skill of persisting with an endeavour in spite of all hassles.

- Pursuing a standard of excellence in every work.
- Never leave a task unfinished.
- Generating alternatives in any difficult situation.
- Reminding the purpose of task to team in the face of obstacles.

FUNCTIONAL COMPETENCY

1. SOFTWARE DEPLOYMENT- It is the ability to use system thinking in all stages of software development to implementation.

- Understanding of how software can be implemented in current system.
- Feasibility of automation of any work process
- Analyzing the optimal capability of software in any framework.
- Interface between user needs and software developer for better understanding and use of resources.
- At Designation of Head Systems, comprehensive set of behavioural skills are essential as system's perspective and holistic view is a key. Dealing with internal customers in organizations, understanding their needs and guide subordinates for automation are the

requirement. Technical vision is necessary but soft skills and managerial skills weigh heavy on technical competencies. Person should be aware of technical up datings but imbibing every new technology is not essential.

MANAGERS AND ADDITIONAL MANAGERS (IT)

COMPETENCIES REQUIREMENT
BEHAVIORAL COMPETENCY SET

1. INITIATIVE- The ability to seize new opportunities and take advantage in development of business.

- Take anticipatory action to avoid problems before they happen.
- Acting before being forced to by external environment.
- Displaying proactive approach in taking action with awareness of consequences.

2. OPTIMISM- The ability to operate from ray of hope rather than fear of failure.

- Persistent in achieving results despite any hassles and setbacks.
- See setbacks as due to manageable rather than a personal flew.
- See the positive side of every situation and circumstance.
- Work with full charm in work and confidence.

3. LEADERSHIP SKILLS- the ability to provide vision to the teams, inspiring and guiding individuals to goal accomplishment.

- Plans for the teams and delegating work to them.
- Making every individual move towards mission.
- Channelizing team towards increasing productivity.

4. INTERPERSONAL UNDERSTANDING- The art of developing and maintaining positive relationships with others with proper understanding of other's perspective.

- Understanding the attitudes, interests and needs of others.
- Knowing what motivates others
- Understanding reasons for others behavior in particular situation.
- Giving regard to others feelings, emotions and moods.

5. QUEST FOR LEARNING- the urge to continuously find, imbibe

- **and use systematically information and knowledge.**
- Continuously seeking out information on any new updating
- technology.
- Observe the pattern of system and learn from the same.

- Translates new concepts into new applications.

TECHNICAL COMPETENCIES

1. PROBLEM UNDERSTANDING AND SOLVING- The ability to understand any issue in current state from all perspectives and finding applicable solutions. Distinguishing symptoms from causes of any issue.

- Anticipating ideas to resolve the issue quickly.
- Understand the needs of internal customers of organization and apply systems approach to find a workable solution by technology.

2. UNDERSTANDING OF NEW TECHNOLOGY- The ability to understand and appreciate the new tools and techniques with hybrid applications.

- Bent of mind to imbibe new technology.
- Appreciate use of new tools in current system to improve business performance.
- Awareness of environment in terms of networking, databases, storage systems etc.

1. SYSTEMS APPROACH- The ability to integrate all components of a system with support of information technology and see the effects in totality.

- Don't divide the process into sub processes.
- Find solution with integration approach.
- Holistic way of understanding any problem scenario to find solution.
- In competence mapping self appraisal is also an important feature for it provides a perspective from employees' point of view. It communicates his contributions, accomplishments and reflections on various facilitating and inhibiting factors which played a role on attaining or otherwise of the goals he set for himself.
- Analysis of performance of the employee through mutual discussion is a very crucial aspect where the design of the Competency Mapping format is of less importance than the process of conducting it. Reporting officer should not let their own biases creep in, put the subordinate at ease, set a constructive tone, listen to subordinates' self appraisal, present his own evaluation of subordinates' on the job performance,discuss areas of differEnce of opinion and arrive at mutually
- agreed workable solutions for realizing future goals and for the fulfillment of professional goals of the subordinate and the Application of performance management practices that enable organizations to improve the performance and bring in a performance driven culture is the need of the hour rather than
- Competency Mappings only.No doubt without the commitment of the top management it would just be very very difficult to bring this sort of change.

- This in fact calls for a cultural change wherein emphasis is not only given to the outcome or the end result but also on the process and effort made to achieve the result. While discussing of the process and effort we need to focus on the eadershipstyle, his approach of consulting others, his ability to learn, his approach as a team member, his effort in planning his days and week, and his overall orientation for subordinate development. For this what can be done is that once in a month or two an effort can be made by the supervisor to sit with his subordinate and have a face to face interaction in a non threatening atmosphere. What I have personally observed that it changes the motivation level of an individual onsiderably and in fact the employee makes all out effort to achieve the Organizational goals.

If you want the employee to do something, you must tellhim/her exactly what you want: what jobs or tasks are mostimportant, what skills and behaviors are required andacceptable, what goals should be accomplished, and what resultyou expect. There are two (2) primary ways to accomplish this:providing the employee with a job description and setting goalsand performance expectations.

Goals should be **SMART**:
·**Specific**.
·**Measurable**.
· **Attainable**.
·**Realistic**.
·**Time-limited**.
Remember: initiating and maintaining positive communicationabout work expectations and work performance is management's responsibility

4.4 Practicing Talent management in IT industries of India:
While for most of the Indian MNCs were the preferred employer of choice until now, all this changed in a matter of a year and a half as Indian IT companies managed to contain attrition and retain employees. The increase in retention rate (from 81% in FY09 to 87% in FY10) saw Indian companies managing to satisfy their employees on key parameters like salary, appraisal, and job content and managing slow down .A quick look at the best employers survey list shows some familiar names .

In FY11, the IT industry grew 19%, up significantly from the 8% growth that it recorded in FY10. Hiring was back in big ways. And so was attrition, according to DQ-CMR Best Employer Survey 2011. Attrition jumped from 13% last year to 19% this year. The higher attrition rate means more jobs and more exertion for firms to create workforce. Yet the sporadic news of layoffs from certain quarters continued to embitter the mood. But as FY11 drew to a close, the apprehensions of the return of the recession had by and large subsided.

Since the attrition rate jumped up, the year was of a strong HR exercise. They faced the challenge to maintain the workable workforce pool in their organizations. It was a time they had to solve employee issues quite persuasively, so that they would not hop jobs.

The attrition rate measured is based on the employees in any organization from April 2010 to March 2011. It was not a vanilla ride for companies, as they continue to lose their talent to their competitors. In the larger picture, we notice that a number of top executives took charge at their competitors. If we take stock of DQ Top200 companies, close to 70 companies have seen significant changes in their senior (C-level) leadership, including CEOs/MDs

The companies which encountered the highest levels of attrition in the IT industry included NIIT Technologies (#1), Citrix (#2), L&T Infotech (#3), Dimension Data (#4) and Synechron Technologies (#5), etc. They were faced with the challenge of maintaining a reasonable size of workforce. A strong application development and managed services player, NIIT Technologies was the worst hit by attrition as a number of employees succumbed to its competitors. Similarly other Best Employer companies had a lot of their employees hopping jobs more often than not.

Hence, managing attrition was a task to reckon with. The companies like Tulip, iGate, and Pitney Bowes, etc efficiently handled their workforce challenges thereby experiencing the least attrition. They ably and persuasively showed value to their employees, handled salary as well as work flexibility issues.

As understood, the pressure was mainly on HR departments. In the survey, conducted by the DQ it was revealed that the employee scores have gone up for the companies, whereas HR scores have dipped. Employee scores that influenced the rankings largely, however, speak of the attention paid to them. When overall HR scores are taken into consideration, the companies lose marks. On the HR parameter, Capgemini India scored most, followed by Mahindra Satyam and Synechron Technologies, whereas on the Employee parameters HCL clinched the top spot followed by Rolta and iGate.

In last few years or especially after the recession, the employee trust in Indian IT companies has gone high. They have proved their capability in addressing the market challenges and managing the slowdown in a much better way than the MNC counterparts. This is the reason that top 3 places in the DQ-CMR Best Employer Survey 2011 are held by HCL Info systems, Rolta India and iGATE, which are Indian MNCs. They have scored high on preferred employer of choice parameters, matching employee expectations, which otherwise was not a cakewalk. In addition, they have kept their retention rate higher than competitors and addressed issues pertaining to salary, appraisal, and job content.

The economic recession of 2008-2009 is a fading memory, with a steady 8% plus GDP growth in 2010-11, showing promise of the heady days of 2007-08, when the economy was briefly poised to cross the barrier of 10% GDP growth. Yet it has been a season of discontent .Inflation has forced many employees, particularly below managerial levels, to postpone major decisions like asset creation. Though India inc has somewhat reluctantly opened its purse mostly in terms of variable pay .while most organizations are hiring, not many are talking about doubling about employee numbers in 2-3 years. Things are better, but even the best employers are not immune to cynicism about governance and talent management. The young have now joined the workforce. The data reveals that 73% of the workforce in India inc. is less than 35 years of age. In the year 2010, it was found from a survey that the overall perception of the employees 'positive perceptions about their organization has gone down by across the board and for the first time in the 25 best workplaces. It can be deducted that employees 'expectations have gone up post recession period in the organization. In the best workplaces, it was evident that the organization linked their business to their people, thus enabling the People-service-Profit chain; be it Google that says its core value is, "we want to work with great people, or HCL technologies who talk about their people-first culture. These are focused group of organizations with a sharp focus on the bottom line, but they know that attracting and retaining the right people is the key to achieve the business results. They are able to link their people philosophy with their strategy and structures for employee collaboration, with clear measures.

The IT and ITES organizations which were a part of the study focused on key "differentiators" to create a great place to work for and attract the best talent in the Industry.

1. Equity- Fair share of profits /fair pay and creating "special and unique" benefits. Majority of the companies gives profit sharing on a monthly basis to all employees.

2. Reliability- management's actions match their words/management delivers on their promises and gives straight answers. Agilent, Scope, Accenture are some of the organizations that have a transparent feedback process for managers and recognize those whose teams gives them high scores in this area.

3. Impartiality-people avoid politicking /managers avoid playing favorites and promotions go to the deserving people. Everyone in the organization can calculate their own increments. The CEO's salary is capped at 40 times the entry level salary.

4. Caring- Flexibility, work-life balance and creating a fun place to work is another area whose importance has grown manifold in recent years with increase of younger employees in the workforce.

The above differentiators were more difficult to achieve than arranging engagement parties and numerous other activities that organizations do to attract and retain the employees. The workplaces designed and implemented such systems and processes that enable their senior managers to deliver the above. Absence of work in these areas cannot be compensated by doing more in other areas. The focus of these organizations is to equip the people managers, at all levels, with the skills required to engage with employees to build trust, pride and camaraderie, which create a great work place for their respective teams. The best workplaces have institutionalized the process of seeking employee feedback and linking the people manager's 'scorecard' to his performance review. One of the biggest challenges in organizations in India is inadequate skills of people managers and lack of incentive to be great people managers. Therefore it is imperative for the organization to build the pillars of the organization by creating great people managers. A common mistake many organizations make is prematurely communicating to the external world what a great employer they are, without doing the groundwork about their systems and processes which create a great place to work for. In organizations with strong employer brands there is very little dissonance between what employees experience internally and what the organizations communicates externally. In a study conducted by the great place to work Institute, India shows that the following factors have a disproportionate impact on overall employee sentiment in an organization:

1. Attracting talent for key positions – employees believe they are working in a great place to work if they see great talent joining their organization. People want to associate themselves with outstanding talent.

2. Equity-treated fairly across different levels. As a rule, employees in organizations with less visible hierarchy, greater egalitarian spirit and more equitable power distribution, tend to have a more positive perception. The CEO of Intel in India sits in exactly the same cabin that everyone else has, travels by economy class like any other employee and has a laptop that is older than the ones given to entry level employees.

3. Creating a fun place to work – statistical analysis only confirms which should be obvious, that a young India and a young workforce want to enjoy their work-life and their time to work.

Last four years research strongly indicates that creating practices, policies, processes and managerial capabilities to build equity, impartiality, reliability, caring, sense of fun at work and ability to attract high quality talent is the way to go. And thinking through and articulating "people philosophy and its nexus to business results," and systematically institutionalizing these practices phase by phase will make this journey more success prone.

Every organization today has to be deeply concerned about selecting and retaining competent, committed people - also known as talent. Accurately describing what talent looks like in a specific organization in specific jobs is the first major step in creating an effective approach to HRApplications.

Competency technology allows an organization to implement HR Applications or Talent Management system that integrates Staffing, Performance Management, Succession Planning, and Development in a way that increases the percentage of outstanding performers in the workplace

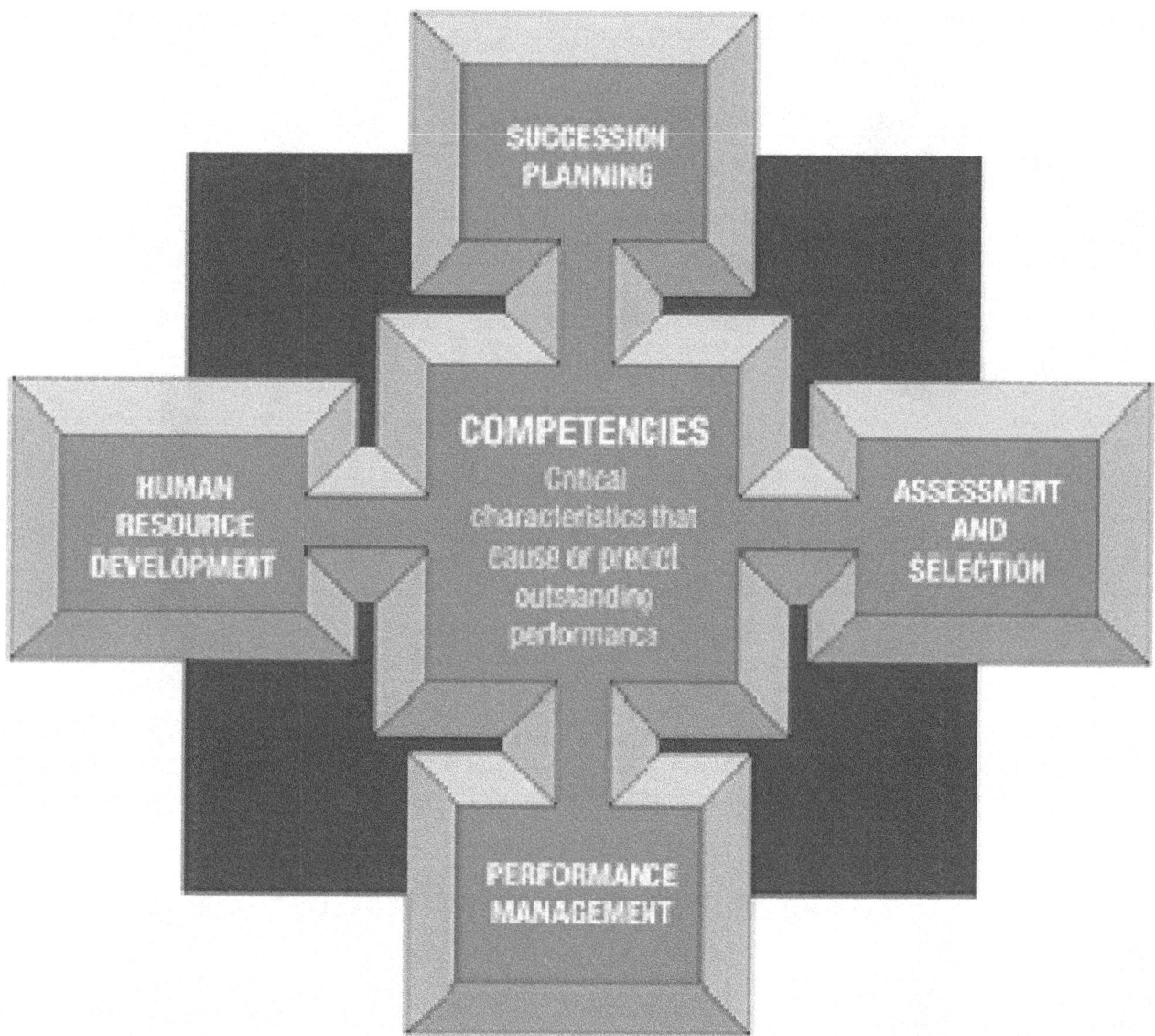

FIG :4.1 TALENT MANAGEMENT SYSTEM

TALENT MANAGEMENT : IN PRACTICE

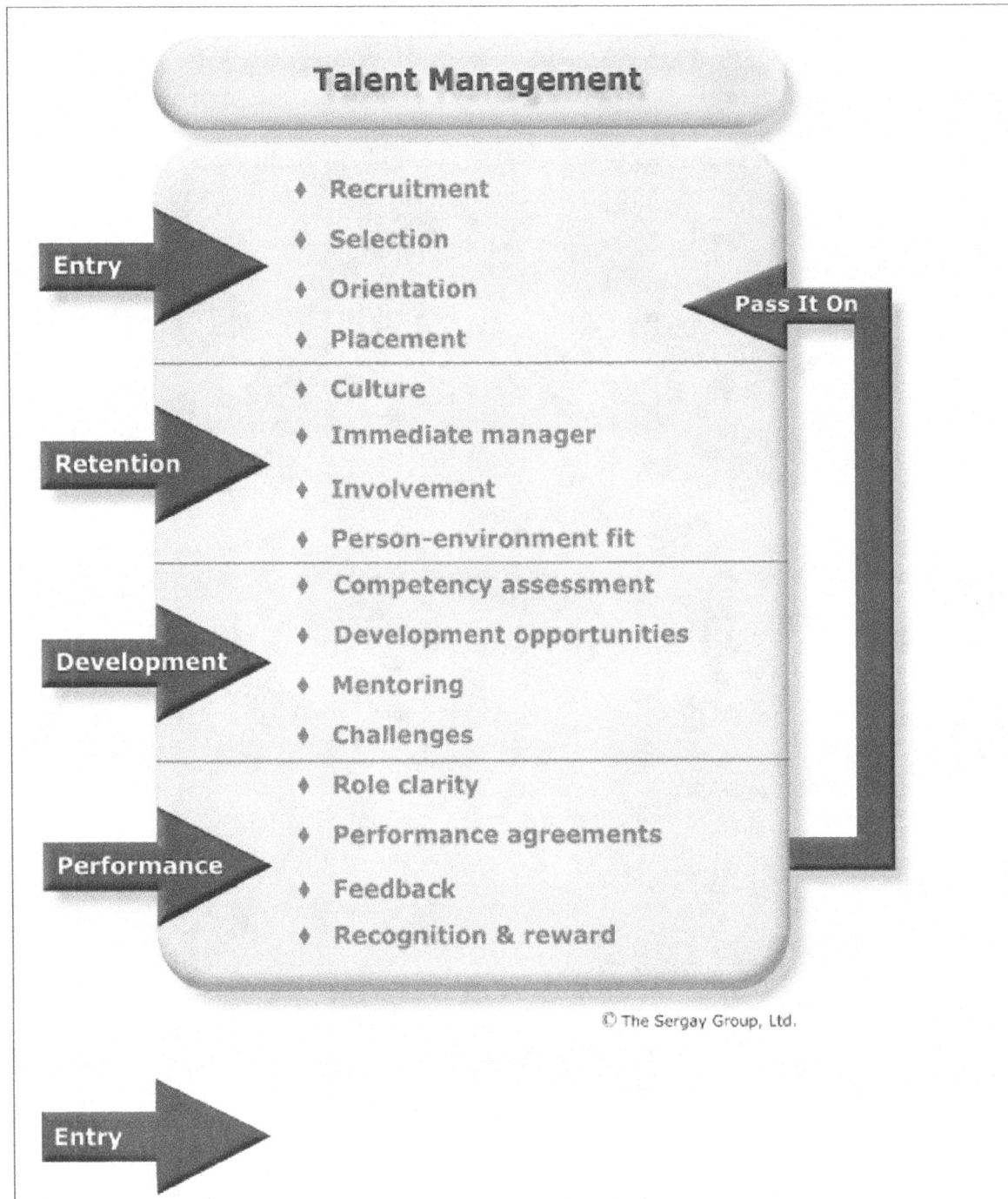

Talent Management

Entry
- Recruitment
- Selection
- Orientation
- Placement

Retention
- Culture
- Immediate manager
- Involvement
- Person-environment fit

Development
- Competency assessment
- Development opportunities
- Mentoring
- Challenges

Performance
- Role clarity
- Performance agreements
- Feedback
- Recognition & reward

Pass It On

Entry

© The Sergay Group, Ltd.

Determine the key leverage skill sets required by the organization in order to move into the future. The organization's strategic plan should give an indication of these, as well as what constitutes the core competence that will ensure a future for the organization. This will all, in turn, direct you to what talent you should be sourcing.

- The organization should source the required people from the appropriate avenues.

- Organization should ensure to have very detailed job descriptions that include specific competencies required.

- Apply behavior-based interviewing to select the best candidates.

- The ability to retain talent starts from the quality of the first point of contact.

- Organization should carefully consider the way they orient a new employee into the culture of the organization, the work area, and the specific job.

- Assist a new employee to transition into the organization and to be able to produce a quality deliverable within the first three months of tenure. This will go a long way to ensuring that the placement will be successful.

Retention →

Retaining the talent will not solely depend on what the organization pays them. It has been found from exit interviews that many high performing individuals will leave an organization for the same or, in some cases, even less remuneration if other needs of theirs are not being met.

- The culture, the way things are done around here, plays a huge role in creating a work environment that will draw individuals in or repel them. The culture is created through the systems, processes, technology, structure, leadership, and behaviors of people and teams in the organization.

- Congruity in values between the organization and the employee will also exert influence on an individual's decision to commit to an organization.

- The most important relationship for any individual in an organization is the relationship with one's immediate manager. Ensure that your managers have the skills to constructively lead their direct reports and their teams.

- Involving individuals in decision-making in their areas of responsibility. Involve high performers in cross-functional projects. Allow people to feel that they are making a difference to the organization

- Organization should ensure that each new employee is the right fit for the organization's culture, and then ensure fit with the work area, and then the actual job. Revisit this person-environment fit, as people and circumstances change and some adjusting or repositioning may be required for best results.

Development

Development is about growing people to meet both their own and the organization's needs. Development plays a large part in talent management. No organization can afford to promise a person a particular job through development. At best, the organization can offer the promise of making a person more eligible to be part of a pool of talent who would be looked at when positions open up, and then only if the existing skills match the position requirements.

❖ Competencies need to be broken down into their four components:

❖ Knowledge (what you know)

❖ Skills (what you know how to do)

❖ Behaviour (what you do)

❖ Attitude (what you are willing to do)

❖ Assess every employee's competency profile. This would include establishing if there are any competency deficiencies that are responsible for the gaps that exist between the actual and desired current performance, as well as gaps between current competencies and possible future performance needs.

❖ Avoid getting trapped into only developing weaknesses; focus on keeping strengths at the cutting edge.

❖ Create opportunities for development through different methods; such as, training, job shadowing, and job rotation, involvement in projects, cross-functional exposure, and teamwork.

❖ Organization should ensure that the training provided is linked to the strategic needs of the organization.

❖ Mentoring can play an important role in developing others, as well as strengthening relationships. This goes a long way to influencing feelings of belonging to an organization.

❖ Build in stretch deliverables for high potential individuals to produce, as being challenged by what they do often meets individual's personal needs.

❖   Link talent development into the performance management system.

Performance

Identifying potential is one component of talent management, but actual performance reflects on usable talent. Sound performance management practices are crucial.

❖   Clarify roles throughout the organization, ensuring alignment with the strategy, as well as across functions.

❖   Involve individuals in setting their own performance agreements. These agreements need to be firm on objectives to be met, deliverables to be produced and at what quality standards, actions to be taken, and the deadlines.

❖   People need to be held accountable for what they deliver, but against performance agreements that function as working documents so that adjustments are made to them as circumstances dictate.

❖   Feedback is essential - ongoing, objective and constructive.

❖   Positive reinforcement, when done with genuineness, goes a long way to making people feel recognized.

❖   Tap into what would make talented individuals within your organization feel rewarded; it is not necessarily always about money or upward mobility.

Identify high performance individuals who display characteristics favored by the organization. Use this pool of talent to help transition new employees into the organization. This will speed up acculturization, and ensure the entrenching of desired ways of operating. It has also been found that the better the first experiences of a new employee, the more likely the individual is to be retained by the organization and the quicker performance results can be achieved.

Talented individuals can also serve as mentors throughout the organization and it can be seen as recognition or as a reward to do so. Innovations by talented individuals can be introduced into systems, processes, and approaches in the organization in the pursuit of continuous improvement. They should also be recognized for this.

Ultimately, talent management that is based on respect and transparency will go a long way to ensure that you access, select, empower, and retain top talent for your organization.

4.4.1 Talent management at Accenture

Accenture is a global management consulting, technology services and outsourcing company, with net revenues of US$19.70 billion for the fiscal year ending August 2011. Committed to delivering

293

innovation, Accenture collaborates with its clients to help them become high-performance organizations.

For Accenture, the emphasis is on trying to help businesses improve their performance. The world's largest consulting firm, Accenture offers management consulting, information technology and systems integration, and business process outsourcing services to customers around the globe. The company divides its practices into five main operating groups: communications and high technology, financial services, government, products, and resources.

The Accenture UK website identifies six core values that define who they are and how they operate:

Exceptional talent: Accenture has more of the world's most talented people assembled under one roof than any other organization. It's stimulating and turns out to be productive.

Continuous learning: Accenture being a knowledge-based enterprise, joining Accenture means committing oneself to lifelong learning and personal development.

High-quality work: The people at Accenture are driven to provide new solutions on how to improve businesses and work with clients to help them seize new opportunities.

A collaborative approach: openness and collaboration are integral to the way it works. To enable its clients to a higher level of performance, it develops a deep understanding of all aspects of their business and how they interconnect.

An entrepreneurial spirit: Accenture was created by entrepreneurs with a vision of the future. It's driven forward by future focused individuals who are eager to share in the success of a global business leader.

A diverse workforce: Accenture believes in creating a diverse workforce by encouraging people from wide range of cultural, educational and geographic backgrounds.

As professional services organizations, Accenture's focus is on making sure that its approach to talent is one which is aligned to its need to ensure that it has the best people with the right skills for its clients. There is remarkable clarity about what the organization requires of its people, what skills are needed, what is expected of them on client projects and what they need to do to ensure they continue to develop. At the heart of this is a process of performance management that is thorough and rigorous and manages the line between delivering for the organization whilst also delivering for the individual.

Accenture could be described as 'an up or out culture'; one where people have a choice to flourish or are supported to make the choice to leave. There is a strong commitment to the development of its people that supports that choice. It regards its whole population as talent ,as this is its main asset when supporting its customers . A strong feature of their approach is their performance management process which is seen as the key factor in its success at managing talent.

While the success of project delivery is measured in terms of total team contribution, individual contribution is also measured and compared to peers. This forms the basis for career progression. There is no structured process of fast streaming or developing high potentials, it is very much down to the individual to make their own decisions about opportunities they want to pursue and the speed with which they are promoted.

Talent dimensions:

Dimension1: Size of the talent pool

Everyone in Accenture is defined as talent. The label of 'talented' is seen as unhelpful in an environment where meritocracy is valued. Within the organization the use of the word 'talent' as attributed to individuals is very limited However, it is worth remembering that 10% of the organization is counseled out every year.

Everybody has access to the same opportunities in terms of careers, coaching and counseling. It is difficult to be a stable contributor within the organization since its performance management process drives individuals to grow and develop; falling into a stable contributor category will ultimately lead to being managed out of the organization.

Dimension-2: Entry criteria

As everybody is defined as talent and the sub division of this talent pool is done by job grade, entry is through promotion. There are annual promotion cycles where those people who are eligible for promotion are considered against their peers. They are considered in relation to their readiness for the next job grade as well as the business need for new entrants within the next job grade. There is a lot of support for individuals to reach the next job grade. This is particularly provided through the counselor relationship, the training and development as well as the access to stretching client work. The process of laddering whereby people are ranked against their peers is described as rigorous time consuming and at the heart of ensuring that the system is seen to be, open and fair.

The ease of entry into the most senior positions in the company is more difficult. The promotion from senior manager to senior executives is seen as less transparent than promotion to the more junior grades. There are a larger number of people at the senior levels waiting for potential promotion. it is unclear to some where they sit within this talent pool and what needs to be done to break through to the most senior levels.

Dimension 3: Accenture is aware that in their world which needs to ensure that every one in a consulting capacity is sufficiently talented there is no use for the labeling of people as talented or not. At junior levels the decision to promote talent is very clear and sits with the collective project leaders, whilst calibration is ensured by the HR and independent assessors. It is less clear within Accenture how the future leaders of the business are selected and developed.

Dimension: 4

Because the talent pool is defined as everybody, the definition of talent is relatively permanent. It is unusual for people to be demoted to lower grades-they are normally managed out . This does not however mean that everyone in the talent pool is expected to be a future leader of the organization. However the success of the organization is very much defined by its ability to provide its clients with a 'fit for purpose' intervention. In this respect those individuals that are successful will have to be able to flex according to changing client requirements. Therefore the definition of talent is very much influenced by the client requirements.

Dimension 5: Recruitment as a source of talent

This is highly dynamic organization where people are expected and encouraged to move through promotion grades. If an individual remains too long in a grade they are eventually managed out of the business. Therefore there is constant process of spotting the right talent both internally and externally. In addition to practice leaders being responsible for spotting talent the Accenture website is a source of talent-it is an accessible and focused way of providing potential new recruits with a sense of what working in Accenture may be like.

Dimension 6: Transparency

Talent management at Accenture could be described as being extremely transparent. Often this transparency and openness stems from how well the processes of performance management are operated rather than explicit conversations about how people are seen. In reality what this means is that people often infer more about how they are seen than they are actually told. This manifests itself in terms of the projects that they get resourced on and the regularity with which they are laddered in the top, or bottom quartile.

The requirements for performance are well articulated and understood throughout the organization. There was no sense that people didn't understand this or in fact that the organization needed to do more.

Developing talent

Dimension 7:

The career path for each individual is clearly laid out and structured. Each job grade is accompanied with guidelines in terms of time expected in grade, and what people can expect to remain within this grade for this period of time if they are performing in relation to their peers. Some individuals that consistently outperform their peers from a holistic perspective can be accelerated through the grades- although the flex is still within very narrow parameters around the guidelines.

Dimension 8:

Accenture openly says that one of its vital areas of focus is to ensure that they have the best people for their client projects and that the only way of doing this is to have a rigorous approach to personal development and make it clear that learning is key success factor not only for individuals but also for success of the organization. Consultants describe the opportunities they have the appropriate level of information to do their job.

In attracting people to work for Accenture an ability to learn is one of the key areas of focus and its development activities support this.

Dimension 9: There is plenty of support for individuals, however they are expected to make the most of this but always within a context that they are expected to perform .Failing to do this will result on them exiting the company.

Dimension10: influence on career

The decision to progress within the organization is very much in the have had as much opportunity possible to realize your potential. Anyone who works hard and shows a willingness to grow is supported and rewarded, whether they are a high flier or not.

People stay with Accenture because they regard it is as an opportunity to grow and learn within an environment which is externally highly regarded and professional .The downside of this for the organization ,and an upside for individuals ,is that they are subject to regular offers from rival consultancies as well as other organizations.

Dimension11:

The openness and fairness associated with the performance management process is largely a feature of the way in which individual's performance is calibrated and assessed against their peers. It is seen as a considerable strength of the process that an individual's final performance rating is the subject of multiple inputs from project leaders that have been connected to that individual throughout the year.

Dimension12: organizational values

The culture of the organization is customer and results focused. The organization has a strong performance ethos; people are expected to work hard on behalf of the organization and in return the organization will invest in them and their future. It is high performance-driven environment.

There is high level of currency placed on the ability of an individual to adapt to different situations. The organization's recruitment and resourcing processes emphasize the need to spot this ability. Adaptability is described in some ways as being more important than technical skills. There is also a strong emphasis on bringing difference and diversity into the organization. The talent pool is well represented by people from very diverse backgrounds both in terms of ethnicity and profession .This is regarded as a significant strength of the organization and is encouraged in its recruitment practice.

Performance management is operated with huge dedication and practice .It is described in the organization as being open and fair. As a result individuals have clarity about their position in the talent pool. Promotion cycles are run regularly and with the support of career counselors individuals are expected to make their own progression.

The process of resourcing people onto projects is done to ensure first ,that the client has at its heart and understanding that the capability of its people are its business. Development is open and available through a variety of access points including online and regular career point skills training.

A key factor in the culture is related to the willingness of each individual to learn. Individuals that are capable of learning and launching themselves into challenging, stretching experiences are highly valued. The organization's processes and culture support these types of people.

Dimension 13:

The level of risk that the organization is prepared to take is medium. There is no high potential fast track and therefore the process for spotting and fast tracking outstanding talent relies on the performance management process. Since the environment is highly performance driven it is vital that success at the client level is ensured which may in some situations discriminate against high levels of risk being taken.

Structures and systems to support talent management:

Dimension 14: performance management

Performance management is done with great rigor at Accenture and forms the backbone of the process. This tends to be done on the evidence –based approach. Project managers who are asked for concrete examples of people's performance rather than what they think or feel. Project managers who are not good at performance management lose people. The project managers understand that a key part of their role is to ensure that at the start of every project each individual has the necessary level of clarity about what needs to be achieved.

Associated with the performance management process is a culture where feedback is not only hugely valued but where it is regularly used as part of an individual's development.

Dimension 15: the process of performance management is highly structured. It is well understood and the checks and balances that exist make sure that it is seen as fair and robust. Specifically the roles of counselor, independent assessor, people advocate and HR is charged with this . There is also a high level of compliance within the practice to ensure that these processes are adhered to.

Dimension16: Technology is used widely as a tool for accessing development. Every individual has access to my learning.com which is an online tool for development options. This also provides access to the variety of tools, systems and methodologies that form the basis of the consulting practice.

Dimension17: The human performance practice is engaged in constant review process of its approach to its own talent. Through the support and challenge of robust line ,HR and people advocates, the issues associated with organizational and individual performance are regularly reviewed.

Dimension18: ownership of talent is distributed throughout the organization .There is no formal process of fast streaming or high potential programme that is owned centrally. Therefore the ownership of talent is largely devolved to the rigor of the process; In particular the clarity with which people understand in relation to their peers and then secondly the support they get from their counselor.

The process of performance management is operated by project leaders who have the responsibility to ensure that the appropriate level of data is gathered in respect to each individual. For each performance cycle there is a three month window of gathering data –this is held as being one of the key responsibilities of project leaders and they are held accountable for ensuring this is done rigorously. Individuals are aware that this process is ongoing and are encouraged to make sure that they are well represented. As a check to the progress, independent assessors also review that the quality and consistency of the laddering to make sure that the fairness and transparency is upheld.

4.4.2 Talent management process of Wipro:

Employer Branding: Azim Premji was keen on preserving values of the organization, which made it to tick in rough times. As the company grew and diversified, Azim premji sought to keep its core values constant. In one case, Wipro's refusal to pay a $10,000 bribe to activate a power station initially adopted for reasons of personal conviction, Premji gradually realized these values were good business policy. They helped Wipro attract quality employees and customers, as well as better suppliers and partners. Wipro's early focus on quality and integrity, the company enabled the company to be better prepared to counter the foreign competition that entered India after economic liberalization in 1991. Wipro was one of the few Indian companies that could confidently compete globally. From 1973 to 1997, only minor changes were made to the "set of beliefs." However, in 1995, Premji and his team felt the company needed to revisit its fundamental beliefs and become more customer focused. Starting in 1998 with the help of Shombit Sengupta, a Paris-based consultant, Wipro went through an 18 month self- examination and market research exercise. At the end, the company rearticulated its beliefs through a Promise statement and laid out a five year vision. At the same time, it adopted a new logo-a multi colored Sunflower-as a symbol of Wipro's single corporate identity. The promise statement emphasized four values: human values, Integrity, innovative solutions and value for money.

Premji thought the explicit statement of these values ,while very general and hardly novel would heighten the pressure on Wipro to live up to them- through both legal and end –user exposures. The exercise, he believed was important to temper the growing concern with the bottom line and to strengthen the "emotional glue that engages people and keeps them together in an organization. "Emotion plays a very large component in the way people run their lives, and we need to be sensitive to the fact," he noted. He felt the values were a reminder" to treat people as unique-both employees and customers –not to brand them." and to consider things "from the human point of view." For Azim Premji Wipro was softer on people decisions than perhaps commercially expedient."

Developing People: Premji's early turn to professional development set the tone for the future. DileepRanjekar, corporate executive vice president, Human resources, attributed Wipro's growth in large measure to its processes for selecting and developing people. At Wipro the first thing was to put efforts to understand the people from all angles –not just from the current job point of view, but also from the angle of what the person can become. In selecting employees Wipro looked for both technical competence and good fit with values. In 1994-95, the company began making use of its "Wipro Leader" attributes in hiring and development activities.

Competencies Defined: The seven attributes: **customer focus ,high energy ,self confidence , ownership ,aggressive commitments , commitments ,commitment to excellence and ability to build star performers –were also used as the basis for 360 –degree evaluations of all team leaders** , conducted yearly and tracked over time.

With the rise in recruiting and leadership demands, Wipro had developed a number of tools to aid in its hiring and development activities. For instance, a "preference inventory" was used to assess to candidate's needs, preferences, and expectations in given role- and thus to help focus the discussion during interviews. In 1999, competency models tailored to different positions and businesses were introduced as tools for selection, training and development. These models helped determine what skills an individual might need for a given job or performance level. In addition to the 360-degree evaluations, managers could also get feedback through "skip level" assessments –team members evaluations communicated through an external facilitator.

Wipro had traditionally placed strong emphasis on learning and development. Wipro invested some 5% of its personnel costs in training, and all managers were expected to devote seven days a year to training.

In 2000, Wipro offered an array of opportunities to learn technical and managerial skills. Premji made a point of dropping in for casual lunches and dinners at many of Wipro's own programs, such as its leadership series, which included five different courses –one for each level from entry leader to strategic leader. The human resources function kept tabs on new developments and training needs. In 2000,Ranjan Acharya, Vice president ,Corporate Human Resources ,was heading up a team of eight people investigating the new competencies needed by Wipro leaders- cross cultural ,personal productivity ,teaming and so on. In June 199, Wipro has begun using the Software Engineering Institute (SEI) people Capability Maturity Model (P-CMM) to help managers improve their effectiveness in managing people, developing talent, and building teams. The SEI was a Carnegie Mellon university based program sponsored by U.S Department of Defense. Through an accelerated learning program, the company hoped to develop more project managers from the large pool of programmers in the software services division.

The talent pipeline

The key issue which emerged from the roundtables had to do with staffing. All the operating units complained of being short on software professionals, and as a consequence having to turn clients away. The recruiting process, they charged, was not generating sufficient number of new employees. On the technology side, the resume inflow was insufficient and candidates for software project management positions were in short supply. In other areas, there were too many resumes for the HR function to read and process.

Another part of the staffing problem had to do with how people were being deployed. In 1999, the company hired aggressively in anticipation of more business, which did not materialize resulting in a utilization rate of 60% versus an ideal of 70-75%. Furthermore, even though the company had low utilization rate, it had been refusing business from customers because of a shortage of available employees at a particular time or location .Year 2000 became critical for the employees. There was large scale employee attrition. Since 1996, the biggest source of attrition was people with two to four years' experience going overseas ,especially to the United States where IT professionals were in great demand .Over 70% of the employees who quit Wipro did so to go to overseas, especially United States, both for employment(50%) and higher education (20%) . Another source of attrition accounting for some 15-20% of Wipro's losses ,were opportunities in India –start-ups, some 300 smaller software companies ,and U.S companies.

The HR managers of the organization spotted that when people were engaged and working on challenging assignments, there were very little attrition. Wipro had to walk the fine line between customer's needs, only part of which was e-commerce work, and keeping employees happy. Another important learning was to provide learning opportunities to the employees so that the employees feel that their ideas are listened to and they are valued by the organization.

Employee retention strategies:

To improve retention, the company ensured the employees got the right work environment and right projects to prove their mettle and eventually get the right compensation packages. The company tried to ensure a strong link between performance and rewards for its top 20-25% performers, and its objective was to have less than 5% turnover from the top 10% of performers. Every time somebody from the top 10% quit Wipro, the information was up the ranks. For grades 3 and above, the top grades of the 10 –level systems, the information went all up to the chairman. Wipro kept track of people's reasons for leaving through exit interviews. In these interviews, employees were also asked what they liked and did not like about the company. The interviewees' names were kept confidential. All answers were analyzed and the compiled results were sent weekly to the senior management team in HR.

To improve internal customer service, The HR department set goals and objectives with clear accountability for all service functions. They also developed internal customer service measures and feedback mechanisms. Previously the company had employee perception surveys once every two or three. Then they implemented employee perception surveys once every two or three years. They implemented the "**dipstick**" survey of 12 simple questions to see how employees were doing every 6 months. To strengthen the relationships among employees, Wipro initiated employee celebrations and events ,started several special interest groups such as employees of a particular "batch" or entering cohort known as "batch mates", and created occasions for everybody to get together with their families.

In an effort to attract and retain key talent, Wipro put in place a stock option program in Oct.1999. Although Wipro had first issued options in 1984, and was the first company in India to do so, only a handful of people had been involved and amounts were small. Wipro also used "shadow options "for a few select individuals since 1993. Under the October 1999 plan, 2,000,000 options were issued and eligibility was extended to high-performing managers in grades5 and above – in total about 90% of senior and middle management and 30% of the total employee base. The decision to grant options was based on individual's performance, their criticality, their market value and their potential. The average grant was 1000 options at a strike price of Rs.1, 086, vesting over a five year period, though the top 10% of performers at all levels received sizeable grants two to two and half times above the meridian.

4.4.3 Talent management at TCS:

TCS pioneered several best practices in the Indian IT industry. Senior management always kept a record of the intellectual assets present in the company and which projects they were working on. TCS decided on its manpower requirements after taking into consideration the views of the senior consultants who provided information on changes in technology and the demand in new skills . Based on the information the HR department would decide on it recruitment strategies.

It gave utmost importance to its human resource function and believed in the school of thought "good ideas can come from any level of the organization and teams can do better than the individuals.

Recruitment at TCS:

TCS believed that recruiting the right people was the secret of success of any organization. TCS followed the waterfall recruitment process (figure-4.3). The company viewed recruitment as an ongoing process. To bridge the corporate-campus gap, TCS conducted faculty development programmes across the country. The process started from accrediting institutions from which students were recruited. For any institute to be accredited, it needed to comply with a set of parameters which included standard of entrance tests, library, faculty and availability of computers. Various research initiatives were being undertaken by TCS in partnership with institutes, not only in India but across the globe. Such relationships with universities were basically for globalizing the workforce.

Figure: Waterfall recruitment process

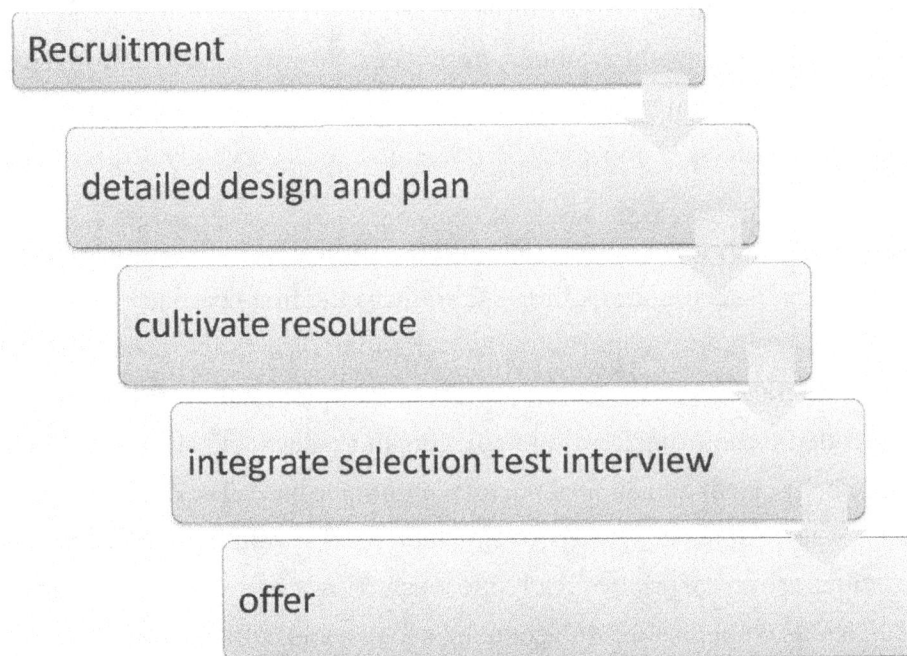

Recruitment

detailed design and plan

cultivate resource

integrate selection test interview

offer

Source: Gwelani Geeta, "Journey to Excellence,"september2000.

The recruitment team was trained in various interview techniques. Most of the interviews were structured to determine individual's orientation towards IT. Forming a part of interview panel was at least one psychiatrist and one language expert. Along with his/her technical knowledge, the candidate's attitude and language skills was also gauged. TCS had also built a robust holistic programme, which included faculty development programmes, workshops and annual conclaves for the professors and teachers which helped them to groom fresher at the entry level itself.

Within TCS, the intranet had announcements about the various positions and requirements. The TCS website also listed the jobs. Being an equal opportunities employer ,the age limit was judged on competency. TCS considered competency as critical knowledge and skills producing key outputs in performance.

TCS conducted written tests, technical and management interviews for selecting trainees and persons with less than two year of experience, but for laterals it did not have written tests. The process included short listing based on certain eligibility criteria pertaining to the student's academic record and domain/specializations, aptitude tests with group discussions. The attributes they typically looked at included technical excellence, analytical skills, professionalism, good communication skills, reality, willingness to work beyond boundaries and team work.

Even though TCS was hiring in large numbers, The HR team believed that hiring was a challenge. The hiring of experienced professionals took place through the year, while campus offers for freshers were conducted according to placement seasons at colleges. The experienced professionals were to be hired under business and practices such as SAP, BI, KM; etc. Off campus recruitments for fresher were conducted periodically for any additional requirements.

Training:

The company had been investing more than 6% of its revenue in training. In recognizing the potential strength of people and groups, TCS helped the participants learn and retain communication skills that could be used in everyday workplace experiences, training was highly interactive and was specifically and uniquely designed for large, medium or small businesses, public agencies, nonprofit organizations, and professional and community groups.

TCS training also built both the individual's and organization's potential to work through conflicts. It was accomplished by improving their decision making skills, teaching them collaborative techniques and helping them recognize and implement the many processes involved in positive change.

Benefits of the TCS training programs:

- Improved workplace environments as they are safer and more productive
- Lessened the chance of costly, destructive and personally damaging litigation
- Reduces misunderstandings, grudges and unresolved conflicts so they no longer undermine the group's or team's ability to work together.

- Decreased the recruitment and staffing cycle time and related costs for training and development.
- Increased the core competency skill base by adding value to the organization.

In 1997,it set up a state of art training centre , "Technopark"at Thiruvanthanapuram and invested INR five billion to make it one of the best. It offered training both to new recruits and TCS staffers. The centre provided its employees with three kinds of training programmes-technology, attitudes and management.

TCS has been presented with golden peacock Training award in recognition of being the biggest state of art training centre in Asia.

Retention and Attrition

TCS has a Manpower Allocation Task committee (MATC) which determined the career path for employees. MATC was supported by a system that helped in identifying not just competencies for a role but also the level of competency needed to fit. The committee was responsible for the allocation of every individual to projects depending on the set of competencies and the level of capability in these competencies. The value proposition that they offer to the employees is an aspiration based career across project management, technology, domain and sales streams. This is enabled by ongoing competency development, differentiated compensation and various work life balance initiatives, as well as the chance to work in different markets and geographies in our network of 169 offices in 35 countries. This had helped TCS attract and retain employees at all levels. TCS also emerged as the best employer in the Indian IT industry in the Best Employer survey 2006.

4.4.4.Talent Management practice at Infosys:

Infosys believes in the progressive reality that HR is much more than a support function. As a matter of fact it views HR as a springboard to drive business. HR plays a strategic role at Infosys that requires dealing with business issues. The challenges thrown up by the fast changing Business environment has also opened a window to a plethora of opportunities like dramatic shift in costs through global talent sourcing and de-risking through global task distribution, achieving global operational excellence through a judicious mix of technology and service models.

Solving the talent paradox is not an impossible task .but it requires an integrated, strategic approach to talent management, from planning to sourcing to training ,development and retention. Insightful and integrated talent management practices can not only help an organization overcome a talent shortage ,but also deliver financial results that will win the approval of all the stakeholders.

At a time when organizations are debating the strategic importance of their human resources ,Infosys human capital figure in its balance sheet affirming their asset value. As a knowledge driven organization, Infosys recognizes the key role of its human assets in sustaining and increasing it's of competitiveness.

In addition to ensure that talent is optimally harnessed to stay ahead of the curve, innovation is the constant process at Infosys. One such initiative is the Infosys Leadership Institute (ILI) with its vision of making its leadership and managerial development integral to business. The mandate of ILI is to:

- Enhance managerial capabilities for increased customer satisfaction
- Develop leaders to take the organizational vision forward.
- Partner with customers to build high performing multicultural teams.

ILI's dedicated campus in India offers a unique atmosphere that encourages thinking, learning and executing. Through multiple initiatives like Pravesh(a continuous learning program for first-time project managers) and Global Business Finishing school(a learning initiative to make every new entrant into Infosys ready for the job in quick time).ILI has ensured that Infosys maintains its edge in talent over competitors for superior business results.

Recruitment

With changing employee demographics in the flat world, the entire recruitment and deployment landscape has changed. It has become essential to source talent where it is most cost effective and deploys it where it creates maximum value. To achieve this objective, Infosys has developed an innovative workforce management strategy – the global talent program. This is a sustained effort by any company to recruit from campuses outside of India and develop the skills of a global work force through training assignments in India. Post training, these resources are deployed by Infosys in their home countries. Increased profitability, reduced costs, increased market share, improved customer service, higher stock value, increased productivity and higher retention rates – these were the criteria that the **Optimas team** looks when evaluating the initiative which led to the initiative winning the **Optimas Award in the Global Outlook category for 2007.**

Employee engagement:

Infosys keeps its employees engaged and enthusiastic in demanding 24/7 work environment necessary to serve its global clientele. A key challenge is countering competition that eyes Infosys trained personnel. To meet these challenges ,a wide variety of programs foster an environment that provides the best aspects of universities but with professionalism that a work place requires. These programs have helped stem attrition, which is below the industry average and has made Infosys top employer of choice.

There is an innovative **online employee and manager Self service delivery** vehicle by:

Analyzing existing processes and applications

Creating online information architecture for consistent, location and time independent access to information for all employees.

The outcome of the self delivery solution was it could provide an interactive application giving employees access to and control over information, independent of time and location constraints. It also increased responsiveness and faster decision making through inline communication channels, it directly saved employee time through automated HR tasks and saved empowered the employees.

The Infosys value proposition:

1. Leverage talent as the strategic differentiator

   - Align people strategy with business strategy to drive business results in an increasingly level playing field.
   - Measure HR contribution to business growth by identifying the right metrics and through continuous improvement.
   - Shift to business performance focused culture.

2. **Acquire and deploy talent globally**

   - Establish the right value proposition require to attract global talent by becoming an "Employer of Choice"
   - Design and implement scalable processes to acquire talent and deploy it where it offers best value.

3. **Scale up to serve increased demands for talent:**

   - Design and implement robust and scalable HR processes to engage ,motivate and retain talent
   - Continuously augment workforce competency by imparting new skill sets and revitalizing existing ones
   - Enable high performance collaborative culture through automated information and self service applications.

4. **Achieve Global operational excellence**

   - Align HRIT strategy to people and Business strategy and leverage it for optimal business results.
   - Identify and leverage appropriate Global Service Delivery Model to optimize operational efficiency and maximize benefits.

4.5 .Critical analysis of competency mapping across IT industries:

Competency implementation is a mammoth task. A competency project succeeds or fails largely by the way it is implemented in an organization. Whenever it has been successful, the success can be attributed to a very clear understanding of not just the competency process and value it adds to the organization but also the way it is implemented.

The competency mapping process followed at CSC and HCL has been more successful compared to the ones followed at Wipro and Infosys. At CSC and HCL there is a standardized competency dictionary on which each individual and job profile is mapped. But when it comes to Wipro and Infosys they believe in more of a flexible model though the Base is Mc Ber model of competency mapping. The Bespoke software can change the competencies as per the requirement of the organization. Though the maturity levels for assessment remains the same. The advantage of this type of model is it can keep pace with the dynamism of the IT industry. But the disadvantage is that the competency dictionary should be carefully crafted every time the role goes for a change. It leads to lot of confusion and doubts in the minds of the employees regarding implementation of the project. CSC follows the "Lominger Card" which has been a very good source of competency dictionary to all employees across different job positions.

The IT industry studied during this research work had one commonality- i.e. each of the organization had a competency development procedure which enabled the employees to gain some time for developing the required competencies over a period of time. And it was observed that a minimum of 20-30% of the weight age is given for acquiring such competencies by each employee during the competency development program. Like Infosys mentions the same in its CDP3.0 framework and CSC does through regular assessment through a prescribed format.

The success of competency mapping implementation requires the following things:

- Getting management Buy in: getting management involved in the process across all job positions in the organization and getting their explicit support in the process of mapping. Therefore it is highly important for the talent management department to prepare a project document, before venturing into competency mapping process.
- Establish rationale for a competency model by calling attention to the direct link of competencies to meeting organizational goals and purposes.
- Bench marking standard competency frameworks and bringing greater clarity while implementing the framework.
- Assessment method also needs to be standardized and discussed with all the employees in the organization.
- Using it not only for competency development but integrating it with other HR processes of the organization.
- Sharing the key project milestones with management. Each milestone needs to be signed off before progressing to the next step.

4.5 Critical analysis of Talent Management practices of various firms:

The following points can be highlighted as **good practice of Accenture's approach to talent management:**

- A rigorous approach to performance management that is undertaken across the organization on a six month cycle.
- A high degree of acceptance that doing performance management well is not only in the best interest of the individual but also contributes to the effectiveness of the organization in client work.
- A high level of openness and transparency of what is expected of individuals in terms of performance grade and also between grades.
- A people's advocate whose responsibility it is to hold the mirror up on balance between

performance and satisfaction.

- Development being the core value of the organization and each individual encouraged and expected to make the most of their opportunities.
- A culture which encourages open and honest feedback to enhance performance and development
- The appointment of career councillors whose objective is to provide a sounding board and constant presence to encourage growth and development.
- Reward system that is linked to performance and supports the messages of skills and competencies to be valued.
- A senior executive development programme that provides stretch and challenge to potential future leaders.

Areas for further consideration:

- Retention of good people: While there is effort within Accenture to creating community that is able to bind the virtual nature of consulting together, there is also high level of turnover that may be considered to be good. However there is a possibility that a good people may also leave the organization. Therefore a little more structured approach to career prospects might be and what the rewards associated with it will add great value.
- To make the employees stay connected there is strict adherence to a process. In Accenture the performance management process is well understood and executed but as a consequence there is possibility that the process prevents sufficient flexibility to cope with outstanding talent.
- The specialist expertise of some individuals may not be fully recognised within a highly dynamic promotion cycle. Career path for experts should be clearly defined and promoted within the organization.
- Leadership development at junior levels also needs to be clearly specified.

Areas of good practice of Wipro's talent management system:

- **Organizational values**: Wipro is known to have a strong organizational culture which is based on a good value system like respecting human values, Integrity, innovative solutions and value for money. This helps Wipro to attract the best talent in the country.

- **Developing people** : At Wipro the first thing was to put efforts to understand the people from all angles –not just from the current job point of view, but also from the angle of what the person can become . They have the career path defined and each employee is mentored on the competencies and the seven attributes: customer focus, high energy, self confidence,

308

ownership, aggressive commitments to excellence and ability to build star performers –were also used as the basis for 360 –degree evaluations of all team leaders.

- **Technology enabled Capability Maturity Model**: to help managers improve their effectiveness in managing people, developing talent, and building teams. This approach presented the flexibility of the competency framework which they could bring to various job clusters.

Areas for further consideration:
- Though Wipro could attract the top talent in the country it was found from the study that retaining the talent was difficult especially in the software developer field.
- It was observed that a systematic job designing and engagement programs of the employees could improve the retention scenario of the organization.
- In performance management systems the employees revealed that transparency on the performance criteria could lead to improve employee capability.
- Though they have job design and fun at work place programs in the work place, but still proper orientation of the employees regarding their competencies and expectation from those competencies could lead to better involvement in the workplace.

Areas of Good practice of TCS:
- Recruitment process of TCS has been very systematic and follows a thorough and detailed approach. This leads to increase in the success rate of attracting the best talent in the country. They systematically interface with the institution and continue interacting with the young minds to know the strengths and weakness of the academic institution. Thereby an HR manager interfaces with the academic institution for empanelment – which means they are on the list of campus visit and recruitment. After various levels of visit they identify the candidate's strength in various small projects after which they are selected for the final round of interview. The scrutinization of candidates in the detailed process can help the organization find the best talent in the industry.
- TCS believes in the strength of imparting world class training to its employees in the functional and technical domain of their job . It has its own In-house training programme which takes care of the effectiveness of the training programme.
- TCS has a Manpower Allocation Task committee (MATC) which determined the career path for employees. MATC was supported by a system that helped in identifying not just competencies for a role but also the level of competency needed to fit in the job profile. Competency development is at its best at TCS. Employees get the best career prospect at TCS.

Areas of good practice of Infosys:

- Innovation is a constant and ongoing process at Infosys. The initiative taken at Infosys to build Infosys Leadership institute (ILI) has been one of the best in its field to churn out future leaders. The mandate of ILI is to-Enhance managerial capabilities for increased customer satisfaction, Develop leaders to take the organizational vision forward, Partner with customers to build high performing multicultural teams.

- The optimas team of Infosys does a commendable work in recruiting and hiring the best talent in the organization.

There is an innovative **online employee and manager self service delivery** vehicle by which the employees can get access to information architecture and analyze the various delivery processes. It also increased responsiveness and faster decision making through inline communication channels, it directly saved employee time through automated HR tasks and saved empowered the employees.

References:

www.csc.com

1.

www.infosys.com

2.

www.wipro.com

3.

www.accenture.com

4.

5. Vaahini team (Accenture)- online newsletter
6. Interviews with the employees of CSC , Infosys, and HCL

Chapter- 5

Employees' perception on Competency Mapping and Talent Management practices

This chapter delineates the research methodology used to fulfill the objectives of the present study. The chapter comprises of the following sections:

1. Research hypotheses.
2. Review of the instruments used to measure the constructs:
   a. Competencies and tools used for IT technical staff
   b. Talent Management practices in IT firms
   c. Employee engagement practices
3. Sample design
4. Data collection
5. Application of Data Analysis
   ANNOVA
   Factor Analysis
   Regression Analysis

Introduction:

Based on the objectives of the study, a couple of hypotheses were formulated which have been tested using primary data.

The sample size that the researcher was aiming to reach was in between 150-200. However 220 questionnaire was administered amongst the 6 IT companies like Infosys, Wipro, Accenture, HCL, CSC and TCS. Only 128 responses were received, on the basis of which the research was conducted.

Section 1: Research Hypotheses:

It has been deliberated upon the relationship between competency mapping and talent management practices. The discussion led to formulation of certain hypotheses which have been tested in the succeeding chapters. A summarization of the entire hypotheses is essential for salient point.

After the questionnaires were collected the data have been analyzed using relevant statistical tools. Three hypotheses were formulated:

H1: The employees of the IT companies significantly hold similar views on the role of preferred competencies as elements of competency mapping.

H2: The employees of the IT companies significantly hold similar views on the role of HR interventions in talent management practices.

H3: Competency mapping effectively contributes to Talent Management practices.

H4 : Effective talent management practices ensures that both the HR and the non HR employees to align with the vision and mission of the organization and it creates an element of excitement to attend to their work.

A number of sub hypotheses have been deduced from Hypothesis 1 and hypothesis 2 for testing.

Hypothesis1: The employees in the IT companies significantly hold similar views on the role of preferred competencies as elements of competency mapping.

1.1 Employees' command over basic facts significantly contributes to competency mapping process.

1.2 Employees' analytical reasoning and problem solving significantly contributes to competency mapping process.

1.3 Employees' continuing sensitivity to events significantly contributes to competency mapping process.

1.4 Employees' initiative significantly contributes to competency mapping process.

1.5 Employees' Result orientation approaches significantly contributes to competency mapping process.

1.6 Employees' ability to see bigger picture significantly contributes to competency mapping process.

1.7 Employees' social skills and abilities significantly contributes to competency mapping process.

1.8 Employees' creativity significantly contributes to competency mapping process.

1.9 Employees' balanced learning habits and skills significantly contributes to competency mapping process.

1.10 Employees' team orientation approaches significantly contributes to competency mapping process.

Hypothesis 2: The employees in the IT companies significantly hold similar views on the role of HR interventions in talent management practices.

2.1 Better employee performance significantly contributes to effective talent management.

2.2 Better workforce planning significantly contributes to effective talent management.

2.3 Planned workforce acquisition significantly contributes to effective talent management.

2.4 Better performance management systems significantly contributes to talent management.

2.5 Planned career development programs significantly contributes to effective talent management.

2.6 Structured succession planning programs significantly contributes to Talent management practices.

2.7 Systematic learning management significantly contributes to talent management.

2.8 Robust compensation management packages contribute significantly to effective talent management.

SECTION 2- REVIEW OF THE INSTRUMENTS USED TO MEASURE THE CONSTRUCTS
Construct 1: COMPETENCIES AND TOOLS IDENTIFIED FOR IT PROFESSIONALS:

The construct competency mapping has been extensively investigated in various IT companies. The prediction towards competency mapping has always been a routinised study where all the companies practicing it felt that it can be used for competency development or performance management practices.

The competency mapping construct has been conceptualised in two different ways. The first conceptualisation involves assessment of various competencies and the tools used to measure the competencies and the second has been to identify the competencies which are mostly preferred by the IT technical staff.

Construct 2: Effectiveness of competency mapping in talent management practices

The construct was designed to understand the effectiveness of competency mapping on various talent management practices. The various talent management practices has been performance, performance management, workforce planning and workforce acquisition ,career development, succession planning ,learning management and compensation management. Competency –based approaches have developed quite rapidly since their introduction 25 years ago. David C.McClleland is credited with introducing the idea of "competency" into the human resource literature. In response to a growing dissatisfaction with intelligence testing traditional job analytic approaches to personnel selection, the competence-testing movement was described by **McClelland** by study of foreign-service officers. **"Testing for Competence Rather than Intelligence"-McClelland's** landmark paper has continued to stir debate even after a quarter century. Competency-based approaches gained popularity and acceptance within the human resources community through the work of McClelland and his associates, particularly **Richard Boyatzis**, past president at the McBer and Company. Boyatzis is credited with popularizing the term in his book "The Competent Manager (**Woodruff,** 1991)".

Construct -3 Work place environments

This part of the questionnaire is designed to know how the Talent Management system contributes to the work environment. The work environment included aligning vision and mission of the organization ,assessing candidates skills in the hiring process,creating a culture that makes employees want to stay with the organization , creating a culture that values employees work , creating an environment where employees are excited to come to work each day, employees ideas are listened to and valued, creating policies that encourage career growth and development opportunities ,identifying gaps in current employees and candidate competency levels, creating and rewarding top employees. The research by Wright and Cropanzano (2000), linking psychological well-being with performance, Donald et.al. (2005) in a study of 16,000 employees found that almost 25% of the variance in reported levels of employee productivity was predicted by psychological well-being, the perceived " commitment of the organization of the employee" and the resources and communication". Using meta-analysis techniques Harter *etal. (*2002) analyzed data from nearly 8,000 separate business units in 36 companies. They found significant relationships between scores on an employee survey and business unit level outcomes, such as customer satisfaction, productivity, profitability, employee turnover and sickness/absence levels. Their research reports are particularly interesting as they illustrate the potential relationships between psychological well-being and employee engagement.

For employees, psychological well-being is linked to important individual outcomes, including a range of mental and physical health issues, with lower levels of psychological wellbeing linked to poorer health. The impact of job strain on the individual has been heavily reported by researcher (Cooper and Quick, 1999). The impact of Job strain on the individual has been heavily reported by researcher Cooper and Quick, 1999. A series of research studies (Ferrie *etal*, 2005; Griffin *etal*., 2007) have explored the relationships between job conditions, individual health and other outcomes in a study of government employees.

In fact, although there is some broad agreement about the type of factors included in "employee engagement", there is a lack of clarity about its definition and measurement, Robinson *etal* (2004, p.9) give a definition of engagement as," A positive attitude held by the employee towards the organization and its values . An engaged employee is aware of business context, and works with colleagues to improve performance within the job for the benefit of the organization…..". In general, the items in most engagement surveys focus on the aspects of engagement that are most obviously related to "positive" employee behavior, and cover established psychological concepts such as organizational citizenship(Organ and Paine,1999) and organizational commitment and attachment(Meyer,1997). For example, the Utrecht Work

Engagement Survey (Schaufeli et al., 2006) concentrates on three factors: vigor, dedication and absorption. The Gallup Workplace Audit (see Harter et al., 2002) focuses on factors such as clarity – knowing what's expected and control (input and opportunity) By and large practitioners and researchers views of engagement embody the three core concepts of Attachment, Commitment and Organizational Citizenship. These concepts reflect a focus on the aspects of engagement that are likely to be most directly involved in driving positive employee behavior. As such, they reflect a focus on "Narrow Engagement" – i.e. the factors that are of most direct interest to employers and organizations, since they describe positive employee behavior that is likely to lead to more effective performance and confer direct benefits on the organization.

Typical questions in (narrow) employee engagement surveys are:

- The goals of my organization make me feel that my job is important.
- I am committed to this organization.
- My opinions are listened to by my bosses at work.
- I am enthusiastic about the job I do.
- At work, I am prepared to work hard, even when things do not go well.

The Narrow Engagement approach reflects a "commitment/citizenship" model of engagement, in which employees' commitment and citizenship are seen as important factors in the overall success of the organization. In addition to this focus on "narrow engagement", many engagement questionnaires also include at least a few items that focus on employee psychological well-being (e.g. "I enjoy my work and feel happy at work") – but, by and large, they do not distinguish between employee psychological well-being and the narrow engagement factors. Of course, narrow (strong commitment and good citizenship) engagement is important for the organization, but in some ways it is less important for employees. There are certainly benefits to employees from being committed to their work and feeling positive about the organization that they work for, but the long-term benefit for employees "themselves" is closely linked to personal psychological well being.

Another study, of 50 global companies, also found that the firms with high levels of employee engagement produced dramatically better results than companies with low levels of In three key metrics –income, income growth and earnings per share –the high engagement organizations performed dramatically better by up to 43%. Most employees however are not very engaged .For example:

- The polling firm's engagement survey data, reflecting the views of millions of (mostly private sector) employees are engaged, while 29% of employees are engaged, while 54% are not engaged and 17% are actively disengaged.
- A consulting firm surveyed more than 17,000 public and nonprofit sector employees and found that only 16% of employees are highly engaged, and 19% disengaged.

The concepts of goal-setting, optimism, and employee engagement as mechanisms to improving employee performance have all been discussed fairly extensively in the management literature. Goal setting has been explored in terms of both motivational impact toward improving performance and as being integral parts of management systems or processes designed to improve performance. Though fewer studies exist concerning optimism in the workplace, evidence certainly exists linking the concept to improvement in worker performance. An article titled "The relationship among goal setting, Optimism, and engagement: the impact on Employee performance" By (Bobby Medlin, USC Upstate Ken Green, Jr., Sam Houston State University, Allied economics International conference, 2008)

Since the Gallup organization's development of the Q12(a survey instrument to measure employee engagement) almost a decade ago, articles in the area of employee engagement –ranging from the benefits of increased employee engagement to ways to improve the level of engagement-has increased and intensified dramatically. Numerous studies (Locke, 1968; Latham and Yukl, 1975; Matsui, et al, 1987; Tubbs, 1986, 1993; Knight et al, 2001; Dweck et al., 1993; Sujan et al., 1994) have pointed to effective goal setting's impact on employee performance. Many management systems or processes (MBO, TQM, and continuous improvement initiatives for example) all feature goal setting as a critical element in improving performance. Gallup's Q12 survey instrument features 12 questions that are used to measure the level of engagement of an employee. Of these twelve drivers of employee engagement, four are related to the idea of goal-goal setting.

Improving individual performance of workers is a critical challenge for all managers. Research indicates that high levels of optimism can lead to improved employee performance. Hiring optimists and creating optimistic subcultures (Green, et al., 2004) are two mechanisms to do this. This study

316

identifies engagement as another means to enhance worker optimism. In addition, it identifies structured, formal goal setting processes as an additional mechanism for managers to improve the level of engagement of their employees.

Engagement can be assessed either indirectly or directly. Indirect assessment involves using data like employee performance, turnover, missed time, accidents, etc., to measure engagement. It isn't a big leap of faith to conclude that an agency with a lot of poor performers, high turnover or excessive employee sick time may have some engagement issues. If we have to establish through this method that high engagement will result in lower turnover, less missed time, better performance, and then this is not the right way of looking at it. Let's us look at high turnover .It could be that an organization with high turnover, but it could also be that an organization with high turnover doesn't pay its employees enough to keep them, or has a poor selection process that results in bad job fits, or has lots of baby boomers who are retiring because it's time for them to move on to the next stages of their lives.

That's why direct measurement, through surveys is the more valid and reliable way to assess engagement. It is more involved than simply looking at already existing data, but it's worth the time and effort to accurately measure engagement.

There are approaches to building employee engagement that are based on strong scientific evidence. For example, one firm's work is based on 30 years of research involving more than 17 million employees. These results, which have been reported in publications such as the Harvard Business Review, have isolated 12 core survey questions that predict employee engagement and therefore work group performance.

- I know what is expected of me at work
- I have materials and equipment I need to do my work right.
- At work, I have the opportunity to do what I do best every day.
- In the last seven days ,I have received recognition or praise for doing good work
- My supervisor ,or someone at work seems to care about me as person
- There is someone at work who encourages my development.
- At work, my opinions seem to count.
- The mission or purpose of my organization makes me feel my job is important.
- My associates or fellow employees are committed to doing quality work.
- I have a best friend at work
- In the last six months, someone at work has talked to me about my progress.
- This last year, I have had the opportunities at work to learn and grow.

In a study conducted by Simeon S. Simon "Essentials of employee engagement" (2008), engagement is linked to three essential forces in the organization-attrition, productivity and profitability. Ultimately the productivity is what is expected by the company from employees. An engaged employee carry out what is expected of him, having the focus and goal clear and bring success to the organization. Profitability is the result of actively engaged workforce.

Section 3: Sample design

The sample design which was used for the study was purposive sampling across the IT organization. Since the study wanted to understand how effectively competency mapping relates to talent management practices in the organization. It made sense to collect responses from the HR personnel as well as technical personnel to give their opinions on the various competencies and the talent management practices.

The six companies selected have proven track record of implementing competency mapping across their various divisions and various departments in the organizations. They are known to have best talent management practices in the organization. These are Infosys, Wipro and TCS among the Indian companies and HCL, CSC and Accenture among the Multinational IT companies.

Section 4: Data collection procedure

The present study uses survey approach for data collection. The survey approach for data collection uses a questionnaire which was administered to the employees of the IT firms. The questionnaire has three sections. Section A dealt with identifying competencies which are mostly useful for the IT technical staff and   Section B dealt with identifying the effectiveness of competency mapping on Talent management practices. Section 3 dealt with the perception that talent management has on work environment. The questionnaire is attached in Table 1 Annexure.

Section 5: Reliability Output

The present author believes that a researcher ought to be careful while considering construct validation as the ultimate test of a measurement instrument's credibility. Firstly, even as construct validity reflects the degree of correspondence between a construct and its measure, its reasons and ramifications have much broader contours. Construct validity is contingent not just upon the measurement instrument but also on the entire measurement procedure and interpretation of data generated (Cook and Campbell, 1976, 1979; Cronbach, 1971). To elaborate further, construct validation is an attempt at giving empirical certification to the physical avatar (the measurement instrument) of an abstract concept. However, the subjectivity inherent in the tool to assess construct validity demand that validation be concerned with generalisability of results across conditions of measurement (Cronbach et. al., 1972) and not just instrument of measurement. Secondly, whether empirical evidence approves or disapproves a measure depends upon the nature of the construct and the hypothesised relationship between it and other variables (Peter, 1981). This brings us back to the notion mentioned earlier in the chapter - the role of theory in construct validation is paramount. Peter (1981) contends that, "it is the theory and nature of construct which not only specify what empirical relationships are worth investigating but also determine whether empirical results support or invalidate a measure." The significance of theory in the construct validation process can be stressed upon by considering it as the fountainhead decision. Construct validation is directly related to the question of "what" the instrument is actually measuring and this "what"(the construct, trait or concept) need to be precisely, specifically and categorically stated so as to give an unambiguous indication of domain included and domain excluded in the definition. Cronbach (1971) suggests that construct validation is an ever extending process of investigation and development. Any acceptance of construct validity of a measure should be preceded by a series of reliability and validity studies.

Reliability:

Reliability is an assessment of the degree of consistency between multiple measurements of a variable Hair et. Al(2000). It differs from validity in the sense that it is not about what is to be measured but about how it is to be measured. A measure can be considered reliable if it would give us the same result over and over again, assuming that the object of measurement is not changing. Peter (1981) defines reliability as the "correlation between a measure and itself." The higher is this correlation; more is the internal consistency of the measuring instrument. The rationale behind this internal consistency is that the individual items in an instrument would all be measuring the same construct and therefore, should be highly inter-correlated (Churchill, 1979; Nunnally, 1979). However, since an entire measure can not be simultaneously correlated with itself, part of a multi-item operationalisation is correlated with the other part to arrive at the correlation coefficient. If all the items constituting a measure reflect a single construct then the responses would be highly inter-correlated whereas a low correlation would denote that some items are not authentic representatives of the construct and therefore, are leading to unreliability (Churchill, 1979). Reliability is essential part of construct validation process since a "valid measure must be composed primarily of systematic variance" and if most of the variance in a measure is systematic; it leads to higher correlation reflecting greater internal consistency (Peter, 1981). This assertion here needs a little elaboration.

Systematic variance is caused by factors that systematically affect the measurement of the variable across the sample whereas random variance is caused by factors that randomly affect measurement of the variable across the sample. While random variance weakens the observed relationships among variables, systematic variance tends to inflate the observed relationships between variables (Bagozzi, Yi and Phillips, 1991). This is the reason why systematic variance leads to high correlations, which is construed as greater internal consistency, and therefore, more reliability of the measure. Some of the recommended measures of reliability include Cron bach coefficient alpha and item-to-total correlations.

If the value of Cronbach's coefficient alpha is below the acceptable level, the researcher can resort to calculation of item-to-total correlation figure. It would facilitate elimination of items with a lower item-to-total correlation figure. The process involves calculation of the correlation of each item with the total score which is then plotted in a decreasing order of magnitude (see http://www.socialresearchmethods.net). Items with correlation near zero and items which produce a substantial or sudden drop in item-to total correlations are likely candidates for rejection.

The present study also conducted the reliability test using the cronbach alpha scores and found that it 0.864 based on standardized 37 items .

Reliability Statistics

Cronbach's Alpha	Cronbach's Alpha Based on Standardized Items	N of Items
.843	.864	37

Section – 5 – ANNOVA

Part –A :   Preferred Competencies   for IT technical staff

TABLE-5.1 Employees' perception on command over basic facts

COMMAND OVER BASIC FACTS				
NAME OF COMPANY	MEAN	S.D	F	Sig
WIPRO	8.27	1.305		
INFOSYS	8.34	1.421		
HCL	8.80	.422		
ACCENTURE	8.21	1.873	.910	.477
CSC	8.94	.250		
TCS	8.29	1.263		
TOTAL	8.41	1.307		

Table5.1 depicts the opinions of the sample employees regarding the competency called "command over Basic facts" of sample respond the selected IT companies. . The result of one way ANNOVA indicates the difference in command over basic facts is statistically not significant. (F-ratio .910 and P= .477). The range of difference between the companies is 8.29 to 8.94. Further investigation indicated that CSC is giving more importance on command over Basic facts as an important competency compared to rest of the companies. CSC has a standard procedure of mapping the competencies as per the role profile of the candidates. Hence the **hypothesis 1.1 that employees' command over basic facts significantly contributes to competency mapping** doesn't hold good.

TABLE-5.2 : employees' perception on analytical reasoning and problem solving

ANALYTICAL REASONING AND PROBLEM SOLVING				
NAME OF COMPANY	MEAN	S.D	F	Sig
WIPRO	9.05	1.026		
INFOSYS	8.55	1.352		
HCL	10.00	.000		
ACCENTURE	8.58	1.017	7.436	.000
CSC	9.75	.447		
TCS	7.94	1.560		
TOTAL	8.88	1.240		

Table5.2 illustrates the opinions of the sample employees on the competency called "analytical reasoning and problem solving skills" of the selected IT companies. It is observed that all the companies have excelled in terms of analytical reasoning measured on a 10 – point scale. The result of one way ANNOVA indicates the difference in command over basic facts is statistically significant. (F-ratio 7.436 and P= .000). It is further observed that HCL and CSC are stressing more on analytical reasoning and problem solving skills of its employees. In fact all the companies have been doing it but HCL and CSC has clear cut written guidelines as to what the competency of Analytical and problem solving skills mean for the role profile of the employees. Therefore each employee in the organization is clear as to how they are measured on analytical skills and problem solving skills.

Hence the **hypothesis 1.2 ,employees' analytical reasoning and problem solving skills significantly contributes to competency mapping holds good.**

TABLE-5.3 : employees' perception on continuing sensitivity to events

CONTINUING SENSITIVITY TO EVENTS				
NAME OF COMPANY	MEAN	S.D	F	Sig
WIPRO	8.05	1.079		
INFOSYS	7.69	1.257		
HCL	9.00	.000		
ACCENTURE	8.00	.943	3.155	.010
CSC	8.56	1.750		
TCS	7.41	1.502		
TOTAL	8.02	1.280		

Table 5.3 reveals the overall opinion scores of the sample respondents on the competency "continuing sensitivity to events" of the selected IT companies. It is observed that HCL and CSC have distinctively paid attention to continuing sensitivity to events as an effective competency. The one way ANNOVA reveals that this competency is statistically significant. (F=3.155, P=.010) this means that that all these companies vary in their approach to this competency. CSC deals with this competency as leading change process in which it stresses the importance of successful execution of the change. The maturity level which is expected is in the level 2. This means the manager is open to information and is aware of what is happening in and around him. Hard information such as figures and facts and soft information such as feelings of the people. As a result successful manager is able to respond in a suitable manner to situations as they arise.

Hence the **hypothesis 1.3, employees'continuing sensitivity to events significantly contributes to competency mapping holds good.**

TABLE-5.4

INITIATIVE				
NAME OF COMPANY	MEAN	S.D	F	Sig
WIPRO	8.35	.857		
INFOSYS	8.10	1.235		
HCL	9.00	1.054		
ACCENTURE	8.42	1.170	2.195	.059
CSC	9.12	1.360		
TCS	8.53	1.281		
TOTAL	8.48	1.164		

Table 5.5 reveals the overall opinions of the sample respondents of the select IT companies on the competency measure of Initiative. It is observed from the table the ANNOVA shows that the scores are statistically significant.(F=2.195 P=.059) . This competency depicts the sense of dedication and commitment to complete the projects on time. It is observed that all the select IT companies do pay more attention to this competency it is CSC and HCL employees revealed that it has greater importance to this competency. As CSC and HCL has clear cut points allocated for such activity, it is with this points the best employee of the month is associated which further leads to a culture of pro activity .

Hence the **hypothesis 1.4 ,employees' initiative significantly contributes to competency mapping holds good.**

TABLE-5.5

RESULT ORIENTATION				
NAME OF COMPANY	MEAN	S.D	F	Sig
WIPRO	8.57	.689		
INFOSYS	8.28	.751		
HCL	9.70	.483		
ACCENTURE	8.47	.697	8.490	.000
CSC	9.44	.892		
TCS	8.65	1.057		
TOTAL	8.70	.883		

The table 5.5 reveals the opinion of the employees of the select IT organization on the competency "Result orientation". It is clearly visible and practiced across all the IT organization as a core competency in a 10 point scale. Further the ANNOVA reveals that it is statistically significant. (F=8.490 and P=.000). The standard deviation on this competency is also very close to each other. All the IT companies are driven by mostly by offshore projects, therefore result orientation is the key competency which can attract their off shore clients. HCL scores highest on these lines, as HCL takes pride in its philosophy of 'Employees First, Customers Second' which empowers its 77,046 transformers to create a real value for the customers. HCL Technologies, along with its subsidiaries, had consolidated revenues of US$ 3.5 billion (Rs. 16,034 crores), as on 30 June 2012 (on LTM basis).For example, at CSC it is currently modernizing the world's largest supply chain, with a $4.5 billion inventory of 6 million items involving 50,000 vendors. They are also building what will likely be the world's largest health IT program, which means creating the most extensive virtualized data center ever implemented. As projects like these demonstrate, CSC is one of the few IT services providers in the world with the skill to handle intricate technical refinements, one day, and the commitment to help you efficiently deliver a massive transformation project, the next day.

Hence the **hypothesis 1.5 ,employees'result orientation approaches significantly contributes to competency mapping holds good.**

TABLE : 5.6

ABILITY TO SEE BIG PICTURE				
NAME OF COMPANY	MEAN	S.D	F	Sig
WIPRO	7.54	1.169		
INFOSYS	7.72	1.032		
HCL	8.70	.483		
ACCENTURE	8.47	.841	3.484	.006
CSC	8.25	1.238		
TCS	7.94	1.197		
TOTAL	7.95	1.121		

Table 5.6 reveals the opinion of the employees of the select IT companies on the competency "ability to see big picture" has been very high. The mean scores vary from 7.54 to 8.70, which is not high as a difference. Further it is observed Through ANNOVA that the scores are statistically significant (F-3.484, P=.006).

Hence the **hypothesis 1.6 ,employees' ability to see big picture significantly contributes to competency mapping holds good.**

TABLE-5.7

SOCIAL SKILLS AND ABILITIES				
NAME OF COMPANY	MEAN	S.D	F	Sig
WIPRO	7.03	1.301		
INFOSYS	6.48	1.405		
HCL	6.60	.516		
ACCENTURE	7.42	1.742	1.469	.205
CSC	6.62	1.500		
TCS	6.47	1.586		
TOTAL	6.80	1.437		

Table 5.7 reveals the overall scores taken from the opinions of the sample IT companies' employees on the competency "social skills and abilities" has been very average. The mean scores vary from 6.60 to 7.42, which is high as a difference. Further it is observed Through ANNOVA that the scores are statistically not significant (F-1.469, P=.205). This shows that there is not much of an agreement on the competence of social skills and abilities of the organization.

Hence the **hypothesis 1.7 ,employees' social skills and abilities significantly contributes to competency mapping does not hold good.**

TABLE-5.8

CREATIVITY				
NAME OF COMPANY	MEAN	S.D	F	Sig
WIPRO	7.86	1.032		
INFOSYS	7.24	.951		
HCL	7.70	.483		
ACCENTURE	8.63	.955	5.301	.000
CSC	7.62	.619		
TCS	7.59	1.121		
TOTAL	7.76	1.018		

Table 5.8 reveals the overall scores taken on the opinions of the employees on the overall scores of the select IT companies in the competency "Creativity". It is found from the one way ANNOVA that it is statistically significant (F=5.301 P=.000). As these are all IT companies Creativity forms the core competency of the organization.

Hence the **hypothesis 1.8 ,employees' creativity significantly contributes to competency mapping holds good.**

TABLE-5.9

BALANCED LEARNING HABITS AND SKILLS				
NAME OF COMPANY	MEAN	S.D	F	Sig
WIPRO	8.81	1.023		
INFOSYS	7.48	1.271		
HCL	8.70	.483		
ACCENTURE	8.79	.787	6.024	.000
CSC	8.12	1.628		
TCS	7.59	1.622		
TOTAL	8.25	1.322		

Table 5.9 reveals that the overall scores of the select IT companies in the competency "Balanced learning habits and skills". It is found from the one way ANNOVA that it is statistically significant (F=6.024 P=.000). As these are all IT companies Creativity forms the core competency of the organization.

Hence the **hypothesis 1.9 ,employees' balanced learning habits significantly contributes to competency mapping holds good.**

TABLE- 5.10

TEAM ORIENTATION				
NAME OF COMPANY	MEAN	S.D	F	Sig
WIPRO	9.03	.957		
INFOSYS	8.34	.769		
HCL	9.30	.823		
ACCENTURE	8.42	.838	3.739	.003
CSC	9.06	1.436		
TCS	8.29	.985		
TOTAL	8.71	1.021		

Table 5.10 reveals that the overall scores taken on the basis of opinions of the employees of the select IT companies in the competency "Team orientation". It is found from the one way ANNOVA that it is statistically significant (F=3.739 P=.003). As these are all IT companies Team orientation forms one of the functional competencies of the organization. In every project based organization team orientation forms one of the key competencies which effectively contribute to the success of the employees.

Hence the **hypothesis 1.10 , employees' Team orientation significantly contributes to competency mapping holds good.**

Out of the above 10 sub hypotheses above 8 have been held good. Therefore the competency factors 1.1 and 1.5 did not hold gold. Therefore the Hypothesis no1 that The employees of the IT companies significantly hold similar views on the role of preferred competencies as elements of competency mapping holds good.

Part-B The perceived effectiveness of competency mapping on Talent management practices :

TABLE-5.11 : Employees' perception on employee performance

EMPLOYEE PERFORMANCE				
NAME OF COMPANY	MEAN	S.D	F	Sig
WIPRO	8.78	1.031	4.105	.002
INFOSYS	7.97	1.180		
HCL	9.00	.000		
ACCENTURE	8.16	.898		
CSC	8.50	.894		
TCS	7.82	1.185		
TOTAL	8.36	1.078		

Table5.11 depicts the opinions of sample respondents of the select IT companies on overall performance. It is observed from the opinions that all the companies have excelled in terms of employee performance measured on 10 – point scale. The standard deviation of performance among the companies is also not very high indicating similarity of performance of the companies under study. The result of one way ANNOVA indicates the difference in performance is statistically significant. (F-ratio 4.105 and P= .002). The range of difference between the companies is 7.82 to 9.00. Further investigation indicated that HCL is giving more importance on competency mapping on the global delivery framework while TCS is more emphasizing on ITES. HCL is having a reward system to back up the performance of the employees.

The hypothesis 2.1 that better employee performance significantly contributes to talent management holds good.

WORKFORCE PLANNING				
NAME OF COMPANY	MEAN	S.D	F	Sig
WIPRO	7.03	1.213	2.002	.083
INFOSYS	6.79	1.320		
HCL	7.80	.422		
ACCENTURE	7.42	.902		
CSC	6.75	1.183		
TCS	7.47	1.419		
TOTAL	7.12	1.208		

Table5.12 describes the opinions of sample respondents on workforce planning. It is observed that all the companies have high scores in terms of workforce planning measured on 10– point scale. The standard deviation of workforce planning among the companies is also not very high indicating similarity of workforce planning of the companies under study. The result of one way ANNOVA indicates the difference in workforce planning is statistically significant. (F-ratio 2.002 and P= .083). The range of difference between the companies is 6.75 to 7.80. Further probing into the analysis made it very clear that all the companies took enough care in their workforce planning process. But it is HCL followed by TCS which topped the table. It was understood after discussing with the employees that the bench strength which these two companies maintained was also qualititative compared to the other IT companies. They had a very good way of engaging the people in the initial days of their career by giving them live projects to work on the internal system process. This made HCL and TCS have an edge over other companies.

The hypothesis 2.2 that better workforce planning contributes to talent management holds good.

TABLE 5.13

WORKFORCE ACQUISITION				
NAME OF COMPANY	MEAN	S.D	F	Sig
WIPRO	7.24	1.211	1.737	.131
INFOSYS	7.17	1.284		
HCL	7.80	.422		
ACCENTURE	8.05	1.177		
CSC	7.31	1.448		
TCS	7.53	1.007		
TOTAL	7.44	1.209		

326

Table 5.13 illustrates the opinions of employees on overall workforce acquisition of various companies. It is observed from the table that Accenture has the advantage of having a very good workforce acquisition practice compared to the rest of the organizations. The standard deviation of the companies showed less deviation. The one way ANNOVA results further proved that there is no significant difference in opinions of employees of the companies in their approaches. (F=1.737 P= .131). The table further illustrates there is visible difference in their approaches to workforce acquisition. Accenture's focus is on making sure that its approach to talent is one which is aligned to its need to ensure that it has the best people with the right skills for its clients. There is remarkable clarity about what the organization requires of its people, what skills are needed, what is expected of them on client projects and what they need to do to ensure they continue to develop.

The hypothesis 2.3 that planned workforce acquisition significantly contributes to talent management does not hold good.

TABLE: 5.14

PERFORMANCE MANAGEMENT				
NAME OF COMPANY	MEAN	S.D	F	sig
WIPRO	8.86	1.032		
INFOSYS	8.21	1.082		
HCL	10.00	.000		
ACCENTURE	7.84	1.259	6.988	.000
CSC	9.19	1.424		
TCS	8.41	1.176		
TOTAL	8.63	1.241		

Table 5.13 illustrates the opinions of employees on overall workforce acquisition of various companies. It is observed from the table that Accenture has the advantage of having a very good workforce acquisition practice compared to the rest of the organizations. The standard deviation of the companies showed less deviation. The one way ANNOVA results further proved that there is no significant difference in opinions of employees of the companies in their approaches. (F=1.737 P= .131). The table further illustrates there is visible difference in their approaches to workforce acquisition. Accenture's focus is on making sure that its approach to talent is one which is aligned to its need to ensure that it has the best people with the right skills for its clients. There is remarkable clarity about what the organization requires of its people, what skills are needed, what is expected of them on client projects and what they need to do to ensure they continue to develop.

The hypothesis 2.3 that planned workforce acquisition significantly contributes to talent management does not hold good.

Table 5.15

CAREER DEVELOPMENT				
NAME OF COMPANY	MEAN	S.D	F	sig
WIPRO	7.84	1.167		
INFOSYS	7.41	1.119		
HCL	7.60	.516		
ACCENTURE	8.42	1.387	2.012	.082
CSC	7.62	.619		
TCS	7.76	1.251		
TOTAL	7.77	1.138		

Table 5.15 illustrates the opinions of employees on overall career development of various companies. It is observed from the table that Accenture has the advantage of having a very good career development procedure followed by Wipro compared to the rest of the organizations. The one way ANNOVA results further proved that there is significant difference in the opinions of employees of different companies in their approaches (F= 2.012,P= .082). Further probing with the employees and learning forum i.e the Vahini team of Accenture it was found that the career path for each individual is clearly laid out and structured. Each job grade is accompanied with guidelines in terms of time expected in grade, and what people can expect to remain within this grade for this period of time if they are performing in relation to their peers. Some individuals that consistently outperform their peers from a holistic perspective can be accelerated through the grades- although the flex is still within very narrow parameters around the guidelines.

The hypothesis 2.5 that better career development practices contributes to talent management holds good.   TABLE: 5.16

SUCCESSION PLANNING				
NAME OF COMPANY	MEAN	S.D	F	sig
WIPRO	7.41	1.257		
INFOSYS	6.34	.769		
HCL	6.30	.483		
ACCENTURE	7.79	1.686	7.177	0.00
CSC	6.25	.577		
TCS	7.35	1.272		
TOTAL	6.98	1.267		

Table 5.16 depicts the opinions of employees on overall succession planning of various companies. It is observed from the table that Accenture has the advantage of having a very good succession planning procedure. The one way ANNOVA results further proved that there is significant difference in the opinions of employees of various companies in their approaches (F= 7.177 P= .000). At Accenture the decision to progress within the organization is very much in and each employee has the possibility to realize one's potential. Anyone who works hard and shows a willingness to grow is supported and rewarded, whether they are a high flier or not. The projects are identified to enable the individual to grow.

The hypothesis 2.6 that structured succession planning significantly contributes to talent management holds good.

TABLE: 5.17

LEARNING MANAGEMENT				
NAME OF COMPANY	MEAN	S.D	F	sig
WIPRO	8.16	1.323		
INFOSYS	7.62	1.425		
HCL	7.00	.000		
ACCENTURE	7:47	1.541	1.839	.110
CSC	7.31	.479		
TCS	7.82	1.845		
TOTAL	7.70	1.366		

Table 5.17depicts the opinions of employees on overall learning management of various companies. It is observed from the table that Wipro has the advantage of having a very good learning management procedure. The one way ANNOVA results further proved that the differences of opinions of employees of six IT companies on learning management is statistically not significant (F= 1.839 P= .110).

The hypothesis 2.7 that better learning management contributes to talent management holds good.

TABLE: 5.18

COMPENSATION MANAGEMENT				
NAME OF COMPANY	MEAN	S.D	F	sig
WIPRO	8.05	1.290		
INFOSYS	7.55	1.660		
HCL	9.00	.000		
ACCENTURE	8.68	.946	2.587	.029
CSC	8.00	1.789		
TCS	8.24	1.200		
TOTAL	8.12	1.397		

Table 5.18 depicts the opinions of employees on overall compensation management practices of various companies. It is observed from the table that HCL has the advantage of having a very good compensation management procedure. The one way ANNOVA results further proved that the opinions of employees of the companies on compensation management practices is statistically significant (F= 2.587, P= .029).

it has been further observed that HCL employees were very happy as the compensation is basically linked to the performance of the employees. They have a very good reward management procedure which is linked to performance of the employees on a yearly basis. The company has a very good procedure of recognizing the employee's performance and recognizing the effort of each employee by giving certificate of best employee of the month.

The hypothesis 2.8 that robust compensation packages significantly contributes to talent management holds good.

Therefore it can be observed from the findings that 6 out of 8 sub hypotheses formulated from Hypothesis 2 have been found to be significant. Therefore it can be proved that hypothesis 2 The employees of the IT companies significantly hold similar views on the role of HR interventions in talent management practices holds good.

5.19

Aligning employees with vision and mission

			aligning employees with vision and mission						
			10	5	6	7	8	9	Total
Type	HR	Count	3	0	0	2	18	33	56
		% within Type	5.4%	.0%	.0%	3.6%	32.1%	58.9%	100.0%
	Technical	Count	1	2	6	26	31	6	72
		% within Type	1.4%	2.8%	8.3%	36.1%	43.1%	8.3%	100.0%
Total		Count	4	2	6	28	49	39	128
		% within Type	3.1%	1.6%	4.7%	21.9%	38.3%	30.5%	100.0%

Analysis:
The table reflects that 58.9% of the HR managers perceive that talent management systems have 90% contribution in aligning employees with vision and mission of the organization. 43.1% of the technical personnel feel that talent management effectively contributes to aligning employees with vision and mission of the organization.

Interpretation:
It can be inferred from the above table that the HR managers feel that Talent management system definitely provides greater alignment with the vision and mission of the organization. Strategic literature largely emphasizes the internal resources of business as the source of competitive advantage. This "resource based perspective (Boxall, 1996) views a firm as a bundle of resources. Such resource must possess four qualities for advantage to be maintained like Value, rarity, inimitability and non substitutability. The technical personnel also feel the same about the talent management system.

5.20

hiring process

			hiring process					Total
			6	7	8	9	10	
Type	HR	Count	0	2	14	27	13	56
		% within Type	.0%	3.6%	25.0%	48.2%	23.2%	100.0%
	Technical	Count	3	27	32	3	7	72
		% within Type	4.2%	37.5%	44.4%	4.2%	9.7%	100.0%
Total		Count	3	29	46	30	20	128
		% within Type	2.3%	22.7%	35.9%	23.4%	15.6%	100.0%

Analysis:

The above table reflects that 48.2% of the HR managers feel that Talent management system effectively contributes 90% to the hiring process; and 44.4% of the technical people rate talent management to be effective upto80% of the times.37.5% of the technical personnel also rate it 70%.

Interpretation:

It can be inferred from the above table that fifty percent of the HR managers feel that talent management significantly contributes to the systematic attraction, identification, development of those individuals with high potential and who are of particular value to an organization. Gutheridge et.al.argue (2008) ,talent management is very much a business issue: "demographics, globalization and the characteristics of knowledge work present long term challenges that reinforce the argument for putting workforce planning and talent management at the heart of the business strategy and for giving those issues a bigger share of senior management's time." The technical managers feel it contributes to 70-80% of the time. The reason being that they feel talent management is more of identifying talent within the organization rather than acting as a base for further searching of the talent.

5.21

Join the organization

			join the organization						
			5	6	7	8	9	10	Total
Type	HR	Count	3	0	10	22	21	0	56
		% within Type	5.4%	.0%	17.9%	39.3%	37.5%	.0%	100.0%
	Technical	Count	8	10	33	15	1	5	72
		% within Type	11.1%	13.9%	45.8%	20.8%	1.4%	6.9%	100.0%
Total		Count	11	10	43	37	22	5	128
		% within Type	8.6%	7.8%	33.6%	28.9%	17.2%	3.9%	100.0%

Analysis:

The table suggests Talent management system has a significant role in enabling the employees to join the organization. 39.3% & 37.5% of the HR personnel perceive that talent management contributes 80-90% in helping the employees to join the organization. Whereas 45.8% of the technical personnel feel that the contribution of talent management to employees joining the organization is 70-80%.

Interpretation:

It can be inferred from the table that very few HR managers feel that the talent management system can create a base for employees to join the organization. However 46% of the technical people feel that talent management system can create an employer brand which can act as a base for attracting candidates to join the organization. An employer brand is a set of attributes and qualities –often intangible-that make an organization distinctive, promise a particular kind of employment experience and appeal to those people who will thrive and perform to their best in its culture (Walker, 2007). There is growing evidence that the criteria used by younger workers in particular to select their future employer include the chance for learning and growth. This is possible if the organization has talent management system.

Table5.22

Recognizes employees work Cross tabulation

			recognizes employees work						Total
			5	6	7	8	9	10	Total
Type	HR	Count	1	0	14	27	14	0	56
		% within Type	1.8%	.0%	25.0%	48.2%	25.0%	.0%	100.0%
	Technical	Count	8	7	28	24	4	1	72
		% within Type	11.1%	9.7%	38.9%	33.3%	5.6%	1.4%	100.0%
Total		Count	9	7	42	51	18	1	128
		% within Type	7.0%	5.5%	32.8%	39.8%	14.1%	.8%	100.0%

Analysis:

The HR personnel of the IT firms were of the view that talent management system contributes 80-90% of the times to recognize employees work. The technical people felt that it contribute to 70-80% of the times towards recognizing the employee's work.

Interpretation:

Motivating and inspiring performance from young employees requires managers, executives and HR to work together. Employers can engage the potential commitment of young people by redefining work in terms of projects which offer variety and learning. More flexible working patterns may be attractive and this may involve restructuring work processes. Talent management system of identifying Super keepers, keepers of an organization and recognizes the work of the employees. Eldridge and Miles (2008) suggest that the organizations need to be tactical in their approach to retention, and recognize the more personalized expectations of employees. Planned actions can be put in place for other groups. This gives the understanding that Talent management system does recognize the effort put in by employees in the organization. In assessing candidates relevant and effective methods are used like assessment centers, behavioral interviews, psychometric testing so that recognizing the effort of the employees in specific activities and the areas where they are confident to carry out their tasks.

Table 5.24

Excited to come to work

			excited to come to work						Total
			4	5	6	7	8	9	
Type	HR	Count	1	0	0	2	20	33	56
		% within Type	1.8%	.0%	.0%	3.6%	35.7%	58.9%	100.0%
	Technical	Count	3	2	6	38	19	4	72
		% within Type	4.2%	2.8%	8.3%	52.8%	26.4%	5.6%	100.0%
Total		Count	4	2	6	40	39	37	128
		% within Type	3.1%	1.6%	4.7%	31.3%	30.5%	28.9%	100.0%

Analysis:

The above table suggests that 58.9% of the HR managers perceived that with effective talent management system the employees feel excited to come to work and this contributes to 90% of their excitement to come to work. Whereas the technical people felt that effective talent management system contributes 70% towards employee's excitement to come to work.

Interpretation:

The observation reveals that though HR managers feel that with effective talent management system employees feel excited to come to work, but the technical personnel differ in their views regarding this component. Technical people feel it is the Job content which excites them to come to work rather than only the Talent management system of identifying competencies and channelizing their efforts towards more productive work. They agree to the extent that if there is a good talent management system then the process for identifying the right fit for the job is possible.

TABLE 5.25

TABLE5.27

Type * retention Cross tabulation

			retention						Total
			5	6	7	8	9	10	
Type	HR	Count	1	6	14	18	16	1	56
		% within Type	1.8%	10.7%	25.0%	32.1%	28.6%	1.8%	100.0%
	Technical	Count	3	1	17	28	14	9	72
		% within Type	4.2%	1.4%	23.6%	38.9%	19.4%	12.5%	100.0%
Total		Count	4	7	31	46	30	10	128
		% within Type	3.1%	5.5%	24.2%	35.9%	23.4%	7.8%	100.0%

Analysis:
The above table suggests that 32.1% of the HR managers feel that talent management system contributes to 80% of the retention of the employees. But the responses range from 70-90%. Whereas 38.9% of the technical people also feel that it contributes to 80% of the times towards retaining the employees.

Conclusion : The HR and the technical personnel of the sample IT companies agreed on the factor that effective talent management practices helped the employees' to align with the vision and mission of the organization, makes the employee join the organization and creates the excitement to come to work.This proves the hypothesis No.4 that effective talent management practices ensures the employees to align themselves with vision and mission of the organization and it creates an element of excitement to come to work. It further also helps the employees to identify the gaps in career development and growth. However both the HR and technical personnel differ in their opinions on the factor that with better talent management practices employees'ideas are listened and valued and recognized for their work.

Factor Analysis

R Kamineni (2005) administered the 18-item Richins and Dawson (1992) scale of materialism in a survey on students in Australia. The data was factor analysed using principal component analysis with varimax rotation. The analysis identified the factors as success, happiness and centrality which accounted for 58% of the total variance in comparison to Richins and Dawson's (1992) original study wherein the same three factors were identified and deemed to be conceptually valid in correspondence to existing theory.

A factor analysis can be carried out not only to identify the underlying dimensions, called factors, from among a large number of variables Hair et. al., (1998) but also to verify if the dimensions conceptualized, or derived from preceding empirical research, are actually supported by the data. This notion is strengthened by Peter's (1981) observation, "if a construct were hypothesised to have three dimensions, a factor analysis of a purported measure of the construct which produces three meaningful factors could be interpreted as supportive evidence of construct validity." It is also in agreement with the premise that construct validation is concerned with generalisability of the output over different conditions of measurement (Cronbach et.al., 1972). Therefore, if the factor analysis of a construct using a different set of respondents, repeatedly leads to the same set of underlying dimensions, it may be construed as supporting evidence towards construct validity of the instrument.

Even though factor analysis has found more use towards determination of the Underlying dimensions of a construct then as a tool to confirm or refute components isolated by other means, it can be used to confirm the conceptualised dimensions (Churchill, 1979).

APPLICATION OF DATA ANALYSIS

The analysis of the data generated through this survey has been divided into four different sections for the purpose of exclusivity and systematisation. At the outset, the **Section one** of the data analysis pertains to assessment of internal reliability of the measuring instruments for the constructs - Talent management, competency mapping and engagement of the employees.. The reliability of these

334

measuring instruments has been determined by calculation of Cronbach's alpha coefficient and item-to-total correlation.

The **second section** of the data analysis measures the variance across all industries on all the dimensions of competency mapping, Talent management and talent engagement.

The **third section** contains factor analysis of the talent management dimensions administered in the questionnaire. The objective was to reduce the dimensions which may be useful for subsequent analysis.

The **fourth section** of the data analysis contains regression analysis to establish the relation between competency mapping and Talent management practices of the sample organization

TABLE: 5.29

KMO and Bartlett's Test

Kaiser-Meyer-Olkin Measure of Sampling Adequacy.		.569
Bartlett's Test of Sphericity	Approx. Chi-Square	356.735
	Df	28
	Sig.	.000

The Kaiser-Meyer- Olkin measure of adequacy was 0.569 which proved that the data generated through the questionnaire was adequate for factor analysis. (Hair et. al. 5th ed., p. 99). The measure of sampling adequacy values, obtained for each variable individually, also fall in the acceptable range, as given in Table 5-61.

Rotated Component Matrix[a]

Table: 5.30

Variables	Factors		
	1	2	3
performance	.764	.234	.105
workforce planning	.160	.814	.164
workforce acquisition	.229	.913	-.075
performance management	.883	-.011	-.036
career development	.240	.147	.785
succession planning	-.213	.339	.715
learning management	.074	-.262	.824
compensation management	.670	.432	.106

Extraction Method: Principal Component Analysis.

Rotation Method: Varimax with Kaiser Normalization.

a. Rotation converged in 5 iterations.

TABLE: 5.31

Factors	Name of the factor	Eigen value	Percent of variance explained	Cumulative percentage
1.	Manpower management	1.00	24.964	24.964
2.	Manpower acquisition	1.94	24.288	49.252
3	Manpower development	1.86	23.287	72.539

These factors collectively explained 72.539% of the total variance. Individually, the factors 1, 2, 3, measured 24.964% 24.288% and 23.287% of the variance. The Factor 1. Which is named as Manpower management consisted of components of performance, performance management and compensation management? Factor2 which is named as Manpower acquisition consisted of workforce planning and workforce acquisition. Factor 3 consisted of career development, succession planning and learning management.

Table: 5.32

Factor Matrix

FACTORS		
FACTOR -1- MANPOWER MANAGEMENT	FACTOR-2 MANPOWER ACQUISITION	FACTOR-3- MANPOWER DEVELOPMENT
PERFORMANCE	WORKFORCE PLANNING	CAREER PLANNING
PERFORMANCE MANAGEMENT	WORKFORCE ACQUISITION	SUCCESSION PLANNING
COMPENSATION MANAGEMENT		LEARNING MANAGEMENT

A principal component analysis was carried out on the data matrix. In order to decide on the number of factors to be extracted, the latent root criterion was used. In this technique, only factors having latent root criterion or Eigen values greater than one are considered to be significant wherein Eigen value is the column sum of the squared factor loadings for a factor. An orthogonal (varimax) rotation method was used to simplify the factor variable structure. The rotated component matrix obtained consisted of three factors as given in the above table.

To summarise, the items pertaining to performance, performance management and compensation management were grouped under one factor to reduce the co linearity among the components. Similarly factor2 combined components like workforce planning and acquisition. Factor 3 combined the components of career planning, succession planning and learning management.

Relationship between competency mapping and Talent Management

For the purpose of establishing the relationship between competency mapping and talent management -the statistical tools which are used for analyzing the data is factor analysis and regression analysis. Among the various talent management components which are practiced in the organization, a factor analysis is run through the components and after that the extracted factors are regressed on the competency variables. The regression analysis was done to establish the linkage between the various competencies and talent management practices in the organization. The purpose of linking the competencies to the talent management practices in the organization was to understand the important competencies and its role in talent management practices in the organization. The pilot study helped in selecting the competencies that were significantly contributing towards competency mapping in the organizations.

Regression Analysis:

Regression analysis can be understood from the following regression equation:

Y= alpha (constant) +B1x1 + B2 x2 + B3 x3

Where X1 refers to factor1; i.e., manpower management
    X2 refers to factor2; i.e., manpower acquisition
    X3 refers to factor3; i.e. ., manpower development

    B1 refers to the beta value of each competency.

Table – 5.33-a. Regression analysis for Factor –Manpower Management

Model Summary[b]

Model	R	R Square	Adjusted R Square	Std. Error of the Estimate	Change Statistics					Durbin-Watson
					R Square Change	F Change	df1	df2	Sig. F Change	
1	.672[a]	.452	.405	.77125614	.452	9.650	10	117	.000	1.221

a. Predictors: (Constant), team orientation, command of basic facts, ability to see bigger picture, creativity, analytical reasoning and problem solving, result orientation, initiative, continuing sensitivity to events, balanced learning habits and skills, social skills and abilities

b. Dependent Variable: REGR factor score   1 for analysis 1

Table-5.33.b.

Coefficients[a]

Model	Unstandardized Coefficients B	Std. Error	Standardized Coefficients Beta	t	Sig.	Collinearity Statistics Tolerance	VIF
1 (Constant)	-4.752	.997		-4.766	.000		
command of basic facts	.039	.058	.051	.668	.506	.816	1.226
analytical reasoning and problem solving	.228	.076	.282	3.013	.003	.534	1.872
continuing sensitivity to events	-.140	.073	-.180	-1.924	.057	.538	1.859
initiative	.217	.078	.252	2.786	.006	.572	1.749
result orientation	.105	.101	.093	1.041	.300	.590	1.694
ability to see bigger picture	.027	.078	.030	.347	.729	.615	1.627
social skills and abilities	-.035	.073	-.050	-.479	.633	.427	2.344
creativity	-.285	.089	-.290	-3.203	.002	.572	1.748
balanced learning habits and skills	.348	.077	.460	4.507	.000	.450	2.222
team orientation	.017	.097	.017	.172	.864	.483	2.072

a. Dependent Variable: REGR factor score   1 for analysis 1

Collinearity Diagnostics[a]

Model	Dimension	Eigenvalue	Condition Index	Variance Proportions										
				(Constant)	command of basic facts	analytical reasoning and problem solving	continuing sensitivity to events	initiative	result orientation	ability to see bigger picture	social skills and abilities	creativity	balanced learning habits and skills	team orientation
1	1	10.848	1.000	.00	.00	.00	.00	.00	.00	.00	.00	.00	.00	.00
	2	.046	15.344	.00	.06	.03	.00	.01	.00	.00	.22	.00	.01	.00
	3	.026	20.527	.00	.34	.02	.11	.01	.00	.00	.03	.03	.03	.01
	4	.022	22.130	.00	.13	.00	.11	.06	.01	.18	.01	.03	.02	.01
	5	.016	26.228	.00	.00	.01	.18	.11	.01	.19	.06	.00	.14	.03
	6	.012	30.597	.01	.00	.05	.00	.02	.14	.01	.06	.38	.10	.02
	7	.008	36.037	.12	.21	.06	.03	.12	.00	.05	.01	.07	.24	.21
	8	.008	37.761	.00	.00	.15	.24	.45	.05	.13	.03	.08	.29	.00
	9	.007	38.586	.06	.01	.66	.10	.06	.00	.12	.41	.01	.07	.03
	10	.004	49.254	.03	.21	.00	.21	.07	.49	.30	.01	.15	.00	.38
	11	.003	59.144	.77	.03	.02	.02	.09	.31	.02	.17	.24	.10	.31

a. Dependent Variable: REGR factor score   1 for analysis 1

It is observed from the above tables that the regression score on the factor 1 i.e., Manpower management reveals that manpower management is highly influenced by the competencies like analytical reasoning and problem solving , continuing sensitivity to events, initiative, creativity, balanced learning habits and skills.

Further it also reveals that manpower management is significantly related the competencies like analytical reasoning and problem solving , continuing sensitivity to events, initiative, creativity, balanced learning habits and skills .

Table: 5.34a_Regression analysis for Factor-2-manpower acquisition

Variables Entered/Removed[b]

Model	Variables Entered	Variables Removed	Method
1	team orientation, command of basic facts, ability to see bigger picture, creativity, analytical reasoning and problem solving, result orientation, initiative, continuing sensitivity to events, balanced learning habits and skills, social skills and abilities	.	Enter

a. All requested variables entered.

b. Dependent Variable: REGR factor score   2 for analysis 1

Model Summary[b]

Model	R	R Square	Adjusted R Square	Std. Error of the Estimate	R Square Change	F Change	df1	df2	Sig. F Change	Durbin-Watson
1	.685[a]	.469	.424	.75917464	.469	10.335	10	117	.000	1.535

a. Predictors: (Constant), team orientation, command of basic facts, ability to see bigger picture, creativity, analytical reasoning and problem solving, result orientation, initiative, continuing sensitivity to events, balanced learning habits and skills, social skills and abilities

b. Dependent Variable: REGR factor score   2 for analysis

Coefficients[a]

Model		Unstandardized Coefficients B	Std. Error	Standardized Coefficients Beta	t	Sig.	Collinearity Statistics Tolerance	VIF
1	(Constant)	-1.696	.981		-1.728	.087		
	command of basic facts	-.025	.057	-.033	-.437	.663	.816	1.226
	analytical reasoning and problem solving	.026	.074	.032	.348	.729	.534	1.872
	continuing sensitivity to events	-.147	.072	-.188	-2.044	.043	.538	1.859
	initiative	.348	.077	.405	4.545	.000	.572	1.749
	result orientation	-.050	.099	-.044	-.507	.613	.590	1.694
	ability to see bigger picture	.130	.077	.146	1.700	.092	.615	1.627
	social skills and abilities	-.102	.072	-.146	-1.418	.159	.427	2.344
	creativity	.212	.088	.216	2.423	.017	.572	1.748
	balanced learning habits and skills	.244	.076	.322	3.208	.002	.450	2.222
	team orientation	-.420	.095	-.429	-4.421	.000	.483	2.072

a. Dependent Variable: REGR factor score   2 for analysis 1

It is observed from the above table that the factor2 i.e., Manpower acquisition is highly influenced by the competencies like continuing sensitivity to events, initiative , ability to see big picture , creativity ,team orientation, balanced learning habits .

It further proves that manpower acquisition is closely related to the competencies of continuing sensitivity to events, initiative , ability to see big picture , creativity ,team orientation, balanced learning habits .

able: 5.35a. Regression Analysis for Factor 3 Manpower Development:

Model Summary[b]

Model	R	R Square	Adjusted R Square	Std. Error of the Estimate	R Square Change	F Change	df1	df2	Sig. F Change	Durbin-Watson
					Change Statistics					
1	.672[a]	.452	.405	.77111342	.452	9.658	10	117	.000	1.537

a. Predictors: (Constant), team orientation, command of basic facts, ability to see bigger picture, creativity, analytical reasoning and problem solving, result orientation, initiative, continuing sensitivity to events, balanced learning habits and skills, social skills and abilities

b. Dependent Variable: REGR factor score 3 for analysis

Coefficients[a]

Model		Unstandardized Coefficients B	Unstandardized Coefficients Std. Error	Standardized Coefficients Beta	t	Sig.	Collinearity Statistics Tolerance	Collinearity Statistics VIF
1	(Constant)	3.036	.997		3.045	.003		
	command of basic facts	-.076	.058	-.099	-1.311	.192	.816	1.226
	analytical reasoning and problem solving	.006	.076	.008	.084	.933	.534	1.872
	continuing sensitivity to events	-.032	.073	-.041	-.441	.660	.538	1.859
	initiative	-.318	.078	-.371	-4.094	.000	.572	1.749
	result orientation	-.088	.101	-.078	-.873	.385	.590	1.694
	ability to see bigger picture	-.334	.078	-.375	-4.294	.000	.615	1.627
	social skills and abilities	-.093	.073	-.133	-1.272	.206	.427	2.344
	creativity	.452	.089	.460	5.080	.000	.572	1.748
	balanced learning habits and skills	.265	.077	.350	3.434	.001	.450	2.222
	team orientation	-.130	.097	-.133	-1.347	.181	.483	2.072

a. Dependent Variable: REGR factor score 3 for analysis 1

341

Collinearity Diagnostics[a]

Model	Dimension	Eigenvalue	Condition Index	Variance Proportions										
				(Constant)	command of basic facts	analytical reasoning and problem solving	continuing sensitivity to events	initiative	result orientation	ability to see bigger picture	social skills and abilities	creativity	balanced learning habits and skills	team orientation
1	1	10.848	1.000	.00	.00	.00	.00	.00	.00	.00	.00	.00	.00	.00
	2	.046	15.344	.00	.06	.03	.00	.01	.00	.00	.22	.00	.01	.00
	3	.026	20.527	.00	.34	.02	.11	.01	.00	.00	.03	.03	.03	.01
	4	.022	22.130	.00	.13	.00	.11	.06	.01	.18	.01	.03	.02	.01
	5	.016	26.228	.00	.00	.01	.18	.11	.01	.19	.06	.00	.14	.03
	6	.012	30.597	.01	.00	.05	.00	.02	.14	.01	.06	.38	.10	.02
	7	.008	36.037	.12	.21	.06	.03	.12	.00	.05	.01	.07	.24	.21
	8	.008	37.761	.00	.00	.15	.24	.45	.05	.13	.03	.08	.29	.00
	9	.007	38.586	.06	.01	.66	.10	.06	.00	.12	.41	.01	.07	.03
	10	.004	49.254	.03	.21	.00	.21	.07	.49	.30	.01	.15	.00	.38
	11	.003	59.144	.77	.03	.02	.02	.09	.31	.02	.17	.24	.10	.31

a. Dependent Variable: REGR factor score   3 for analysis 1

It is observed from the above table that the factor3 i.e., Manpower development is highly influenced by the competencies like   initiative , ability to see big picture , creativity , balanced learning habits .

It further proves that manpower acquisition is closely related to the competencies of initiative , ability to see big picture , creativity , balanced learning habits.

342

Chapter- 6

SUMMARY AND CONCLUSIONS

The extensive research into the competency mapping practices of Indian IT companies need to be put succinctly ,yet in a lucid manner to make the readers understand the importance and role of competency mapping on Talent management practices in the Indian IT organizations. This chapter is an endeavor in the above mentioned direction and consists of six sections. The chapter begins with an overview of the study in order to give a brief narrative of the entire research. It is followed by the researcher's interpretation of the significant findings derived out of the research. The third section offers a precise and objective description of the research results. Thereafter the limitations of the study within which interpretations ought to be imbibed. This is followed by a major section contributing to the major contributions of the study and the benefit it can render to the field of academic research. Academic research is fruitful only if it can, in some way, contribute towards an improvement in industrial practices. Therefore a considerable portion of this section is devoted to the utilitarian value of the present research to marketing practitioners. And finally, the author has suggested directions for members of academic fraternity to ensure further development in this area of research.

OVERVIEW

The present study was aimed at understanding the scope of competency mapping and the role it has in the talent management practices. Competency mapping has been widely debated in not only in the industry forums but also in the academic forums as well. Especially it is a widely accepted phenomenon in the Indian IT sector. However, the researcher believes that though theoretically the concept of competency mapping is widely adopted in most of the IT industry, it could still be used in more tangible and logical forms if it is thoroughly integrated with the talent management practices in the organization, thus improving the work environment.

The researcher is of the opinion that the literature related to competency mapping in the field of Human resources management is here to stay and therefore needs to be empirically researched and show that an integrated approach of various talent management practices starting with competency mapping can surely play a vital role in improving the work environment. Two of the works on competency mapping like McClleland (1965) and Berger and Berger(2000) had a significant impact in drawing the scales of measurement.

Talent management has become the strategic priority for every organization in the present scenario. In order to create continuous value to stakeholders and to maintain competitive advantage, organizations must proactively manage their human capital. The shift therefore has been from efficient operations and low cost products to outstanding customer service and innovation which in turn demanded to build capabilities in the organization's human resource base. The customer centricity strategy invites employees to contribute their unique ideas and experiences in providing service to the customer. The organizations can propel towards high performance if they build in those distinctive capabilities that are key drivers for organizational success. The pace of growth of every country has been significant .within the next 20 years by most projections there will be these developing countries who will take the

344

lead. A whole new middle class is emerging with huge disposable income which has increased the spending power of this group. Adapting to this scenario requires right resources and capabilities. The idea of talent as the force that powers companies is taking centre stage. People are the key to add value to any of the organizational processes.

Modern organizations own and employ fewer of the basic inputs of the production-land, materials capital and support services than they did 20 years ago, now with the advent of new technology organization has been able to make a shift from redundant work processes to a more evolved approach in which there are interdependent parts and the production is divided not only in the units where it is produced but across the value chain altogether. As a result of this transformation there has been a shift in the source of value. Earlier the source of value was always tangible assets of the company but in today's context it is equally beneficial to attach it to the intangible assets of the organization- your employees. Branham (2005) found that recognizing the key employees on which your organization depends and attempting to understand how to better meet their needs is highly important for the organization. The organizations must multiply talent by combining and recombining knowledge, skills and competencies throughout the organization to generate superior levels of effort, imagination, creativity, learning, adaptability and performance from the entire workforce. A virtuous cycle of talent multiplication is set in motion starting with defining the organizations talent needs, discover the sources of talent, and develop the talent potential and lastly deploy the talent strategically.

The preceding discussion led to the formulation of the Hypothesis – H1- competency mapping effectively contributes to Talent management practices…… At the outset, the present study expected there is significant relationship between the preferred competencies and talent management practices. However, the present author arrived at findings based upon secondary data which suggests that competency mapping is highly used as a method/tool for performance management at a high degree alone rather than using it for all talent management practices.

Major findings:

1. It was observed that the reliability scores tested on Cron bach alpha was 0.862 which suggested that the questionnaire had high internal consistency scores. Therefore it was proved to be useful for further analysis of the answers.

2. Further ANNOVA revealed that the competencies which were listed to be highly preferred competencies across all the selected IT companies are analytical reasoning and problem solving, continuing sensitivity to events, creativity ,initiative, balanced learning habits, ability to see big picture, team orientation to be highly significant as a competency to be used for competency mapping.

3. ANNOVA also revealed that employee performance, workforce planning ,performance management , career development, succession planning, compensation

management were found to be significant as a talent management practice. However workforce acquisition and learning management is not significant.

4. After conducting factor analysis it was clearly visible that three factors could be constructed on the basis of the above method; i.e., Manpower management- which comprised of employee performance, performance management and compensation management formed the first factor. The second factor was manpower acquisition which comprised of workforce planning and workforce acquisition. The third factor is called as Manpower development includes career planning , succession planning and learning management.

5. The competencies when regressed on the three factors it was found that there were certain core competencies which were influencing the effectiveness of the talent management practices. Manpower Management was greatly influenced by analytical reasoning, continuing sensitivity to events, initiative, creativity and balanced learning habits and skills. Manpower acquisition was significantly related to creativity, balanced learning habits and skills, ability to see big picture and team orientation. Manpower development was influenced by initiative ,ability to see big picture ,creativity ,balanced learning habits and skills.

6. It can be further concluded from the findings that Manpower management which includes performance management, employee performance and compensation management in the IT companies greatly depends on the employee demonstrating the competencies of analytical reasoning and continuing sensitivity to events. These two competencies form the threshold competencies which has causal relationship with Manpower management. However the functional competencies which contribute to the effectiveness of manpower management are initiative, creativity and balanced learning habits.

7. It was also found from the study that Manpower acquisition which includes workforce planning and workforce acquisition greatly depends on the employee demonstrating the competencies of team orientation as a threshold competencies whereas creativity ,balanced learning habits and skills and ability to see big picture form the functional competencies of the manpower acquisition process.

8. The threshold competencies of the Manpower development were initiative as a competency. Employees demonstrating this competency had an edge over others in the IT sector. The functional competencies are ability to see big picture, creativity and balanced learning habits.

9. It was observed that the work environment also significantly influenced by the talent management practices. To measure work environment practices several parameters were used ;which included aligning employees with vision and mission ,encourages employees to join the organization, excited to come to work, employees ideas are listened and valued and employees are enabled to identify the gaps in their competencies ,so that there can be competency development.

10. The part c of the empirical analysis revealed that both the technical and HR personnel felt that the talent management practices effectively contributed to aligning the employees to vision and mission of the organization, attracts the prospective employees for the organization, and makes the employees excited to come to work and further helps in identification of gaps.

Contributions of the study:

The present study emphasizes competency mapping can be used in other talent management practices such and identifying the threshold and functional competencies required for each of the talent management practices. However there has been dearth of empirical studies to present the study of competency mapping and talent management practices and presenting it as an integrated approach. In this regard the present study may be considered as a small step towards developing a deeper understanding of a dynamic and dialectic construct that competency mapping is. The finding generated out of the study has better utilitarian value.

BIBLIOGRAPHY

Anstey, Edgar (1989). *Reminiscences for wartime Army psychologists*", The Psychologists, vol. 2, November, pp.475-78.

Berger, L.A. (2004c). **Four steps to creating a talent management system.** In D.R Berger &L.A. Berger. The Talent management handbook, ch.2 .New York : McGraw Hill.

Boyle, S.J. Fullerton and R.wood (1995). **'Do assessment/development centers use optimum evaluation procedures? A survey of practice in UK organizations'** International journal of selection and assessment, pp.132-40

Burgoyne,J.G. and R.Stuart (1976) . *"The nature ,use and Acquisition of Managerial skills and other attributes'*,Personnel review ,5(4) , pp.19-29

Boyatzis,Richard E. (1982), *"The competent manager"*. New York, NY: Jhon wiley ,

Boyatzis ,Richard E. ., Scott.s.Cowen ,and David A. Kolb . (1995) , *"Innovation in professional education*". San Francisco, CA.

Bipp, Tanja. , (Mar2010), International Journal of Selection & Assessment, Vol. 18 Issue 1, p28-39

Bersin, Josh,(Jun2006),Performance Management, Training, Vol. 43 Issue 6, p7-7, 1p;

Best Practices for Performance Management. HRMagazine, Oct2006, Vol. 51 Issue 10, p16-16
Cooper, Kenneth carlton (2000) .**Effective competency modeling and reporting,** New york : AMA publications.

Chavan, Meena, (2009), The balanced scorecard: a new challenge. Journal of Management Development, Vol. 28 Issue 5, p393-406

Cernuşca, Lucian1 luciancernusca@gmail.com Dima, Cristina2 cristina@data.no Source:Revista da Faculdade de Ciências Humanas e Sociais; 2007, Issue 4, p162-171

Corbitt, Terry, Mar2004, Business Performance Management Systems, , Vol. 48 Issue 3, p22-23.

Dubois D. (1993) **competency based performance improvement, A strategy for organizational change,** Amherst, Mass: HRD press.

De Waal, André; Kourtit, Karima; Nijkamp, Peter. (2009) International Journal of Operations & Production Management, Vol. 29 Issue 12, p1242-1265.

Davis, Patricia; Rogers, Robert W, (Summer2005) *"Getting the most from your performance management system",* Vol. 34 Issue 2, p13-16.

Dobson, Phillip; Myles, John; Jackson, Paul. (Apr-Jun2007), *"Making the Case for Critical Realism: Examining the Implementation of Automated Performance Management Systems"* Information Resources Management Journal, Vol. 20 Issue 2, p138-1

Furnham, Adrian., (2004) European Business Journal 2nd Quarter, Vol. 16 Issue 2, and p83-94,

Gunaratne, K. Asoka; Du Plessis, Andries J. Journal of Global Business & Technology, Mar(2007) , Vol. 3 Issue 1, p17-28,

Hay Mc Ber, (October 1997) **Competency Study Database**
Hair, J.F., R.E. Anderson, R.L. Tatham, and W.C. Black (1998), Multivariate Data Analysis, 5th ed., Pearson Education

Hsi-An Shih; Yun-Hwa Chiang; (2006) Chu-Chun Hsu. International Journal of Manpower, Vol. 27 Issue 8, p741-763, 23p, 3

Mc Clleland ,David C(1973) . *"Testing for competency Rather than Intelligence"* , American Psychologist,28 ,January , pp.18-20.

McClleland ,David C. " *Identifying competencies with the behavioural event interviews"* Psychological science .Vol.9,no.5, September 1998

Management charter initiative 1990.

Management issues News Online (2006) *Employee engagement gives big boost to the bottom line, 7 June* (online) http:// www. Managementissues.com /2006/8/24/research/ employee-engagement –gives –big boost to the bottom-line .asp (accessed 21 july 2012)

Maslow ,Abraham H (1943) *A theory of motivation, Psychological Review* 50,pp 370-96

Mc Kinsey (2005) – *"Addressing china's Looming Talent shortage"* report- October

Martone, David, (Autumn2003) A Guide to Developing a Competency-Based Performance-Management System Employment Relations Today (Wiley), Vol. 30 Issue 3, p23-32.

Mei-I Cheng; Andrew Dainty; David Moore., (Jan2007), *Implementing a new performance management system within a project-based organization: A case study* International Journal of Productivity & Performance Management, Vol. 56

Marchand, Marie; Raymond, Louis. (2008)International Journal of Operations & Production Management, , Vol. 28 Issue 7, p663-686

Morgan, Robert, Compensation & Benefits Review, (Sep/Oct2006), Vol. 38 Issue 5, p22-27.

Hamel,Gary and C.K prahalad (1994) .**Competing for the future**, Boston: Harvard Business school .

McKinsey study (1997) **The War for Talent,** Report-October

Martin .,et.al(2000) **competency mapping –its impact on organizational success.**

Naqvi, Farah,(Jan2009), . ICFAI Journal of Management Research Vol. 8 Issue 1, p85-94,

Nath, Rabindra; Raheja, Rajat.(Apr-Sep2001) Journal of Services Research, , Vol. 1 Issue 1, p25

Bersin, Josh.,(Jun2006), "**Performance Management Training**". Vol. 43 Issue 6, p7-7, 1p;

Resource Management International Digest, (Aug2004), "*Pay for performance* report.Vol. 4 Issue 8, p1-15, 4p

Spencer ,Legde M. and Sigme M. spencer (1993) . *competence at Work* ,Newyork : Jhon Wiley & Sons Inc.

Hartley, Darin E.T+D, (Apr2004) *Significance of clarity in setting goals on the performance of the workforce Tools for Talent.*

T.V. Rao* and Sumeet Varghese TVRLS, February (2009), Ahmedabad, Indian Human Resource Development, 15–34 .Vol. 12, No. 1

Woodruffe,c, (2003). *To have and to hold: Getting your organization onto talented People CVs* .Training Journal ,May :pp: 20-24

Kaplan, RobertS and Norton,David P(2004) *Strategy Maps : converting intangible assets into intangible outcomes,* Harvard Business SchoolPress , Boston, Mass

Wright, Robert P.; Cheung, Frenda K. K. (2007), Personnel Review, Vol. 36.

Yuk Lan Wong; Snell, Robin Stanley. (Winter2003). Journal of General Management, Vol. 29 Issue 2, p53-69.

Websites :

11. www.dqindia.com June,2009 issue

12. www.dqindia.com Dec ,2010issue

13. www.dqindia.com June ,2012 issue

14. www.infosys.com

15. www.wipro.com

16. www.csc.com

17. www.accenture.com

18. www.hcl.com Learning forums:

1. Vaahini team (Accenture)

2. Interview excerpts from the employees.

QUESTIONNAIRE
Interview schedule for HR Managers/ technical managers

PART A

This part of the questionnaire is divided into two sub sections. The first section is designed to know the preference of HR managers of the select Competency mapping methods for managing employee performance. The second section is designed to know their preferred competencies for the IT technical staff in order of importance.

Profile

NAME: _

POSITION:

NAME OF THE COMPANY:

GENDER:

AGE:

NO. OF YEARS IN COMPANY:

_____

_

INSTRUCTIONS FOR FILLING UP THE QUESTIONAIRE:
- Please tick the appropriate choice you feel is the best suited
- Please give reasons wherever required
- Please answer all the questions.
1. Please rank the following methods used for Competency mapping according to your preference, you feel, is effective in Managing employee performance.(8 being the highest and 1 being the lowest.

   a.   Assessment/Development Centre

1	2	3	4	5	6	7	8	9	10

b. **360 Degree feedback**

1	2	3	4	5	6	7	8	9	10

c. **Role plays**

1	2	3	4	5	6	7	8	9	10

d. **Case study**

1	2	3	4	5	6	7	8	9	10

e. **Structured Experiences**

1	2	3	4	5	6	7	8	9	10

f. **Simulations**

1	2	3	4	5	6	7	8	9	10

g. **Business Games**

1	2	3	4	5	6	7	8	9	10

h. **Any other**

1	2	3	4	5	6	7	8	9	10

2. **Please rank the following competencies for the IT technical staff, in order of preference(1 being lowest and 10 being highest)**

a. **Command of basic facts**

1 2 3 4 5 6 7 8 9 10

b. **Analytical Reasoning/Problem solving**

c. 1 2 3 4 5 6 7 8 9 10

d. **Continuing sensitivity to events**

1 2 3 4 5 6 7 8 9 10

e. **Initiative**

1 2 3 4 5 6 7 8 9 10

f. **Result Orientation**

1 2 3 4 5 6 7 8 9 10

g. **Ability to see bigger picture**

1 2 3 4 5 6 7 8 9 10

h. **Social skills and abilities**

1 2 3 4 5 6 7 8 9 10

i   creativity

1   2   3   4   5 6 7 8   9 10

j   balanced learning habits and skill

1   2   3   4   5 6 7 8 9 10

K   team orientation

1 2   3   4   5 6 7 8 9 10

PART B

This part of the questionnaire is designed to know how much effective is Competency Mapping in Managing Talents in organisations, as Perceived by the HR managers/technical staff.

1. Competency mapping effectively contributes to better employee performance

    1   2   3   4   5   6   7   8   9   10

2. Competency mapping effectively contributes to Workforce Planning

    1   2   3   4   5   6   7   8   9   10

3. Competency mapping effectively contributes to Workforce Acquisition.

    1   2   3   4   5   6   7   8   9 10

4. Competency mapping effectively contributes to Performance Management.

    1   2   3   4   5   6   7   8   9 10

5. Competency mapping effectively contributes to Career Development

    1   2   3   4   5   6   7   8   9 10

6. Competency mapping effectively contributes to Succession Planning.

    1   2   3   4   5   6   7   8   9 10

7. Competency mapping effectively contributes to Learning Management.

    1   2   3   4   5   6   7   8   9 10

8. Competency mapping effectively contributes to Compensation Management.

    1   2   3   4   5   6   7   8   9 10

PART C

This part of the questionnaire is designed to know how the Talent Management system contributes to the work environment.

1.   The Talent Management System has contributed to aligning employee with the mission and vision of your Organisation.

   1   2   3   4   5   6   7   8   9 10

2.   The TMS has contributed to Assessing candidates skills earlier in the hiring Process

   1   2   3   4   5   6   7   8   9 10

3.   The TMS has contributed to Creating a culture that makes employees want to stay with the organization

   1   2   3   4   5   6   7   8   9 10

4.   The TMS has contributed to Creating a culture that makes individuals want to join the organization

   1   2   3   4   5   6   7   8   9 10

5.   The TMS has contributed to Creating a culture that values employees work

   1   2   3   4   5   6   7   8   9 10

6.   The TMS has contributed to Creating an environment where employees are excited to come to work each day

   1   2   3   4   5   6   7   8   9 10

7.   The TMS has contributed to Creating an environment where employees ideas are listened to and valued

   1   2   3   4   5   6   7   8   9 10

8.   The **TMS** has contributed to Creating policies that encourage career growth and development opportunities

     1   2   3   4   5   6   7   8   9 10

9.   The **TMS** has contributed to Identifying gaps in current employees and candidate competency levels

     1   2   3   4   5   6   7   8   9 10

10. The **TMS** has contributed to Creating Rewarding top performing employees

     1   2   3   4   5   6   7   8   9 10

THANK YOU FOR YOUR CO-OPERATION

BLACK EAGLE BOOKS

www.blackeaglebooks.org
info@blackeaglebooks.org

Black Eagle Books, an independent publisher, was founded as a nonprofit organization in April, 2019. It is our mission to connect and engage the Indian diaspora and the world at large with the best of works of world literature published on a collaborative platform, with special emphasis on foregrounding Contemporary Classics and New Writing.

www.ingramcontent.com/pod-product-compliance
Lightning Source LLC
Chambersburg PA
CBHW080555030426
42336CB00019B/3202